The Antimodernism of Joyce's
Portrait of the Artist as a Young Man

2003

RICHARD FALLIS, *Series Editor*

The
Antimodernism
of Joyce's
Portrait of the Artist
as a Young Man

WELDON THORNTON

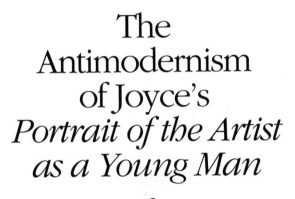

SYRACUSE UNIVERSITY PRESS

Permission is gratefully acknowledged to quote various excerpts from *The Critical Writings of James Joyce* by James Joyce, E. Mason and R. Ellmann, editors. Copyright © 1959 by Harriet Weaver and F. Lionel Monro, as administrators for the Estate of James Joyce, renewed © 1987 by F. Lionel Monro. Used by permission of Viking Penguin, a division of Penguin Books.

The paper used in this publication meets the minimum requirements of American National Standard for Information Sciences—Permanence of Paper for Printed Library Materials, ANSI Z39.48-1984. ∞™

Library of Congress Cataloging-in-Publication Data

Thornton, Weldon.
    The antimodernism of Joyce's Portrait of the artist as a young man
/ Weldon Thornton. — 1st ed.
        p.   cm. — (Irish studies)
    Includes bibliographical references and index.
    ISBN 0-8156-2587-1 (alk. paper). — ISBN 0-8156-2613-4 (pkb. :
alk. paper)
    1. Joyce, James, 1882–1941.   Portrait of the artist as a young
man.   2. Modernism (Literature)—Ireland.   I. Title.   II. Series:
Irish studies (Syracuse, N.Y.)
PR6019.O9P653   1993
823'.912—dc20   93-5484

Weldon Thornton is professor of English at the University of North Carolina, Chapel Hill. He is author of *Allusions in "Ulysses": An Annotated List* and *J. M. Synge and the Western Mind,* and coeditor (with Robert Newman) of *Joyce's "Ulysses": The Larger Perspective.*

Contents

Figure

Preface

*I*t is a singular tribute to Joyce's genius that at the completion of this project of several years, dealing with a book I have read and discussed in class innumerable times for more than thirty years, I find myself excited at the prospect of going back through this novel. My intensive work on *Portrait* has given me a fuller sense of its density of texture and the range of its cultural evocativeness. It has given me as well a new appreciation of the inexhaustible richness of Joyce's presentation of the "individual" psyche. I sense now more than ever the appropriateness of Seán O'Faoláin's saying of this novel, "Enter these enchanted woods ye who dare."

Weldon Thornton

Chapel Hill, North Carolina
May 1992

Acknowledgments

I owe thanks to those friends, students, and colleagues who have discussed this novel and these issues with me and who read and criticized parts of the manuscript.

The Department of English of the University of North Carolina at Chapel Hill provided me with very helpful leave time in the Spring term of 1991.

My thanks also to Frances Coombs for her indispensable advice and assistance in formatting and printing my manuscript.

I am also grateful for permission to quote from the following books: *Transparent Minds: Narrative Modes for Presenting Consciousness in Fiction,* by Dorrit Cohn (Princeton: Princeton Univ. Press, 1978); and *The Genealogy of Modernism: A Study of English Literary Doctrine 1908–1922,* by Michael Levenson (Cambridge: Cambridge Univ. Press, 1984).

Abbreviations

The following works are cited in the body of the text by the abbreviations indicated below.

CH   Deming, Robert H. ed. *James Joyce: The Critical Heritage*. 2 vols. New York: Barnes and Noble, 1970.

CW   Joyce, James. *The Critical Writings of James Joyce*. Edited by Ellsworth Mason and Richard Ellmann. New York: Viking Press, 1959.

D   Joyce, James. *Dubliners*. Edited by Robert Scholes and A. Walton Litz. New York: Viking Press, 1969. The Viking Critical Edition.

JJQ   *The James Joyce Quarterly*

JJII   Ellmann, Richard. *James Joyce*. Revised edition. New York: Oxford Univ. Press, 1982.

Letters I, II, III   Joyce, James. *Letters of James Joyce*. Three volumes. Vol. I edited by Stuart Gilbert (1957); vols. II and III edited by Richard Ellmann. New York: Viking Press, 1966.

MBK   Joyce, Stanislaus. *My Brother's Keeper: James Joyce's Early Years*. Edited by Richard Ellmann. New York: Viking Press, 1958.

P   Joyce, James. *A Portrait of the Artist as a Young Man*. Edited by Chester G. Anderson. New York: Viking

Press, 1968. The Viking Critical Edition. (When there is no ambiguity, references to *Portrait* are indicated by a page number, with no abbreviation.)

SH ———. *Stephen Hero.* Edited by Theodore Spencer, John J. Slocum, and Herbert Cahoon. New York: New Directions, 1963.

U ———. *Ulysses.* The Corrected Text, edited by Hans Walter Gabler et al. New York: Random House, 1984. (Cited by episode and line number.)

Workshop Scholes, Robert, and Richard M. Kain. *The Workshop of Daedalus: James Joyce and the Raw Materials for "A Portrait of the Artist as a Young Man."* Evanston: Northwestern Univ. Press, 1965.

The Antimodernism of Joyce's
Portrait of the Artist as a Young Man

1

Introduction

*T*his book stems from two sources. The first is several decades of teaching, reflecting on, and writing about the works of James Joyce. The second is an equally long-standing interest in certain themes of Western thought, especially those involving our culture's compulsion to give a formal account of all aspects of reality, and its strange deference to a simplistic schema of ideas that is incapable of doing justice to our experience. One result of my several years's exploration of this latter interest is a manuscript entitled "The Roots of Modernism: A Study in Cultural Temperament" that is much closer to cultural criticism or intellectual history than to literary criticism. My epigraph for that manuscript is Goethe's proverb Stephen Dedalus thinks of in *Ulysses:* "Beware of what you wish for in youth because you will get it in middle life" (*U,* 9.451). In that manuscript I argue that the modern Western world view—"the Modernist Syndrome"—involves a view of reality the Western psyche has been tending toward and even striving to bring about, explicitly and implicitly, for hundreds, perhaps thousands, of years. Drawing mainly upon ideas sanctioned by "empiricism" and by the Enlightenment, we have in the present century succeeded in effecting this modernist world view, and our success has now raised the question of whether we can live with what we have wrought—whether, that is, the Modernist Syndrome permits a full and rich view of reality and of human nature.

In "The Roots of Modernism" I identify certain temperamental orientations or biases of the Western psyche that have provided the impetus behind our persistent cultivation of the modernist mind-set. Although most of these temperamental traits have surfaced in the Western mind only in recent centuries, their roots go much deeper, for some of these dispositional biases can be traced back to the earliest stages of Greek or Hebrew thought. These cultural orientations function in the Western psyche much as personality traits or Carl Jung's "dispositions" or "orientations" do in the individual psyche; they function, that is, as selective orientations toward the world, implicitly sanctioning certain perspectives upon reality, certain attitudes or ideas, and denigrating others. In "The Roots of Modernism" I illustrate how these orientations have contributed to the development and the authority of the modern Western worldview.

I began work a few years ago on "The Roots of Modernism" partly to resolve the confusion that surrounds the use of the terms *modern* and *modernism,* both in literary criticism and in discussions of Western culture generally. Reading books and attending conferences on literary modernism, I recognized the confusion and contradictoriness in the use of the terms *modern* and *modernism,* reflected, for example, in the label *modern* being applied to movements as substantially different as Romanticism and nihilism, or phenomenology and behaviorism. In order to resolve this confusion within discussions of *literary* modernism I had first to determine how the term can justifiably be used in Western intellectual history.

I soon realized it was not feasible in so broad an endeavor to use works of literature to illustrate my ideas about intellectual history. Because literary texts involve indirection and irony in dramatizing their themes, because they so subtly exemplify the ideas and attitudes of their milieu, my use of such texts as evidence in a philosophical argument would have required me either to oversimplify the works, or to turn aside for detailed analysis of the texts themselves. To illustrate the difficulties surrounding the use of literary works in a philosophical analysis, I refer briefly in "The Roots of Modernism" to the theme of individualism in Joyce's *Portrait of the Artist.* The modernist idea of "discrete individualism"—i.e., the idea that the individual is self-contained and self-determining—is undoubtedly a central theme of that novel. But in my view, Joyce's purpose in the novel is not to celebrate such individualism; on the contrary, it is to show how superficial and insufficient this understanding of the individual psyche is. Demonstration of that claim about Joyce's handling of individualism in the novel, however, would have deflected me from my discussion of sources and expressions of atomic individualism in Western intellectual history and would require a book to itself. This is that book.

My argument here is that Joyce's *Portrait of the Artist* is, in some meaningful senses of the term, antimodernist. In Stephen Dedalus, Joyce depicts an intelligent, sensitive young man who is strongly influenced by various ideas and assumptions of the Modernist Syndrome—ideas that Joyce himself weighed and found wanting. Though Joyce treats Stephen sympathetically, he reveals in a number of ways the insufficiencies of Stephen's implicit view of reality and of the self. Furthermore, *Portrait* reflects this distance between Joyce and Stephen, not simply in its tone or in certain differences of aesthetic opinion between author and character, but in its very structure and verbal texture, because the structure itself embodies Stephen's implicit view of reality, and the verbal presentation of his consciousness persistently involves a deeper individual and cultural psyche than Stephen himself can comprehend.

From early in his career, Joyce saw the need to dramatize within his works the conflicting perspectives the twentieth century inherited in the subject-object, mind-nature dichotomy—a dichotomy expressing itself in literary terms mainly in symbolism vs. naturalism. Joyce saw the essential falseness and pernicious effects of this dichotomization, and prepared himself to effect a synthesis of these two perspectives. In *Portrait* the need for this synthesis is fully dramatized through Stephen Dedalus, who is enamored of such a dichotomy, while Joyce reveals the incompleteness of Stephen's view.

Thus I see Joyce as "taking the measure" of Stephen, but I add two things to this long-established perspective on the novel.[1] First, I set my views about Joyce's "antimodernist" aims in *Portrait* within the context of certain deep-running currents of Western thought, within the context of certain of Joyce's underlying ideas, and within the implications of the genre of the *Bildungsroman*. Second, I show how profoundly Joyce takes the measure of Stephen's individualism, even of his implicit view of the nature of reality and of the psyche. The distance between Joyce and Stephen goes beyond such superficial matters as Stephen's emotional transports upon certain epiphanic occasions or the quality of his writing in the villanelle; rather the irony goes to the very core of Stephen's modernist conception of his world and of his self—i.e., to his penchant for dichotomizing the world into "inner" and "outer," and to his aspirations to self-knowledge and self-determination, aspirations virtually all commentators have presumed Joyce shares with Stephen. Thus the sources of the irony I demonstrate run along largely unexplored lines—lines contrary to much earlier Joyce criticism,

Part One

❧

Contexts

2

Literary Modernism

My title asserts the antimodernism of a writer who is regarded as an exemplar of literary modernism (and more recently of postmodernism as well), and so some clarification is called for. I do not presume here, however, to resolve the vagueness, idiosyncrasy, and contradictoriness that characterize current discussions of literary modernism. My more modest aim in this chapter is to explain certain relevant sources of the confusion in regard to modernism, and to clarify my own understanding of the term, especially in regard to those philosophical issues that bear upon what I am calling Joyce's antimodernism.[1]

Some Sources of Confusion

Let me list, in order of their increasing relevance for my purposes, five sources of the confusion that pervades current thinking about literary modernism, and elaborate on each. The first is inherent in the word *modern*. The term has an inherently temporal implication (with a modicum of perennial meaning), but we would endow it with substantial, a-temporal meanings; some of the confusion stems from the impossibility of exorcising this temporal or perennial aspect. Second, confusion about literary modernism results from the variety, the internal tensions and contradictions, and the complex evolution of the ideas we label with this term. There simply is no single phenomenon, no single idea or attitude, that we can label "literary modernism," and yet most studies, however modestly or cautiously they

7

may begin, aspire eventually to locate some quintessential modernist quality. Such monolithic proclamations do little to advance our understanding
of this complex cultural phenomenon. Astute critics have long discriminated among modes or phases of literary modernism, and some recent
studies show that modernism consists of a congeries of loosely related
movements or individuals whose views are not coordinated or even logically compatible—but the procrustean generalizing tendency is still strong.
A third source of confusion is the lack of a clear sense of the underlying
philosophical issues that literary modernism emerges from and reflects—
the issues at the core of what has been called "the crisis of modernism."[2]
Characterizations of literary modernism always involve implicit philosophical issues, and yet articulation of these issues is often simplistic, confused,
and inconsistent; as a result we find utterly antithetical philosophical
stances—e.g., phenomenology and behaviorism—described as modern. A
fourth stumbling block—especially when discussion turns to the modernity
of specific writers, works, or techniques—involves the subtleties and dra-
matizations that are always involved in the literary presentation of abstract
themes. Simply because a writer dramatizes modernist ideas or situations
does not mean that he or she sanctions them, and yet critics often disregard
this crucial discrimination when affixing the "modernist" label to writers,
works, or techniques. A fifth complicating factor is the attempt to characterize literary modernism retrospectively, from the vantage point of a presumably achieved postmodernism, or (more tendentiously) to regard "true"
modernism as a harbinger of structuralism or deconstruction. Attempting
either to take the measure of modernism or to appropriate it to their program, some contemporary theoreticians describe modernism in ways that
bear little resemblance to earlier, less tendentious accounts, thus rendering
a clear understanding of modernism all the more difficult. Such attempts to
see modernism as the precursor of structuralism or deconstruction are especially relevant to this study, because Joyce's works have so often been
subjected to this retrospective reconstruction—i.e., the postmodernism that
is presumably found in *Finnegans Wake* is assumed to reveal the true
nature of Joyce's earlier modernism.

1. Modernism—Substantial Concept, or Chronological Label?

One underlying source of confusion about modernism may seem too
simple to take seriously—i.e., the time-bound nature of the words *modern*

and *modernism*. The inherently temporal aspect of the word is rooted in its etymology and is reflected in dictionary definitions. According to the *OED*, *modern* is an adaptation of the late Latin *modern*-us, which comes from *modo*, meaning "just now." If we refer to the popular *Webster's New Collegiate Dictionary*, we find a series of definitions and discriminations that are almost—though not quite—sheerly temporal:

1 a: of, relating to, or characteristic of a period extending from a relevant remote past to the present time b: of, relating to, or characteristic of the present or the immediate past: CONTEMPORARY.

[And in its synonymic discrimination *Webster's* says:] MODERN, RECENT, LATE shared meaning element: having taken place, existed, or developed in times close to the present. In spite of the common element of meaning these words are seldom freely interchangeable without loss of precision. MODERN may date anything that is not ancient or medieval . . . or anything that bears the mark of a period in time nearer than another . . . or, less clearly, may apply to whatever is felt as new, fresh, or up-to-date. . . . In all these uses a change or contrast in quality or character is implicit.

While this definition is essentially temporal—i.e., "the present time" is constantly changing—the last part of the synonymic discrimination points to a modicum of perennial meaning, that of *contrast* with what has gone before. To be modern, that is, first of all means simply to be recent, but it also means to stand over against the past—which of course renders the term applicable to any era and especially appropriate to one that sees itself as challenging what preceded it. This ubiquitous temporal sense of the term clouds attempts to give it any substantial meaning.

For the past half-century we have tried to exorcise these embedded elements of mere chronology (i.e., "recent") or of generic meaning (i.e., contrast with what preceded); we have tried, that is, to use the term *modern* substantially, to designate a specific set of early twentieth century cultural and artistic attitudes. But while historical specificity comes naturally to terms such as "eighteenth-century" or "Victorian," *modern* inherently resists attempts to find some set of characteristic attitudes and ideas, analogous to those designated by terms such as neoclassicism or Romanticism.[3] Nor have we had better success in defining the "modern period," both because of the perennial aspect of the term and because it can be used on such different levels of generality. In the broad context of history of ideas, involving a time-frame such as Medieval, Renaissance, and Modern, the modern period begins in the early seventeenth century. In a more specifically literary context we think in terms of Romantic, Victorian, and Modern, in which case the modern period would begin around the turn of the twentieth century.[4]

But even if we could agree upon the chronological boundaries of the modern period, it would only tempt us to a simplistic, mechanical "solution" to the problem of deciding which writers are modern. Given a sheerly chronological standard—e.g., that literary modernism ran from 1910 to World War II—we could say without question that James Joyce is a modern writer, because he lived and wrote—or at least *published*—virtually all of his works during the designated modern period. (Joseph Conrad, though, would become a problematic case.) We do not need to argue about whether Thomas Carlyle is a *nineteenth-century* writer; but whether Carlyle is a *Romantic* writer is another matter, for we define Romanticism in terms of certain themes, techniques, and life-attitudes. Because this is the case, we can even acknowledge that a writer who lived during the "Romantic period" can best be understood as an antiromantic, because the writer's themes are uncharacteristic of or opposed to the Romantic view of reality. And so any sheerly chronological designation of modernism would simply defer the problem of our finding a substantial characterization of "modern" literature. The appeal of a simplistic chronological solution to the problem of modernism can be detected behind some discussions that limit themselves to a designated period. While all such chronological designations presumably begin from some sense of the nature of modernism—i.e., the dates chosen are not utterly arbitrarily—the substantial issues often seem neglected, so that we feel that the proposed dates were arrived at in order to avoid reflection and discrimination.[5]

Simplistic as it may seem, then, inherently temporal connotations of the term *modern* do continue to cloud thinking about the issues of modernism. Still, we must try to use the term substantially—i.e., to establish for literary modernism a characteristic set of techniques and attitudes and aims. Such use of the term should enable us not only to say that certain writers or themes are modern, it should permit us to recognize that someone who lives in the "modern period" may exemplify antimodern ideas and attitudes, and even to discriminate between modern and antimodern elements within the work of a given writer.

\

2. The Complex, Multi-faceted, Evolving Nature of
Literary Modernism

Literary modernism is difficult to characterize because it has varied so much from writer to writer and from phase to phase. Some critics have recognized that the movement consisted of strands and of phases, and have explored its mixed and evolving nature. In *A Genealogy of Modernism: A Study of English Literary Doctrine 1908–1922* (1984), not only does Michael Levenson confine himself to what he acknowledges is a single strand— Pound, Hulme, Ford, Lewis, Eliot—but within that group he describes historical changes that involved complete reversals of attitude in regard to such issues as the relationship between art and society, the relationship of poetry and prose, the nature and desirability of *vers libre,* and the attitude toward history and toward individualism. Similarly Maud Ellmann, in *The Poetics of Impersonality,* proclaims the logical inconsistencies of Eliot and Pound concerning the idea of impersonality, and apparently even disdains attempts to "straighten things out."[6]

This does not of course mean that we must forego a coherent account of literary modernism; on the contrary, these careful studies of limited aspects of modernism, acknowledging and tracing contradictions and changes of attitude, promise some real clarification of the issues. This possibility is illustrated by what is perhaps the most successful and far reaching discrimination among modes of modernism—Matei Calinescu's intelligent and well-informed *Five Faces of Modernity: Modernism, Avant-Garde, Decadence, Kitsch, Postmodernism* (Second edition; Durham, N.C.: Duke Univ. Press, 1987). In any event, recognizing the mixed, developing nature of modernism should make us wary of attempts to identify the movement with one group or with one idea or theme, such as Meisel's "belatedness" or Perl's *Nostos.*[7]

3. Confusion about the Philosophical Issues Underlying Modernism

Literary modernism continues to be incoherently characterized because we remain unclear about what the underlying issues of philosophical modernism are, and about which of these issues have most affected literary modernism. The problem has two aspects. First, there is confusion and even contradiction as to which philosophical ideas and attitudes are modern, reflected in the fact that movements as contradictory as phenomenology and behaviorism both continue to be described by that term. Second, there is no clear understanding of which philosophical issues impinged most strongly on literary modernism and how they did so—i.e., on such broad questions as the writers' attitudes toward the self or the existence of public values or the nature of art, or on such specific technical matters as point of view or modes of psychological presentation. While philosophical modernism and literary modernism are not identical, there are ineluctable congruences between them, and until we are clearer about what these are, we cannot possibly achieve more than a superficial understanding of literary modernism.

As long as we continue to describe as "modernist" philosophical ideas or schools of thought that are diametrically opposed, there is little hope of our being able to arrive at a coherent account of a literary modernism which inevitably grows out of and reflects those underlying ideas. If philosophical modernism did begin with the ideas of Bacon and Descartes and Locke—as most intellectual historians say that it did—how can we possibly label as modern Rousseau and most of the Romantics whose ideas obviously run counter to the ideas of those seventeenth-century thinkers? Yet we do commonly refer to Rousseau and to the Romantics as moderns, or as presaging modernism. Similarly, if the Lockean idea of the mind as a *tabula rasa* is a characteristically modernist idea—and Locke has been said to be the father of modern philosophy—what then are we to label the interest in the unconscious that is characteristic of many writers and thinkers of the past 150 years but that directly challenges the Lockean model? How can both Locke and Wordsworth be modernist?

We should not expect help in articulating the underlying issues of philosophical and literary modernism from the writers themselves, even the more abstract and programmatic ones such as Pound and Hulme or those trained in philosophy such as Eliot. These writers were too close to what was happening, chronologically and personally, to be able to provide a coherent articulation of what they were struggling with. And of course we do not value creative writers primarily for their capacity to formalize what they are living through. One theme of Joyce's *Portrait* is this very question of how much articulate understanding of himself and his milieu is required of the writer, and, perhaps surprisingly, Joyce suggests the need for relatively little.

One study of literary modernism that explicitly raises philosophical issues is Sanford Schwartz's *The Matrix of Modernism: Pound, Eliot, and Early Twentieth-Century Thought* (Princeton: Princeton Univ. Press, 1985). But in its focus on the philosophers who themselves lived in the midst of the modernist milieu, such as Bergson, James, Bradley, and Nietzsche, Schwartz simply does not delve deeply enough or trace the issues back far enough to provide the clarification that we need.[8] More promise for an in-depth understanding of these issues is held out by Charles Taylor's *The Sources of the Self: The Making of the Modern Identity* (Cambridge: Harvard Univ. Press, 1989), even though it does not set out specifically to cast light on literary modernism. Taylor's book reflects a deep and thorough historical knowledge of the issues behind modernism and offers a clear-minded discrimination of many of the confusions that still enthrall us when we try to think about the interrelationships among language, value, and the self.

4. The Subtlety and Irony of Literary Presentations of Modernist Themes

A fourth source of confusion about what it means to designate a specific writer or work or technique modernist is that the writers who explore "modernist" themes may not themselves sanction what their works present. Good writers necessarily present their themes complexly, indirectly, dramatically, which means that they do not always stand behind the ideas or themes that they dramatize, and that even when an author depicts characters sympathetically, he or she may not agree with their life-attitudes. If we are not capable of making such distinctions between what the author dramatizes and what she believes, or between the views of an author and those of the characters, we are incapable of doing literary criticism. Such distinctions are not easy, but they cannot be ignored. Yet much of the confusion about literary modernism stems from precisely this failure to distinguish between what an author believes or values, and what he dramatizes, perhaps criticizes, in his works. In recent years, almost everyone who quotes Stephen Dedalus' famous dictum about the impersonality of the artist who aspires to be "refined out of existence" points out that the sentiment is Stephen's, not Joyce's. But Joyce criticism has not always made that discrimination, and we still do not make it about other aspects of Joyce's relationship with his various narrative voices, nor do we make it when discussing the characters and situations created by other modern writers.[9]

To illustrate briefly—let us say that "individualism" refers to the modernist idea that the individual is self-contained and self-determining and is capable of a high degree of self-awareness, and that these qualities are to be sought after. This superficial conception of individualism is not confined to recent Western literature, but it has been very influential in our culture, and many of our writers have been presumed to emulate it.[10] Undoubtedly, many twentieth-century novelists have depicted characters who aspire to such autonomous individualism; they include Stephen Dedalus, Hemingway's Nick Adams and Frederic Henry, and Faulkner's Isaac McCaslin. It might appear, then, that these writers (as well as their characters) deserve the label *modern*. But such labeling begs the very important question of the tone in which the writer depicts the character's claim to self-understanding and self-determination—i.e., whether the author sanctions this aspiration or presents it with a degree of irony. In a straightforward philosophical treatise the presumption is that the writer does stand behind the ideas he presents, but that can by no means be taken for granted with works of literature (nor for that matter with the works of philosophers such as Kierkegaard or Nietzsche). The gist of my argument in subsequent chapters is that while Stephen Dedalus subscribes to a simplistic idea of individualism that deserves to be called modernist, Joyce shows us the costs and limitations of such a view, and thus should be seen as antimodernist.

There is an analogous confusion about what is involved in labeling various literary techniques or strategies modern. Is a literary strategy modern simply because it emerged during the "modern period"? Is a technique modern simply because it serves to dramatize or to present a modern theme in a work or a modern attitude on the part of a character, or does calling it modern imply that the technique inherently conveys or epitomizes the modernist world view? If a poet uses fragmentary presentation or ellipsis in order to evoke the disconnected character of modern experience (which he himself may abhor), is he using a *modern* technique? Simply because a writer uses "stream of consciousness," can we presume that the device is used to further modernist ends?[11] Such questions require careful attention because it is easy for us to slide into the view that if a writer uses "modern" techniques then she is a "modern" writer—implying that she subscribes to modernist ideas.

An instance of such blurring occurs even in so perspicacious a work as Michael Levenson's *A Genealogy of Modernism*. In his discussion of Eliot's *The Waste Land* Levenson makes two points. The first is that the poem intentionally dramatizes a situation lacking any "presiding consciousness, along the lines established by Conrad or James," presenting instead a "plurality of voices that sound in no easy harmony" (p. 191); Eliot, in significant contrast to his predecessors, "wrenched his poetry from the self-sufficiency of the single image and the single narrating consciousness" (p. 193). Second, Levenson argues that the poem disdains any specific *point d' appui*, such as European culture: rather, the poem "disallows the special claims of any single system"; it "acknowledges the greatest range of attitudes and faiths, with the consequence that none comes to final dominance" (p. 202). The result is that "history in the poem is not some consistent or continuous inheritance but something that the poem constructs and whose unity can no more be assumed than the unity of personality" (p. 204).

According to Levenson, then, *The Waste Land* is, technically and thematically, supra-individualistic and supra-provincial, and his discussion makes these values sound quite positive and implies that Eliot himself *advocates* the values of this modernist sensibility that he is depicting. But Levenson does not pursue this question of whether the unresolved, less-than-unified, polyglot situation of the poem is one that Eliot is in fact sanctioning, or one that he simply is dramatizing, perhaps even criticizing. Levenson strongly implies that Eliot does stand behind the poem's abandonment of a traditional "central consciousness" and its invoking so great and cosmopolitan a range of attitudes and faiths, but it seems more likely that while Eliot may sympathize with it, he does not admire or stand behind the deracinated, aimless situation of most of the poem's "characters." Levenson acknowledges that Eliot himself "was in flight from *The Waste Land* as soon as he completed it," and acknowledges further that Eliot "would never repeat its most distinctive devices: the severe discontinuities, the sustained mythic parallels, the reliance on Eastern belief and primitive ritual" (p. 206). And as Levenson points out, Eliot soon spoke disparagingly of the poem's accomplishment, and he espoused other, more traditionally European, values in his *Criterion* essays and editorials (pp. 206–12). In a more cautious and ambiguous statement, Levenson refers to the poem as "Eliot's *presentation* of the modernist position" (p. 209; my emphasis), thus leaving unclear whether these most implicit levels of the poem represent something that Eliot himself affirms or disdains. Surely, though, it is important that we know Eliot's attitude toward the deeper as well as the superficial aspects of his poem, since our judgment of that attitude determines what we think we mean when we call Eliot a "modern" writer. Finally, then, Levenson leaves unresolved—virtually unaddressed—the important issue of whether Eliot himself does stand behind the supra-individualistic, cosmopolitan (deracinated?) perspective that the poem embodies.

Another example of ambivalence in regard to the "modernism" of Eliot and of Joyce is John Blades's discussion in his *James Joyce: "A Portrait of the Artist as a Young Man."* Referring to *Ulysses* and *The Waste Land* as two works that stand out as monuments of modernism—which sounds quite positive—Blades then goes on to say that Eliot's poem "confronts and comes to terms with the theme of chaos," and further says that "though it clearly achieves an internal formal sort of order, it only dramatizes chaos, representing it through Eliot's pervasive tone of resignation and, through the poem's polemical ironies, attempts to fix or formulate it while at the same time acknowledging the helpless plight of the individual before the gathering tide of degeneration and nihilism" (p. 177), thus leaving the impression that Eliot's own position is distinctively antimodernist.

Similarly in regard to *Ulysses,* Blades repeatedly describes the novel in accents of apparent praise as modern or modernist, and says that its technical innovations "established both it and Joyce in the foreground of the Modernist movement" p. 186); and of *Portrait* he says that "its enduring significance is as a major landmark in the development of Modernism" (p. 188). Such comments inevitably suggest a favorable disposition toward modernism and leave the impression that Joyce was a proponent, a champion, of it. But Blades also says that "like *The Waste Land, Ulysses* is an attempt to come to terms with the dislocated individual in the Human Age" (p. 177). Even more puzzling is Blades's stance in regard to Joyce's attitude toward his protagonist. Blades is consistently critical of the life attitudes of Stephen Dedalus, who embodies so much of what Blades himself describes as modernist. He says, for example that "one of the novel's chief drawbacks is the character of Stephen himself, especially aspects like his callous pride, lack of humanity and obsessively dogmatic attitude to life" (p. 187), and he says that "next to *Ulysses* and even to *Dubliners, A Portrait* comes through as a sombre, earnest production but lacking most in humour and almost completely in human warmth, a direct consequence of the manifest limitations of its main character" (p. 187; see pp. 64–70 for other criticisms of

Stephen, especially his isolation and withdrawal). Furthermore, Blades never makes it clear whether he believes that Joyce shares his negative evaluation of Stephen. The result is a persistent vagueness in regard to important questions of Joyce's fundamental attitudes toward his work.

Failure to distinguish between an author's *presenting* various situations and his *sanctioning* of them is, then, an ineluctable source of confusion as to which authors, works, and techniques are modern, and in what sense.

5. Postmodernist Perspectives on Literary Modernism

A fifth form of confusion about literary modernism has emerged more recently, from two related but distinguishable sources. The first of these arises simply from the wish of some writers and critics to discover something *after* modernism that stands in contrast to it. This necessitates both positing an end to modernism, and being able to characterize whatever has developed since then with sufficient clarity to give it a name—most often, by default, postmodernism. A second source of this confusion involves more programmatic and tendentious attempts to appropriate "true" modernism into contemporary avant garde theories—e.g., to argue that many of the modernists were in fact proto-poststructuralists or closet deconstructionists. Though these two "retrospective" readings of modernism are closely akin, they are sufficiently different in motive and in effect that they should be discriminated.

Attempting to determine the end-point of modernism and to characterize what has happened since need not per se involve confusion; on the contrary, it would help us to understand modernism if we could establish its termination and recognize truly different subsequent attitudes. But in practice, introducing the idea of postmodernism has compounded the confusion. For one thing, it is by no means clear that modernism has expired and that we require a distinction between it and "postmodernism." Many critics would argue that such attempts would make a distinction where there is no substantial difference. Morton Levitt quite firmly denies the need for the term postmodernism, preferring to see even the most recent literature as an extension of modernism.[12] And perhaps more surprisingly, Ihab Hassan detects a similar skepticism about the demise of modernism on the part of John Barth, saying "even John Barth, as inward as any writer with postmodernism, now argues that postmodernism is a synthesis yet to come, and what we had assumed to be postmodernism all along was only later modernism, in 'The Literature of Replenishment: Postmodernist Fiction.'"[13]

The attempt to gain perspective by putting some distance between ourselves and the preceding generation is understandable, and we should not necessarily regard it skeptically. But those critics and writers who most strenuously insist on a distinction between modernism and postmodernism reflect a reactionism arising from an undue "anxiety of influence." That postmodernist proclamations often betray their immense debt to modernism by their vociferous assertion of difference has been acknowledged even by the champions of postmodernism. As Ihab Hassan has observed, "we come closer to the question of postmodernism itself by acknowledging the psychopolitics, if not the psychopathology, of academic life. Let us admit it: there is a will to power in nomenclature, as well as in people or texts. A new term opens for its proponents a space in language"; and more specifically of the term *postmodernism,* Hassan says "the word postmodernism sounds not only awkward, uncouth; it evokes what it wishes to surpass or suppress, modernism itself. The term thus contains its enemy within, as the terms romanticism and classicism, baroque and rococo, do not" ("Toward a Concept of Postmodernism," pp. 86, 87). Similarly, John Barth says of postmodernism "the term itself, like 'post-impressionism,' is awkward and faintly epigonic, suggestive less of a vigorous or even interesting new direction in the old art of storytelling than of something anticlimactic, feebly following a very hard act to follow."[14] William A. Johnsen also sees postmodernism as simplistically reactionary: "The new sensibility represents an epistemological break with the canonical Moderns, but on a deeper level it is another symptom of our compulsion to be new: postmodernism, out-moderning the moderns. The Contemporary strategies of antimyth, antimetaphor, being against interpretation, and postmodernism, have a deceptively obvious theoretical similarity; all define themselves by rejecting earlier modes of thought, especially modes peculiar to the Moderns of the early twentieth century."[15]

This persistent anxiety of influence forces the proponents of postmodernism to characterize modernism as far more traditional and conventional than it seemed to those who were writing or reading it, and to illustrate postmodernism by extreme devices and attitudes. The result is that much of the revolution in regard to subject matter and technique that high modernism had presumably achieved in the early decades of this century is now deferred and claimed for postmodernism. In the eyes of the postmodernists, modernism turns out to have been quite conservative, even stodgy.

⌐For example, at the time that they appeared, novels such as *Ulysses* and *The Sound and the Fury* were regarded as antitraditional and virtually chaotic; they defied the received rules of narration and involved the reader in the text in ways not required by traditional novels./ But as Carl D. Malmgren explains in his Barthean characterization of modernism, the modernist work, while perhaps superficially challenging, is quite "readerly" and almost conventional, in that it is committed to "the closure system of the West"; "in the modernist work, as in the classic text, 'everything holds together.'".[16] Malmgren goes on to develop an account of the modernist text as "readerly" that would surely have amazed those who were reading (or writing) those texts in the earlier decades of this century. He says, for example, "modernist works . . . offer themselves up to structuration, frequently falling back on the aesthetically satisfying totalization which the formal closure of structure supplies" (p. 14). As his prototypical postmodernist text, Malmgren takes John Barth's *Lost in the Funhouse*, a text which in a variety of ways, including its recurrent motif of "The Irish author James Joyce once wrote . . . ," betrays a striking anxiety of influence and reactionism. Malmgren himself explicitly acknowledges this: "Impoverished or intimidated by the monumental accomplishments of the great modernist tradition, the postmodernist imagination is reduced to 'all tell' and 'no show,' or to hackneyed banality, both of which are conducive to no little 'anxiety of influence.' . . . From the point of view of the hag-ridden postmodern writer, the inescapability of the inter-text is an hysterical/historical burden" (p. 23). The result of such attempts to distinguish modernism from postmodernism is, then, doubly unfortunate, resulting as it does both in a misleadingly conventional and traditional account of modernism, and in a postmodernism that defines itself in terms of a reactionary, hypertrophic "going beyond" whatever was characteristic of modernism.

In addition to these characterizations of modernism by contrast with postmodernism (and vice versa), there is another kind of retrospective view of modernism that takes the opposite tack—but one that is more tendentious and that has a stronger agenda beneath it. This is the attempt to appropriate certain high modern writers and works and strategies to the programs of structuralist or deconstructionist criticism—to read modernism, that is, as a forerunner and validator of these avant garde modes. Usually this approach requires the critic either to argue that there is an underlying, unacknowledged continuity between modernism and deconstruction, or to distinguish between *true* modernism, which is now seen to be the spring-head of deconstruction, and *pseudo*-modernism, which in the view of contemporary theoreticians turns out to have been quite conventional—to have been in fact traditionalism in disguise.

Though an array of examples might be invoked to illustrate this attitude, in the present context it will work best to consider such retrospective views of Joyce and his works. This is appropriate both because no single high modernist writer has been more appropriated by poststructuralists than has Joyce—Derrida has gone so far as to say that without James Joyce deconstruction could not have come into being—and because it will pro-vide a context for my subsequent claims about *A Portrait of the Artist*.

A comment by Richard Pearce in his brief essay "What Joyce after Pynchon?" provides a nice transition from the preceding point about at-tempts to discriminate between modernism and postmodernism and the present point about appropriating modernism (and Joyce) to contemporary theory. There Pearce says "let me begin by arguing that there is no differ-ence between modernism and postmodernism. It is only that revolutionary writers like Joyce had to be read in a conservative way"[17] (1986, p. 43). Pearce argues that once we are able to see Joyce through a post-Pynchon perspective, we can more readily resist the regularizing tendencies that "modernist" reading had fostered in us and recognize Joyce for what he was—a postmodernist before his time. We can, that is, get beyond our "refusing to recognize that *Ulysses* was 'ineluctably constructed upon the incertitude of the void,'" and ask ourselves whether we have been "misled by the mode of reading that masqueraded as modernist writing, that reached its flower in the new criticism, that we are now recognizing as imperialistic and totalizing" (pp. 44, 46).

Pearce's brief essay employs several moves that are typical of recent attempts to appropriate Joyce for deconstruction—the claim that only to privileged present-day eyes can Joyce be seen in his true (revolutionary) light; the implication that what many had naively thought was modernism was in fact imperialism in disguise; and the characteristic attribution to earlier critics of an appalling naivete or a perverse refusal to face reality—the whole cast in a vocabulary of intellectual Realpolitik.[18]

Another similar example, with an Irish slant, is that of Richard Kearney, who in his *Transitions: Narratives in Modern Irish Culture* (Dublin: Wolfhound Press, 1988), accommodates Joyce to the deconstructionist program. Kearney is one of several present-day Irish critics who for various reasons make W. B. Yeats, whom they regard as aristocratic and traditional, a whipping boy, and by contrast see the tougher-minded Joyce as their spiritual mentor. According to Kearney, "whereas Yeats moved back towards a premodern culture, Joyce moved forward to a postmodern one. He opted for a radicalist rather than a revivalist version of modernism; a version which revolted against traditional notions both of cultural identity and literary narrative. . . . He preferred to deconstruct rather than reconstruct the myth of a Unity of Culture" (pp. 31–32). Predictably, Kearney sees *Finnegans Wake* as Joyce's work that most fully manifests his deconstructionist tendencies: "*Finnegans Wake* is a deconstructing, or rather self-deconstructing, narrative which reveals language to be an infinite interplay of multiple meanings" (p. 34). But typically, Kearney traces Joyce's deconstructionism back into his earlier works: "Joyce's deconstruction of the classical conventions of narrative did not confine itself, however, to *Finnegans Wake*. It was already under way in *A Portrait* and *Ulysses*" (p. 35). *Portrait* is "as the self-reflexive title suggests, a parody of the quest-structure of the traditional bourgeois novel" (p. 37), and "in *Ulysses* the narrative quest of the 'artist' son (Stephen) for his 'artificer' father (Bloom) is brought to its absurd conclusion" (p. 39). In an Appendix entitled "Joyce and Derrida," Kearney pursues his deconstructionist reading even more fully, arguing that both *Ulysses* and *Finnegans Wake* manifest Derrida's critique of Western logocentrism, the first mainly through Molly's "woman's reason," the second via "the equally deconstructing, equivocating, decentering language of Anna Livia Plurabelle" (p. 43).[19]

As we shall see in later chapters, Joyce's works are today caught in a tug of war between two opposing critical attitudes—those on the one hand that claim Joyce for deconstruction, and those on the other that see his works as involving discernible values and presenting a critique of the modernist-postmodernist-deconstructionist mentality. Those in the first camp see Joyce as a harbinger of some of the leading ideas of structuralist and poststructuralist theory—e.g., skepticism in regard to the reality of history and of the self, of meaning, of narrative integrity, etc. (Critics within this camp include Steven Helmling, Colin MacCabe, Hélène Cixous, John Paul Riquelme, and Stephen Heath.) On the other hand are those who argue that Joyce never endorsed the austerities and skepticisms even of modernism, much less those of deconstruction. These critics argue that while Joyce does dramatize an

irony

array of modernist problems, and many of his characters are enamoured of various modernist notions, Joyce handles such ideas and characters ironically, invoking in the process such traditional ideas as the continuity of history and the unity of the self and an array of traditional values such as charity and openness to experience, and criticizing xenophobia, mawkish sentimentality, scientistic objectivity, scholarly abstrusiosities, etc. (Critics of this persuasion include Morton Levitt, Marilyn French, Stanley Sultan, Marguerite Harkness, and Joseph Buttigieg.) I take my place in this second group, regarding Joyce's *Portrait of the Artist* as a brilliant dramatization of certain modernist tendencies that Joyce exposes as superficial and specious.

Individual and Cultural Psyche in Modernism

Having discussed various impediments to characterizing modernism, I must now tack in a complementary direction and develop a view of modernism that will clarify and justify my description of Joyce's *Portrait of the Artist* as antimodernist. The aspects of modernist thought that I wish to bring into focus in preparation for discussing *Portrait* involve two main ideas. The first of these is the pervasiveness of the subject/object, mind/matter dichotomy in the modern psyche, a dichotomy that stems from Descartes' distinction between *res extensa* and *res cogitans,* which itself grew out of Galileo's earlier distinction between primary and secondary qualities. While this dichotomy has been extensively discussed, we have not yet fully appreciated the effects that it has had on our world view and on our image of our selves, especially in regard to our attitude toward the ontological status of human consciousness and of the psychic aspects of reality generally. The second aspect of modernist thinking that I wish to focus involves certain skeptical modernist ideas about the individual psyche and the social psyche—ideas that derive from Hume and the Enlightenment philosophes, but that also stem eventually from Descartes and from Galileo. In regard to the individual psyche, these ideas include the notion that the mind is a *tabula rasa* and that self-knowledge is both feasible and desirable. In regard to the social or collective psyche these ideas involve deep skepticism as to the very existence of any such entity, because of the assumption that consciousness exists (if at all) only in individual persons.[20]

Understanding these ideas is essential to appreciating the critique of modernist thinking that Joyce develops in *Portrait.*

The modernist worldview comes down to us from Galileo, from Francis Bacon, from Descartes, Hobbes, Newton, Hume, and the French philosophes, though its roots lie much deeper in the Western psyche—all the way back to Platonic idealism and Greek atomism, both of which in quite different ways reveal a metaphysical bias towards stasis rather than process.[21] This worldview is clearly expressed in the conjunction of seventeenth-century scientific empiricism and Enlightenment rationalism. From scientific "empiricism" (a term whose inherent contradictions we shall examine shortly) we get a corpuscular-kinetic or matter-in-motion view of reality as consisting of small discrete material entities that move about in space in ways that are described by the laws of physics. We are given to understand that the objects of our everyday world—chairs, desks, even our own bodies and brains—consist at bottom of such entities. We are told too that on the atomic scale—the scale that, according to the modernist view, manifests reality most directly—there is no intentionality or consciousness, nor are there any "abstractions" or "ideas." Admittedly we do not ordinarily walk about in a world that we conceive in this way—we walk about in the phenomenological world of objects, qualities, other persons—and yet our respect for science intimidates us into supposing that this naturalistic account describes what the world out there really is. Analogously, the view of "mind" or "psyche" (insofar as the corpuscular worldview permits such a thing) that comes down to us from both British empiricism and from Enlightenment rationalism is that of a *tabula rasa* that has no characterizable nature and no depth, and that receives all of its information through the physiological channels of the five senses. Furthermore, this line of thought assumes that it is both feasible and desirable to be fully self-conscious and self-aware—to articulate and even to be critical of all of one's ideas and assumptions. Finally, this line of thought admits the possibility of mind or psyche only in conjunction with an individual person's body and brain, thus rendering suspect any notion of psychic aspects of ordinary nature (e.g., trees) or any artifact (e.g., a basket), or any notion of a social or collective psyche that is anything other than the additive sum of individual minds (i.e., brains).

The "crisis of modernism" produced by this Modernist Syndrome is essentially a crisis in regard to the status of psyche, and especially of human mentality or consciousness, whether individual or cultural, within the whole of reality. The crisis involves our having implicitly accepted not only a subject/object, mind/matter dichotomy, but also the idea that the only place that mind or psyche exists is in individual persons—and even there in a precarious state. As these ideas and their implications filter down and have broader effect, human beings come to regard themselves as aliens in the universe, and to regard the cultural entities they have brought into being as less than substantial. Human consciousness comes to be seen not as our species's distinctive expression of something present in various forms and modes in every qualitative aspect of reality, but as an utter anomaly or fluke, having emerged at some relatively late stage of the evolutionary process (which is understood as sheerly random, not as involving any emergent or teleological aspect); human consciousness is thus not a blessing but a curse. This is not to imply that these ideas have emerged so clearly as to become settled conclusions; rather they exist as fears, misgivings, whose implications have been clearer to some than to others.

To understand better the Modernist Syndrome's skepticism in regard to consciousness, we should attend briefly to the distinction between primary and secondary qualities that has been so important a part of Western thought for the past several centuries. Though we usually associate this distinction with John Locke (because in his *Essay Concerning Human Understanding* [1690] he elaborated it and integrated it into his larger system), the discrimination was made clear by Galileo. It is not surprising that it was Galileo who introduced this idea; it was virtually predictable that he should, because the distinction was engendered by the increasingly precise observation and quantification that instruments such as the telescope brought about. As it became possible to observe and quantify phenomena more precisely, Galileo felt the need to distinguish between those aspects of reality that are "in the objects themselves" (such as mass and extension—i.e., weight, and length and breadth) and those qualities that exist in the observer's response to reality (such as taste, color, odor). The former, Galileo called primary qualities; the latter, secondary qualities. The primary qualities he presumed to reside in the objects themselves, but of the secondary Galileo said, "I think that tastes, odors, colors, and so forth are no more than mere names so far as pertains to the subject wherein they reside, and that they have their habitation only in the sensorium. Thus, if the living creature were removed, all these qualities would be removed and annihilated."[22] Galileo goes on to say, "I do not believe that for exciting in us tastes, odors, and sounds there are required in external bodies anything but sizes, shapes, numbers, and slow or fast movements; and I think that if ears, tongues, and noses were taken away, shapes and numbers and motions would remain but not odors or tastes or sounds. These are, I believe, nothing but names, apart from the living animal" (p. 311). Of this, his editor and translator Stillman Drake says, "Galileo's revival of atomism is a good illustration of his anti-metaphysical approach. Where Democritus did not escape endowing his atoms with the very qualities they were designed to explain, such as sharpness or roughness, Galileo stripped them of all such qualities and required motion alone to account for all sensation" (p. xxv).

This distinction is worth attending to because it so clearly involves a severance between the "objective, real" world of material objects in motion, and the "subjective, less-than-real" world of the individual's mind, and as such it is the thin edge of the wedge that was subsequently driven deeper into the modern Western mind by Descartes' proclamation of two utterly different substances, matter and mind. If we take Galileo's distinction seriously, we are led to the conclusion that if all observers were eliminated from the scene—or if the planet Earth were destroyed, since it appears to be the sole locus of sensient creatures—what would remain would be matter in motion, utterly devoid of all sounds, colors, textures—in short of all those qualities that are "brought into being" by the mind of the perceiver and that the Modernist Syndrome describes as "merely subjective."

This distinction thus involves issues that have increasingly troubled the Western mind (as they have come slowly to the surface) over the past several centuries. Essentially, there are two questions: the first is whether the "real world" in the absence of an observer truly involves anything other than the quality-less matter-in-motion described by Galileo and by Newtonian physics—a question that has serious implications for our conception of a social or collective psyche; the second is whether, if it exists only in one recently (and randomly) evolved species on one small planet in an out-of-the-way corner of the cosmos, human consciousness represents anything real at all, or whether it is not better understood as a random epiphenomenon.

To attend briefly to the first: if it is true that secondary qualities depend upon an observer, then what is the world "really like," in the absence of all observers? Is it really a world devoid of all sounds, colors, textures—of all qualities? What is any object "as in itself it really is," to invoke a phrase that we shall return to shortly? Further, it is a crucial feature of Galileo's account of primary/secondary qualities that the observer is presumed to be an *individual person*. It is presumed, that is, that the sensorium capable of responding to matter-in-motion in terms of color or odor or sound is in an individual's mind, which has access to the real, material world by means of its senses. Though it has taken Western thought some time to assimilate and realize the implications of this presumption, there is no place in this schema for a "cultural mind" or a "social psyche," since a qualitative response to the movements of minute particles is possible only for an individual mind, by virtue of its existing in a sensorally-endowed physical body. All of us have heard the old conundrum about whether any sound is produced by a tree that falls in a forest if no one is there to hear it; we have heard it so much that it is difficult to take its implications seriously. But according to the corpuscular world view, not only does the tree make no sound if there is no one there to hear it, the entire forest, if uninhabited, is utterly devoid of all qualities of sound, color, texture, and even of "objects" such as "trees," since (as we shall see), the very whatness or *quidditas* of such objects is as dependent upon some psychic observer for their realization as are these perceptual qualities.[23]

As to the second question raised by Galileo's distinction, if consciousness, mind, psyche, is an evolutionary late arrival and fluke—something unique to the recent history of one planet—how seriously can we take its reality? There are those humanists who would claim that the circumstances of origin or the apparent uniqueness of consciousness are beside the point—that what is important is that consciousness does now exist. But if we see consciousness or psyche as coming into being at a late stage in a sheerly material world—one consisting of matter-in-motion and involving no primordial aspect of "psyche"—then we can never regard it as anything but an unaccountable, unreal freak that never interfaces with "reality" in any meaningful way.[24]

There have of course been attempts to maintain the significance, the reality, of human consciousness, even while acknowledging that it exists only in individual persons or that it is an evolutionary fluke. In the late nineteenth century certain writers (e.g., Rimbaud, Pater, Wilde) even claimed to exult in their subjectivity, proclaiming it more real than the physical world that it was divorced from. But more perspicacious thinkers soon recognized such proclamations as either bravado or self-deception, and this attempt to maintain the significance (or even the existence) of an entity that is not sanctioned by the corpuscular world view has become a crucial part of the modernist crisis, one more effect of Descartes' positing two utterly distinct substances. Given our Cartesian heritage, those who reflect most clearly on the implications of this world view will be brought quickest to the conclusion that consciousness is, for all the bravado we may muster, an anomaly, marking human beings not as the "highest" of the creatures, but rather as freaks whose distinctive traits can finally bring them only misery.[25]

Intellectual historian H. Stuart Hughes, in his *Consciousness and Society* (Brighton: Harvester Press, 1979), says that "nearly all of the students of the last years of the nineteenth century have sensed in some form or other a profound psychological change. Yet they have differed markedly in the way in which they have expressed their understanding of it" (p. 34). In my view the profound psychological changes that were surfacing at this time arose from the gradual unfolding of the implications of the ideas of Galileo and Descartes that we have been tracing. These changes were difficult to recognize and characterize because on the one hand they called into question something so basic as human consciousness, and on the other they involved the apparent passing away of implicit cultural entities—the social psyche or collective consciousness—that had never before been fully articulated, much less challenged.[26]

The modernist crisis, which has been gathering momentum for several centuries, is to a large extent a crisis about the status of consciousness, of psyche, in the universe. One effect of this crisis is an inevitable conflict between our wholistic experience as human beings, and what we can articulate of that experience through the schemes of analytical thought that have authority for us. Each of us lives within a continuum of consciousness that is the basis of all our qualitative experience and of all of our values—a "semi-transparent envelope surrounding us from the beginning of consciousness to the end," as Virginia Woolf described it in her essay "Modern Fiction." But the matter-in-motion worldview that modern Western culture implicitly defers to does not enable us to sustain or justify any conception of consciousness, to give any account of psyche, and so the typical modernist lives in constant unease and defensiveness about the reality of the very basis of his or her being. In one sense, then, the modernist crisis involves an unbridgeable gap between our lived experience, and our attempts to "give an account" of that experience within the parameters of a frame of explanation that is utterly antithetical to many implicit features of our experience. Since we are reflective as well as sentient creatures, we do need some degree of congruence between our experience and our understanding. But the schema of ideas that we defer to in the modern Western climate of opinion renders any such congruence impossible.

Viewing our dilemma in this way, we can more readily trace its roots back to David Hume, who in frighteningly clear-eyed fashion pursued the implications of the "new philosophy" that he had inherited from Locke and from Galileo and was led by the logic of his underlying ideas to develop a philosophy that he admitted he could not live by.[27] From his day forward, we have been in the self-contradictory situation of deferring to a schema of thought that in effect denies the existence of mind, and thus has no place whatsoever for the very mind that brings the schema into being. In a naive observer this situation should prompt incredulity— how can we grant authority to an idea-scheme, a world view, that has been generated by our own minds, that claims to have no place for mentality? And while this anomaly may have remained beneath the conscious notice of many people, it has affected the tenor of experience in Western culture in the past several centuries in ways that few persons have totally escaped, and the implicit tensions it involves have dramatically erupted in several of the hyper-sensitive minds that have been among the pioneers of modern Western thought—e.g., Blake, Kierkegaard, Poe, Melville, Nietzsche, Gerard de Nerval.

Lest these issues seem tangential, I want to show how directly they impinge upon literary modernism by exploring a juxtaposition made by Ihab Hassan in his essay "The Critic as Innovator: A Paracritical Strip in X Frames." In that essay Hassan suggests how several of our contemporary attitudes were foreshadowed by Oscar Wilde in his essays, and as a part of this he says "Matthew Arnold, we recall, enjoined critics (in 1864 in 'The Function of Criticism at the Present Time') 'to see the object as in itself it really is.' This precept soon began to shift toward a more subjective focus in the criticism of Ruskin and Pater. But it remained for Wilde to stand Arnold on his head, and scandalously to suggest that the aim of the critic is to see the object as it really is not."[28]

I believe that between these two dicta of Arnold and of Wilde there exists a major watershed of Western thought as regards the place of psyche (roughly, of consciousness) in reality. For when Arnold enjoined the critic to see the object "as in itself it really is," he was of course referring to an object that consisted not simply of matter in motion—not, that is of a physical substrate that involved mass and extension only—but to an object that he presumed "in itself" involved certain qualities, forms, and colors.[29] He was in effect calling upon the critic to avoid any personal idiosyncrasy that might distort his perspective and keep him from doing justice to "the object." In other words, Arnold's adjuration presumed a public object, one with its "secondary qualities" and its object quality very much intact, as it really is in the "social consciousness." For Wilde, on the contrary, there was a terrible presumptuousness or irony in Arnold's behest, since Wilde— much more of a modernist—knew that to try to describe the object "as in itself it really is," would deprive it of all the paraphernalia given it by the subjectivity of the observer; to describe an object as it really is, "objectively," without the enhancements of some one's personal, perhaps idiosyncratic, subjectivity, would require us to talk in terms only of matter in motion, or mass and extension—which, according to Galileo and to Newtonian physics—is all that the object as in itself it really is involves. And for this reason Wilde insisted that what we must do is to describe this paltry objective entity it as it really is *not*—i.e., to describe it as it appears "subjectively" to some individual, idiosyncratic person.

We hear much of the death of God in the late nineteenth century as one of the milestones of modern intellectual history. But casting the modernist crisis in such terms obscures it by rendering it at once too stereotyped and too dramatic. The watershed between the dicta of Arnold and of Wilde is best understood not as the death of God, but as the evanescence of the social psyche, the collective consciousness. That is, when Arnold spoke of the object as in itself it really is, he was not (as Bishop Berkeley was) thinking of the object as sustained by the mind of God; Arnold did not need to invoke God every time he wished to refer to a public object. What he did (implicitly) invoke was a public, cultural/psychic "medium" in which the object existed with all of its qualities, primary and secondary, regardless of whether any individual was observing those qualities. For Wilde (and for modernists generally) there is no such mystical medium sustaining the wholistic object; there are only individual minds-in-bodies, through whose subjective perceptions the mute matter in motion of objective reality is given color and shape and texture. And so the modernist critic must attend not to the mere proto-object given him by nature, but to the subjectively-accoutered object as he finds it in his own private sensorium.

The crisis of modernism, then, was in effect an unfolding crisis in regard to the ontological status of consciousness, of psyche. By no means clearly defined for those who were experiencing it, the crisis involved a progressive skepticism about whether psyche, consciousness, subjectivity really exists anywhere except in individuals—i.e., whether psyche manifests inherent, enduring aspects of reality reflected in nature and in culture, or is merely some evolutionary fluke in the history of our planet and thus some wishful, self-indulgent illusion. At one stage, the crisis expressed itself in a self-assertive and seemingly confident subjectivism or impressionism, as if the resilient subjectivist found nothing to regret in Descartes' severance of *res cogitans* from *res extensa,* preferring to revel in his own domain, and even to show others how to burn with a hard, gem-like flame. But at a subsequent stage it emerged that this subjectivism had been speciously sustained by a public psyche that had been implicitly relied upon as the medium enabling communication among all of the subjectivities; once this medium was called into question (since there was no place for it in the schema of Galileo and Descartes), what had been self-assertive subjectivism necessarily devolved into solipsism. Deprived of the sustaining social-psychic atmosphere it had implicitly relied on, the individual flame guttered out.[30] Furthermore, for clearer-minded persons, it became obvious that without the medium of the cultural psyche—which, once articulated, seemed an unwarranted presumption—not even objects "as in themselves they really are" have any full-scale, qualitative existence (i.e., any existence other than as matter in motion), except when they are being perceived by some individual observer. For how could any rigorous-minded person, scanning the whole of the universe from atom to galaxy, and finding "subjectivity" in only one species on one small planet in some out-of-the-way part of the cosmos, seriously believe that consciousness, individual or social, represented anything but a fluke or an illusion? Though these troubling implications of Galileo's and Descartes' and Hume's thought took several centuries to filter down, they were always present, to be sensed by any sufficiently perceptive mind, and for this reason, the proclamation of subjectivity as a domain separate and sacrosanct—the mind entirely as its own place—has been a rather defensive and pretentious voice in the modern Western intellectual milieu.

One important implication of the matter-in-motion world view, then, is that we (i.e., modernists) have become deeply skeptical about supra-individual psychic (or psychological) perspectives. As a result we feel that

⌐any response to "reality" (i.e., the external world of matter in motion) that involves any attribution of value or of judgment must reflect the perspective of some individual person, because there is no such thing as a "public subjective" perspective. All accounts are either "objective" (a term that, whenever applied to human affairs, embodies deep confusions), or else they are individual and thus subjective and private; there is for the modernist no account that is both valuational (i.e., that involves values, or qualities) and public, because, from the modernist perspective, there is no cultural psyche, no collective consciousness, to sustain valuational or moral judgments.

This skepticism in regard to a cultural psyche, which filtered down into the awareness of many persons—especially it seems of many writers—in the late nineteenth century, has had specific literary effects. We are told that the purported abandonment of traditional omniscient point of view by modernist novelists reflects their recognition that there simply is no "omniscient" perspective. Morton Levitt for example speaks of "the Modernists' endeavor to develop narrative techniques which place modern man in his true setting—principally their development of a point of view that removes the omniscient-omnipotent Victorian God at the center of the narrative and replaces him with limited, representative man" (*Modernist Survivors,* p. 20). But this account of what lies behind the presumed abandonment of omniscient point of view clouds the issues and would make a virtue of something which for reflective persons is a crisis. First of all, the analogy between traditional "omniscient" point of view and an omniscient-omnipotent God, though apparently sanctioned by the term "omniscient," is shaky and imprecise, for it is doubtful that the traditional omniscient point of view ever "stood for" or represented the mind of God. In practice, the "omniscient" point of view, while it did tell more than any one observer could know, never really told all; it confined and constrained itself in a variety of ways, reflecting something more like a conventionalized and localized cultural psyche than the omniscient, ubiquitous God of the Judeo-Christian religion. That is, when modernist critics consider issues of point of view, and when they scrutinize the narrative procedure of pre-modern writers, they ask themselves what perspective the point of view of the novel purports to represent—or more mundanely, where is this observer or commentator standing? And for the modernist critic there are two easily conceivable answers: either the novelist is standing in the perspective of some individual person (which

Levitt with some imprecision equates with "limited, representative man"), or she is standing in the perspective of "God." For as vague or dubious as this latter term may seem, the modernist is far more familiar and comfortable with it than with saying that the point of view represents some "public cultural psyche"—something that he finds very difficult to conceive.[31]

We should realize that what is for us a problem was not even a question for the premodern writer; that is, it is unlikely that Fielding or Austen ever interrogated themselves about the precise perspective that their point of view "embodied," since they lived in a climate of opinion in which various aspects of the "modern crisis"—including the fear that qualitative and interpretive perspectives exist only in individuals—had not yet emerged. Moreover, it is inaccurate and presumptuous to think that the "omniscient" perspective has been eliminated from modern literature. The author in modernist fiction does conceal or efface himself or herself more than did the traditional author, but we should not delude ourselves that there is no authorial perspective. The implicit claim of those who say that omniscient narration is a thing of the past, is that no perspective exists in modernist fiction that we cannot readily triangulate through naturalistic coordinates— i.e., that we cannot equate with the perspective of some "representative man." But this is manifestly not the case—certainly not in Joyce's *Portrait* or *Ulysses*—for in fiction that involves anything other than a very strictly maintained first-person point of view, we still find words on the page that represent some supra-individual authorial perspective or some shadowy narrative persona, that we cannot readily conceptualize within a modernist frame of reference—words that inevitably involve some selective, valuational perspective. We still have, that is, words spoken by, or representative of, some "authorial presence" hovering near (and within) the character that represents something like 1) the old-fashioned omniscient God, or 2) some manifestation of a collective cultural psyche. Before we presume that our present day "humanistic" perspective has freed us from the supernaturalism of the nineteenth century, we should adknowledge that there are many value-laden words on the pages of our novels, evoking some qualitative perspective other than that of an individual character, and we should ask ourselves what we think those words represent.[32]

There is another equally serious problem obscured by Levitt's sanguine assumption that modernist narrative techniques reflect "limited, representative man"—namely, that, as we have seen, all that the post-Humean, modernist perspective really permits is individual, *solipsistic* man. That is, Levitt would presumably answer the question about what a present-day disembodied narrator represents by saying that it is neither God nor the "collective consciousness," but the perspective of "representative man." Sensible as this proposal at first sounds, positing such a thing smuggles in another entity that is supra-personal and that has predictably been challenged by modernist nominalism—i.e., "human nature." That is, according to rigorous modernism (à la Sartre) there is no "representative man," only separate, solipsistic individuals.

Michael Levenson has also discussed some of the purported effects of these philosophical issues in literary techniques, but he seems not fully to appreciate what they involve, especially when it comes to qualitative or valuational statements that are not attributed to an individual character. Levenson begins his *A Genealogy of Modernism* with a close analysis of a paragraph in Conrad's *The Nigger of the "Narcissus"* which involves a shift of perspective from an unattributed "evocative physical description" to the perspective of a narrator. Levenson says that at the outset of this paragraph, "the prose is restrained, the narrative tone detached," there is the typically Conradian close attention to detail, sensitivity to motion, eye for the telling gesture, but that Conrad "clings fastidiously to externals" and restricts his attention to "the directly available sensory surface," so that all is presented as description, with similes serving to suggest psychological attitudes or states. According to Levenson, "it is plain that the conventions of omniscience were breaking down, and that one result was an increased dependence on evocative physical description" (p. 5). As the paragraph progresses, however, the emotion deepens and then the "perspective abruptly alters" to that of an explicit narrator, whose various feelings and values are quite tangibly expressed.

Levenson then makes this observation:

> Once *the leap into consciousness* is made, no need remains for the painstaking *reconstruction* of subjectivity by means of accumulated detail or evocative metaphor. Psychology, emotion, attitude become immediately accessible. There need be no scruples about the text penetrating a consciousness, because the text has become identical with a consciousness. Where an author may not go, the narrator is entitled to tread because, *as a fictional character, he may quite plausibly give utterance to his beliefs, perceptions, inferences.* Conrad no longer hesitates to make direct statements of attitude or to use psychological verbs (e.g. "admired," "loved"). (Ibid., p. 6; my emphasis)

Levenson then quotes for contrast a passage from the end of chapter 61 of George Eliot's *Middlemarch* involving an essentially "omniscient" point of view, of which he says "part of every fiction is *physis,* the elaboration of an external physical space, and part is *psyche,* the construction of an internal psychological space. For George Eliot, as this passage reveals, the two regions open readily into one another: both submit to her narrating eye" (Ibid., p. 7). Levenson then goes on briefly to characterize the point of view of the passage, saying that "the narrator is not another character, but a disembodied presence, moving freely over the dramatic scene, and granted prerogatives not allowed to mere mortals" (Ibid., p. 8; note the deific implication). Returning then to Conrad's *Nigger,* he says "in *The Nigger of the 'Narcissus'* he makes what amounts to a division of narrative labor. The third-person narrator provides the precision of physical detail but hesitates to penetrate the individual psyche which George Eliot had so remorselessly invaded. Only with the shift to the first person is there a comfortable indulgence in moral and psychological speculation. . . . While he is by no means systematic in his alteration between [these points of view], the shifts reveal the pressures upon an omniscience no longer confident that it knows all" (Ibid., p. 8).

While I find parts of this analysis perspicacious, certain aspects of it call for sharper scrutiny. Here again we have the assumption that the shift from Victorian omniscience to the more restricted modes of point of view in modernist (or pre-modernist) fiction involve unease on the author's part about his right to whatever the omniscient perspective was presumed to represent. But if this were in fact Conrad's concern—if it formed his justification for the divided labor of his narrative voices—his solution was superficial and shortsighted. The presumed logic behind Conrad's strategy (according to Levenson) is to be more faithful to the modernist awareness that there is no omniscient perspective, only that of individuals, and for this reason, Conrad's prose changes qualitatively when he takes on the persona of a specific observer, becoming more psychological and valuational. But surely the earlier sentences of the paragraph that Levenson has quoted involve various prestidigations that are virtually equivalent to omniscience— or at least that have no place in a rigorously construed modernist worldview. For not only does that account involve qualities (e.g., momentous, struggle, gravely heavy), it involves an overall qualitative perspective that must finally be consciousness-grounded. In short, when Conrad's unattributed narrator presents an "evocative physical description" of objects, he (and Levenson) is still implicitly assuming Arnold's public "object as in itself it really is." That is, no mere recording instrument in a comparable situation, even one strategically placed by a designing proto-author, could give an account in any way approaching what we are given in these sentences. The account is not only valuational, it is qualitative and perspectival; it is "empirical" (i.e., experiential) in a sense that no instrumental account could possibly be. These opening sentences involve a perspective that by rigorous modernist standards is just as metaphysically dubious as that assumed by Eliot. We may, of course, say that even these opening sentences reflect the consciousness of the We who emerges into tangibility in the fifth sentence. But to say that, of course, would dissolve and undermine the very distinction that Levenson is making between "evocative physical description" and narration via a first-person narrator.[33]

Though Levenson does not invoke Arnold's phrase, his book does show that early modernist writers such as Pound and Ford Madox Ford worried a good bit over whether their task was to describe reality "as in itself it really is," or to be true to their own perceptions, and Levenson shows how some of these modernist writers vacillated from one view to the other. Whether they realized it or not, they were struggling with the question of whether there is in fact any im-personal description of reality that is compatible with the modernist world view, the authority of which was becoming ever stronger. But these writers could hardly afford to acknowledge that if we do follow the mind/matter dichotomy to its logical endpoint, then mind—consciousness—is revealed to be nothing more than an epiphenomenon that can make no meaningful claim to affect, or even accurately to describe, reality. We are left with nothing other than the sensationalist solipsism that Walter Pater had so clearly foreshadowed and Oscar Wilde had expressed in his response to Arnold.

Thus while the influence of the modernist climate of opinion can undoubtedly be traced in the literary techniques of early twentieth century novelists, I challenge on two counts the claim that this fiction disavowed the "omniscient" point of view because that perspective conformed to Victorian belief in an omniscient God. First, it is erroneous to claim that twentieth-century fiction has disavowed omniscience, and especially so to claim that it presents no valuational perspectives except those of individual characters. This overlooks the innumerable modes of authorial presence that pervade this fiction. Second, to construe the modernist crisis as the death of God is inaccurate and overly-dramatic; rather, it involves the

erosion or evaporation of any basis for public valuational perspectives—
i.e., of any collective consciousness or cultural psyche. The question these
authors were so troubled by was not whether Jehovah was still in his
heaven, but whether there is any valuational, qualitative perspective other
than that of isolated individuals—i.e., of whether there is any such thing as
a cultural psyche—or even *culture*—in any meaningful sense.

Another perspective on the issues at stake in the modernist crisis is
provided by our considering the term "scientific empiricism"—a term that
has had authority for several centuries, but that is misleading and even self-
contradictory. The erosion of the term's meaning was implicit in Galileo's
primary/secondary quality distinction. For what empiricism *should* mean is
a perspective upon reality that takes the standpoint of human experience—
i.e., a qualitative and experiential perspective. Originally it was acknowledged that science was grounded in perception and thus depended upon
consciousness and was "empirical" in this qualitative, experiential sense.
This reliance of science upon wholistic perception enabled apologists for
science even as late as T. H. Huxley to say, "all the phaenomena of Nature
are, in their ultimate analysis, known to us only as facts of consciousness."[34]
But by Huxley's time science was already well along in the process of
abandoning human perception and consciousness in favor of instrumental
perspectives that view reality "objectively," without any anthropomorphic
"distortion"—which of course gave impetus to the more general shift of
attitude we have traced between Arnold and Wilde. And once we have
reached the stage where instrumentalism supersedes and disavows fallible
human perceptions, there is no longer any scientific sanction for the perspective of consciousness, which comes to be regarded as "merely subjective" and thus anomalous and solipsistic. We must, then, recognize that the
term "scientific empiricism" hides the treacherous implication that what
science deals in is the empirical, with the implication that the only valid
"empiricism" is that amenable to instrumental science. We are thus deprived of the term for human use—i.e., empiricism no longer really implies
a human perspective—and so we must resort to another term, such as
"phenomenological" (which then becomes metaphysically suspect), to try
to indicate some truly qualitative perspective.[35] According to the characterization of the modernist view of reality that I am proposing, then, the
clearest contemporary expressions of the Modernist Syndrome are behavioristic psychology and computer models of the mind that would call into

Modernist view

question the very existence of consciousness—though there are many other less obvious progeny of Hume among twentieth century intellectual movements.[36]

For our purposes one important implication of this characterization of modernism is that there is an inherent tension between modernist thought and virtually all literature. Given my characterization of the Modernist Syndrome, literature is inherently antimodernist. For it seems clear that very little literature can be written within the parameters of the world view that is sanctioned by scientific empiricism and Enlightenment rationalism. Insofar as we take the *tabula rasa* image of the mind seriously, insofar as we give authority to Hume's ideas that we experience nothing but discrete sensations and that we thus have no experience of causation, insofar as we accept the Enlightenment idea that the contents of our minds can be fully articulated and understood, insofar as we accept the behavioristic idea that human acts have no element of volition and Marvin Minsky's claim that consciousness is nonexistent or an illusion[37]—insofar as we accept these quintessentially modernist ideas, literature has virtually no room in which to work. Especially is it true of great novelists—novelists such as Hardy and Joyce and Lawrence and Woolf, whose works evoke so rich a sense of character and of milieu and of the subtle relationships between human personality and locale—that their works in general and their sense of human personality in particular stand in diametrical opposition to all of the most characteristic ideas and attitudes that comprise the Modernist Syndrome.

Let me now redeem from redundancy this assertion that all writers are antimodernist by clarifying how these writers *are* modern. They are modern not simply in a trivial chronological sense, nor in the sense that they espouse modernist ideas, but in devoting their works to understanding and dramatizing various aspects of the "modern crisis." The modern writer accepts the intellectual and artistic challenge of depicting in his or her characters all of the confusions and frustrations that living in a world dominated by the Modernist Syndrome necessarily involves. Such writers deal with characters whose self-conception is deeply influenced, or distorted, by the implicit authority of empiricist and Enlightenment ideas. Nor is this a merely redundant use of "modern," for relatively few of the writers of our century have seriously accepted these challenges. Every year hundreds of novels are published that blithely ignore the appalling contradictions of twentieth-century life. We value our great "modern" writers precisely for their relentless, courageous exploration of what is most distinctive and troubling about our age.

And in this sense Joyce is indubitably a modern writer. Nowhere is the genius of James Joyce more fully manifested than in his depiction, in *Portrait of the Artist,* of a young man whose psyche is so deeply (and unwittingly) colored by the modernist view of reality. Young Stephen Dedalus, very much a creature of his time, has a conception of reality and of his own psyche that is deeply influenced by the Modernist Syndrome. In this novel Joyce reveals to us the shallowness and insufficiency of Stephen's views.

3

Joyce's Assumptions and Aims

My subsequent discussion of the antimodernism of *Portrait* requires as a context certain of Joyce's underlying ideas and attitudes. These will be gleaned mainly from Joyce's reviews, letters, and notebooks, but I draw as well on the testimony of Stanislaus, and on the recollections of others. While Joyce's fictional works of course provide essential evidence, they must be used circumspectly; though the creative works can demonstrate Joyce's awareness of an issue, or the importance of some theme for him, it is much harder to use them as clear evidence of Joyce's underlying life-attitudes.

Several critics have remarked on how early in his career Joyce seems to have come to a sense of what he wanted to do as an artist.[1] Certainly the achievement of the *Dubliners* stories, all except "The Dead" written between August of 1904 and April of 1906, when Joyce was only 22 to 24 years old, is remarkable. And the January 1904 "A Portrait of the Artist" sketch, though sometimes abstruse, was doubtless a seminal document for him—one that did to some extent guide his work on what became *Portrait* over the next ten years, justifying his use of 1904 as the terminus a quo for that novel. Richard Kain labels 1904 as the *annus mirabilis* (in *Workshop*, p. 116)—though Mary Reynolds applies that term to 1907, adding "It was in 1907 that he found his identity as a writer" ("Davin's Boots," p. 218).

But a careful examination of Joyce's early writing career does not confirm that he was so self-confident or that polished works flowed easily from his pen. The *Stephen Hero* text that Joyce composed from February 1904 to June or July 1906 is by no means sure-handed or well controlled; it is flaccid, vacillating in its perspective and its tone, and reflects a callowness not simply in Stephen Daedalus but in its author. Perhaps this is because the material is so close to Joyce personally, and the thrust of the work so largely autobiographical—by which I mean that in writing *Stephen Hero* Joyce's focus (wittingly or not) was upon exploring and learning about his own development, rather than (as in *Portrait*) upon presenting an interpretation of a type. (The difference in control and sureness of touch between *Stephen Hero* and the *Dubliners* stories that he was writing at the same time is remarkable and needs to be better accounted for.) Also, his letters from Rome in late 1906 and early 1907 reflect serious doubts and misgivings about himself.[2] "The Dead," written for the most part in the spring of 1907, is undeniably a great achievement, personally and artistically. But we can hardly infer that in writing that great story Joyce gained any large measure of artistic assuredness, for the composition of *A Portrait,* which was begun in the autumn of 1907 and progressed well into the next spring, went on very slowly and sporadically over the next several years, and apparently the novel was largely recast as late as 1912–1913.[3]

Joyce's early career, while it involves undeniable evidence of genius, does not present a picture of an artist who at an early stage of his career came into a clear sense of himself and of confidence about his artistry, and in spite of Ellmann's monumental biography, we still have only a limited understanding of Joyce's early psychological and spiritual development. I have, however, no intention of providing such an account here; my more modest purpose is to call attention to certain ideas or assumptions that were important for Joyce, and to show that equally important for Joyce was his realization of what he did *not* need to know in order to become an artist—i.e., his coming to understand that being an artist does not depend upon one's first formulating a full-scale philosophy.

Joyce was guided as to what his art should be by certain leading ideas that enabled him to see through the simplifications and distortions of the Cartesian metaphysic and the Humean epistemology—i.e., of modernism as I have characterized it in the preceding chapter. These ideas were 1) the inextricable unity of "mind" and "matter" and the consequent rejection of any dualism of psyche and physis, of mind and body, whether stemming from Platonism, or from Descartes' division of reality in *res cogitans* and *res extensa;* 2) the idea of potentiality, which sees life in terms of unfolding processes through which persons and societies realize (or fail to realize) in the future certain potentialities inherent in their past and present; 3) the understanding that every act of perception is an act of the mind (i.e., of psyche) as well as of the bodily senses, and that what we know through perception are mental entities—i.e., that we do not perceive "discrete sensations" (in the Humean sense) nor material "objects" (in the matter-in-motion, Newtonian sense): rather, we perceive qualities and natures and meanings. This last idea is the underlying point of Stephen's "aesthetic" in *Portrait*, which is better understood as an account of the perceptual act than as a full-blown aesthetic theory.

∽

The first guiding idea that I wish to elaborate is that Joyce was not a metaphysical dualist—that he did not accept the idea of sheer "matter" or of sheer "mind"—and that he recognized the insufficiency of the conflicting varieties of idealism and of materialism that have been ubiquitous in the Western intellectual tradition. Joyce saw through these dichotomous, dualistic views of reality, whether they took the form of Platonic idealism vs. atomistic materialism, or of Descartes' mind/matter division.

We should not mistake Joyce's persistent evocation of tensions and oppositions within human experience for metaphysical dualism. One of the recurrent themes of Ellmann's biography, as well as a commonplace of Joyce criticism, is that Joyce saw his art as a reconciliation of opposites. Ellmann says, for example, that Joyce may have been attracted to Bruno "because he saw his art as a reconciler of those opposites within his own mind which he would later personify as Shem and Shaun" (*JJ II*, p. 60). Conceiving human experience in terms of such oppositions, however, does not make Joyce a dualist. In his understanding of human experience, whether individual or cultural, Joyce was an "oppositionist," believing, as he said in "Drama and Life," that drama is "the interplay of passions to portray truth; drama is strife, evolution, movement in whatever way unfolded" (*CW*, p. 41). Certainly he believed that patterns of opposition and of oscillation and of cyclic movement pervade human history, and that persons as well as cultures inevitably evoke and then struggle with their own opposites. He believed, that is, as did William Blake and D. H. Lawrence, that such polarized tensions are the very essence of human experience, and that for either side of any of these polarities ever to triumph over the other would be death (as Lawrence so eloquently shows in his essay "The Crown").

We see this "oppositionism" reflected in Joyce's mind and his works in innumerable ways—most often in the antitypical tensions that emerge repeatedly in his characters and that become perhaps the main organizing principle of *Finnegans Wake*. It is reflected as well in his interest in such opposites as Defoe and Blake, on both of whom he delivered lectures in March of 1912.[4] But for all his belief in the inherent tension of human experience, personal and cultural, Joyce did not concur in the post-Cartesian notion of there being two utterly different modes of reality, matter and mind. Joyce's perspective went beyond dualism to the view that reality consists of a unity of mind and matter—Bruno's ultimate principle "related to any soul or to any material thing" (*CW*, p. 134). The "dichotomy" represented by Shem and Shaun is qualitatively, metaphysically different from that between mind and matter. The dialectic within Joyce's worldview, as within that of Blake and Lawrence, is a dialectic of wholistic entities, each of which embodies a unification of "mind" and "body." It is a dialectic of persons, of temperaments, of cultural orientations, not of abstract metaphysical entities.

Bruno was, of course, one of those from whom Joyce learned this "oppositionism." In his review of McIntyre's *Giordano Bruno*, Joyce twits Coleridge for having seen Bruno as a dualist, and says "that idea of an ultimate principle, spiritual, indifferent, universal, related to any soul or to any material thing . . . unwarranted as it may seem in the view of critical philosophy, has yet a distinct value for the historian of religious ecstasies. It is not Spinoza, it is Bruno, that is the god-intoxicated man. Inwards from the material universe, which, however, did not seem to him, as to the Neoplatonists the kingdom of the soul's malady, or as to the Christians a place of probation, but rather his opportunity for spiritual activity, he passes, and from heroic enthusiasm to enthusiasm to unite himself with God" (*CW*, p. 134). Joyce's rejection of materialism is reflected as well in his statement in his review of Burnet's *Aristotle on Education* that "at the present time, when the scientific specialists and the whole cohort of Materialists are cheapening the good name of philosophy, it is very useful to give heed to one who has been wisely named 'maestro di color che sanno' " (*CW*, 109–110), and in his criticism of the "hurried materialism now in vogue" in the lecture on Blake (*CW*, p. 220).[5]

The second idea implicit in Joyce's works is that reality is not static but changes through time, that it inherently involves processes of growth, development, evolution, and thus that it involves true potentiality. So strong is the Western bias in favor of a static view of reality (whether the static entity be abstract Ideas or material atoms) that the modernist mentality implicitly regards change as evidence of an inferior or incomplete mode of reality. This attitude has its origins in Platonism, in which the real entities—i.e., Ideas—are presumed to be changeless, and change or mutability is clear evidence that an entity is not fully real; this attitude is also implicit in atomic materialism, since the particles of matter are presumed to be discrete and without relationships. As a result of this Western bias toward the static, the Modernist Syndrome is baffled by the nature of processes and tends to construe them as a series of discrete states each of which is more real than the presumed process that it forms a part of. Modernist common sense can find nothing within atoms and molecules that corresponds to "potentiality," and so either utterly denies the idea, or presumes that all relationships between past, present, and future are mechanical and deterministic. Finally, then, the modernist bias in favor of a static view of reality means that the idea of potentiality (i.e., of a present state as containing in potentia some other future state) seems mere abstrusiosity.[6]

But here again Joyce, probably by virtue of his Aristotelian orientation, eluded the simplistic predispositions of the modernist view of reality and believed in *potentiality* not simply as an abstraction but as a real aspect of the present, by virtue of which it holds an array of possibilities for the future. Joyce, that is, was able to conceive a real relationship of continuity, of unfolding, of entelechy among events in time (i.e., a real process) without construing it as deterministic. The idea of potentiality is invoked in the opening sentences of Joyce's "Portrait of the Artist" sketch. There, after criticizing our inability to conceive the past "in any other than its iron memorial aspect," Joyce says "yet the past assuredly implies a fluid succession of presents, the development of an entity of which our actual present is a phase only" (*Workshop*, p. 60), and it is this developing entity whose "individuating rhythm" Joyce speaks of discerning in the last sentence of this same paragraph.

Perhaps the most perspicacious statement that Hugh Kenner has made about Joyce's mind and work acknowledges Joyce's belief in potentiality. Kenner says

the sharpest exigetical instrument we can bring to the work of Joyce is Aristotle's great conception of potency and act. His awareness of it helps distinguish Joyce from every other writer who has used the conventions of naturalist fiction. Naturalism as it was developed in France was based on scientific positivism, which affirms that realities are bounded by phenomena, persons by behavior, that what seems is, that what is must be. But Joyce is always concerned with multiple possibilities. For a Zola, a Maupassant, a Flaubert, it is always meaningless to consider what might have been; since it was not, to say that it might have been is without meaning. But in the mind of Joyce there hung a radiant field of multiple possibilities, ways in which a man may go, and corresponding selves he may become, bounding him by one outward form or another while he remains the same person in the eye of God. The events of history, Stephen considers in *Ulysses*, are branded by time and hung fettered "in the room of the infinite possibilities they have ousted" (*U*, 25). Pathos, the subdominant Joycean emotion, inheres in the inspection of such limits: men longing to become what they can never be, though it lies in them to be it, simply because they have become something else.[7]

But Kenner, inescapably committed to a paralytic view of Dublin, subsequently draws back from the implications of his insight and denies Joyce's characters any real possibilities of growth, saying "in Dublin one can only become a Dubliner" (p. 180), and "for Joyce no self is immutable, it is a costume; hence the costume changes in 'Circe' " (p. 180).[8]

This idea of potentiality is so fundamental and pervasive in Joyce that we are likely to overlook its profound implications. As we shall see shortly, it is this sense of the frustrated potentialities of his characters in *Dubliners* that redeems the collection from mere naturalism. It was his frustration with the inertia of his fellow Dubliners that provided the impetus behind Joyce's arguments with Grant Richards over the importance of letting them see a reflection of themselves, so that they might better realize their own latent capacities. A similar note is sounded in Joyce's essay on Ibsen's *When We Dead Awaken*, where Joyce tells us that Rubek "sees that he has not fulfilled the promise" of his early work, or when he says of Rubek, in terms that might be addressed directly to Gabriel Conroy, that "there may be lying dormant in him a capacity for greater life, which may be exercised when he, a dead man, shall have risen from among the dead" (*CW*, pp. 53 and 66). Apparently Joyce's own early play, *A Brilliant Career*, involved a similar situation, to judge from Stanislaus' recollection of the now-lost work. According to Stanislaus, a young doctor, Paul, "renounces the valiant purposes of his youth, and becomes a time-server," only to realize later "that his brilliant career is dust and ashes" (*MBK*, p. 115). The idea of potentiality is of course implicit within every episode of the *Bildungsroman, Portrait of the Artist*, and Stephen himself acknowledges the continuity of his own unfolding (as well as the superficiality of his own self-understanding) when in *Ulysses* he quotes Goethe's dictum, "Beware of what you wish for in youth because you will get it in middle life" (*U,* 9.451).

The third idea—that every perception involves an apprehension of "mental" entities and of meanings—while very much at odds with the modernist view of reality, should seem familiar to readers of Joyce because it underlies the aesthetic theorizing in Joyce's notebooks and in *Portrait,* and it is quite explicitly stated in various writings, including *Stephen Hero.* For our present purposes three points about that "aesthetic" are worth attending to—first, (which I shall develop later), that the aesthetic theory is primarily dramatic—i.e., it is a means of characterizing Stephen, not an opportunity for Joyce to present his own ideas; second, that the aesthetic theory is not so much concerned with the distinctive nature of beauty as it is with the nature of perception; third, that these theories, as presented in the notebooks and in *Stephen Hero* and *Portrait,* reveal congruence on essential points between Joyce and his character(s) Stephen D(a)edalus. This means that while Joyce does take Stephen's measure in many ways, he does not deny him certain fundamental psychological-metaphysical insights—which bodes well for Stephen's subsequent artistic success.[9]

Let us consider the philosophical implications of the discussion of wholeness, harmony, and radiance (i.e., *integritas, consonantia, claritas/quidditas*) as we find it in *Portrait of the Artist.*[10] In order to show that the underlying issue here is perceptual rather than "aesthetic" (i.e., that what Stephen says refers to all objects, not just to beautiful ones) let us apply Stephen's terminology to what happens when an image on a slide transparency is slowly brought into focus on a screen. Initially, the screen is blank, but when the transparency comes into place, what was a white screen presents a blurred image of some *thing,* though at first we cannot recognize even its shape, much less "what it is." This corresponds to the first stage in the process of *apprehension* that Stephen delineates: " 'The first phase of apprehension is a bounding line drawn about the object to be apprehended. . . . the esthetic image is first luminously apprehended as selfbounded and selfcontained upon the immeasurable background of space or time which is not it. You apprehend it as *one* thing. You see it as one whole. You apprehend its wholeness. That is *integritas* " (p. 212). Though Stephen here refers to an "esthetic" image, he also speaks generically of apprehension, showing (especially within the context of the Pola Notebook just quoted) that the process he describes applies to our *perception* of any object. We should note too that Stephen's account presumes an active mind (not a Lockean/ Humean *tabula rasa*) that is engaging a public world of objects amenable to the psychic act of perception (not a Kantian set of mental categories that mind imposes upon some ultimately alien *Ding an sich*)—assumptions which have already taken him far beyond the austerities of Cartesian and Humean skepticism.

As the image on the slide is brought gradually into focus, we discern that it is not just a blurred object against a white background, but an entity with a distinct shape or structure—though we still cannot tell what the entity *is*. We can see now that the object is vaguely ellipsoidal, but with some circular or semi-circular form above it. As the image sharpens, we can sense its structure, and this corresponds to the second stage of the process that Stephen describes: " 'Then,' said Stephen, 'you pass from point to point, led by its formal lines; you apprehend it as balanced part against part within its limits; you feel the rhythm of its structure. . . . You apprehend it as complex, multiple, divisible, separable, made up of its parts, the result of its parts and their sum, harmonious. That is *consonantia* " (p. 212). This stage once again involves an active mind and one for which the underlying notion of "whole" and "part" is a given. What is perceived at this stage is the "structural" relationship of part and whole, though we should recognize that such a "structure" is not merely spatial; in a full-fledged three-dimensional perception it may involve color, texture, perhaps even taste. But as Stephen goes on to explain, the perceptual act is not yet complete.

The crucial part of the perceptual act is yet to come, and finally, as the transparency on the screen is brought clearly into focus, we see what the object *is*—a basket. Approaching this third phase of the apprehension, for which he uses the term *claritas*, Stephen acknowledges that for a time he wondered whether St. Thomas " 'had in mind symbolism or idealism, the supreme quality of beauty being a light from some other world, the idea of which the matter is but the shadow, the reality of which it is but the symbol' " (p. 213). But Stephen explicitly rejects such idealism as "literary talk," and goes on to explain the tangible meaning of *claritas*: " 'When you have apprehended that basket as one thing *[integritas]* and then have analysed it according to its form and apprehended it as a thing *[consonantia]* you make the only synthesis which is logically and esthetically permissible. You see that it is that thing which it is and no other thing. The radiance of which he [St. Thomas] speaks is the scholastic *quidditas,* the *whatness* of a thing' " (p. 213). In other words, the term *claritas* refers not to something mystical, but simply to the distinctive identity or whatness of the object.[11] While each stage of the act of apprehension involves an active mind, this last stage does so most clearly, most fully, because what is apprehended here is obviously not one aspect or another—not merely a Humean discrete sensation—but the distinctive *nature* of the thing. This experience of perception is something not possible for instruments—i.e., it cannot be achieved by anything but a mind—because it is itself "mental," not "material," and thus involves us directly in a dimension of reality that is unaccountable in terms of the modernist metaphysic.[12]

Joyce knew that this same quality of whatness is possessed not simply by objects but by persons, events, situations—but in those more complex cases where *"quidditas"* shades over into "meaning," it requires a more active understanding to discern (and artistic skill to reproject) the "individuating rhythm" of a person or the "meaning" of a series of events. Perhaps the most explicit statement of this crucial idea comes from Stephen Daedalus in *Stephen Hero,* where he tells us that the artist is "gifted with twin faculties, a selective faculty and a reproductive faculty. . . . the artist who could disentangle the subtle soul of the image from its mesh of defining circumstances most exactly and reembody it in artistic circumstances chosen as the most exact for it in its new office, he was the supreme artist" (*SH,* pp. 77–78). Here I would insist with Stephen Dedalus in *Portrait* that what is referred to as the "subtle soul" of the image is not some mystical entity involving "symbolism or idealism" (p. 213), but the dimension of meaning that lies within every experience and which the artist is always attempting to get at in any character, any scene, any series of events. The difference between "Literature" and "Drama" that Joyce proposes in his essay "Drama and Life" is that Literature deals with trivial externals, while Drama deals with underlying laws, with truth, with constancy. Joyce similarly acknowledges that art should get at some *meaning* when he says of his reading of Seamus O'Kelly that he read the stories "patiently trying to see whether the writer was trying to express something he had understood" (*Letters,* II, 196; to Stanislaus, Nov. 20, 1906); or when he says of Marcelle Tinayre's *The House of Sin,* "a simple narration has always singular charm when we divine that the lives it offers us are themselves too ample, too complex, to be expressed entirely"—i.e., that their *gist* has to be conveyed—(*CW,* p. 122); or when he says of Defoe's *The Storm,* "by dint of repetitions, contradictions, details, figures, noises, the storm has come alive, the ruin is visible" ("Defoe," p. 16). In his second essay on Mangan, Joyce says that some poets do not just reveal "to us some phase of the human conscience," but "[sum] up in themselves the thousand contrasting tendencies of their era" (*CW*, p. 175). Similarly, of another of his paradigm artists, William Blake, Joyce says "Blake heard with the ear of the soul . . . he sees with the eye of the mind," and later he describes "the mental process by which Blake arrives at the threshold of the infinite" by comparing it with the process described by Dionysius the pseudo-Areopagite (*CW*, pp. 215, 222). And in his essay on "The Universal Literary Influence of the Renaissance" Joyce says "we might say indeed that modern man has an epidermis rather than a soul. The sensory power of his body has developed enormously, but it has developed to the detriment of the spiritual faculty. We lack moral sense and perhaps also strength of imagination" (*James Joyce in Padua*, p. 21).

In each of these cases Joyce is acknowledging that processes and events and persons involve *meanings* and that the writer must capture and convey those meanings to us. What we value so much, for example, about the opening paragraphs of "A Painful Case," is that Joyce so deftly captures not just the distinctiveness of his character James Duffy, but the crucial qualities of a type and even of a certain mode of life-response that each of us has encountered. Derek Attridge makes essentially this same point when he says that our enjoyment of Joyce lies in seeing Joyce's style "suggest with immense precision a mind, a social milieu, a series of emotions," and that "our readerly enjoyment [in "Eveline"] includes some appreciation of the elegant and economical way in which the phrase ["pleasantly confused"] sums up a complex and contradictory experience" ("Reading Joyce," in *The Cambridge Companion to James Joyce,* ed. Derek Attridge [Cambridge: Cambridge Univ. Press], pp. 6, 7). This "meaningful" dimension of reality is taken for granted in Robert Scholes' statement about Epiphany #33 that in it "Joyce attempts to get at the *essence* of prostitution" (*Workshop*, p. 43; my emphasis). Diego Angeli similarly compares Joyce to "the late impressionists who single out the *characteristic elements* of a landscape or a scene or a human face" (*CH*, I, 116; my emphasis). Similarly, William M. Schutte says of *Portrait* that "the technique which Joyce developed is designed to reveal, not merely to record, the *essential nature* of each of the nineteen presents [i.e., sections of the novel] as it impinges on the consciousness of Stephen Dedalus" (*Twentieth Century Interpretations of Portrait*, p. 12; my emphasis), and Hugh Kenner says of Joyce that "he is scrutinizing existences for their significance" ("*Portrait* in Perspective," pp. 159–60). These critics probably would deny that in talking this way they are being Platonic or mystical—and yet they are acknowledging a dimension of experience and of reality that few modernist critics feel comfortable with and that the materialistically grounded modernist climate of opinion cannot give an account of—namely, the meaning of an event, the whatness of a perception, the "characteristic elements" of a landscape, the individuating rhythm of an evolving psyche. These are the very mysteries within the ordinary that Joyce devoted himself to exploring.[13]

Joyce, then, believed that the artist's purpose is to discern and re-present the gist, the meaning, of the things that he writes about—of the persons, the events, the processes. This is the obvious implication of his saying in his "Portrait of the Artist" sketch that the aim of the artist is to "seek through some art, by some process of the mind as yet untabulated, to liberate from the personalized lumps of matter that which is their individuating rhythm, the first or formal relation of their parts" (*Workshop*, p. 60). Whenever a writer presents a person or a scene he necessarily does so selectively, and the details or perspectives that he selects for presentation are those that he believes will capture something crucial or essential about the event or the person. Young Stephen in *Portrait* is, then, on the right track when he tries to write a poem about his experience with E___ C___ by brooding on the incident in the hope that the common and insignificant elements would fall away; Stephen's problem is that the aspects he rejects as insignificant—the tram, tram-men, horses, the boy and girl themselves—are precisely those that the mature artist Joyce would see as evoking the essence of the experience.[14]

One implication of these ideas is that each of us—including the would-be artist—is constantly involved with the *meanings* of the events around us, with trying to *understand* the persons and events we experience. One question, one issue, that Joyce's works should keep in focus for us is the question of what we think we mean when we refer to the *meaning* of an episode, or the *gist* of an event, or the *essence* of a character or of a social milieu—terms that occur pervasively in the essays even of those critics who claim to see Joyce as deconstructing traditional values. Unremarkable as it may sound, the claim that an act or a series of events should have some gist or meaning is inexplicable in terms of the modernist, matter-in-motion, metaphysic outlined in the preceding chapter. One of Joyce's great virtues is that he did not lose sight of the implications of this mystery implicit within the most ordinary perceptions and events, and even devoted his art to calling our attention to it. Joyce saw that every human act of perception

involves a qualitative aspect that we can give no account of, yet implicitly rely upon. While his fellow Irishman Yeats persistently explored the inexhaustible, mysterious relationship between the visible and the invisible worlds through every possible mode of the occult, Joyce devoted himself to exploring the equally inexhaustible mysteries of meaning implicit in the most ordinary acts of human perception, human speech, and human response to the world around us.[15]

To articulate these "leading ideas" is not to make Joyce into a philosopher or to proclaim him an Aristotelian or a Thomist. While he did undoubtedly respect and return to these thinkers, they served simply to provide the intellectual touchstones, or beacons, that his development as an artist required.[16] Perhaps the most important change that occurred in Joyce's thinking during these formative years was in regard to this question of how fully an artist must understand the processes within himself and within the world around him. What enabled the flowering of Joyce's artistry was not his discovery of certain philosophic or aesthetic principles, but his realization that a great deal of what the artist continually draws upon, in himself and in the world, remains unformalizable and inexplicable, and that the artist need not be a philosopher. For all his intellect and his pride, this pioneer of self-exploration came to see that the artist is not self-generating or omniscient, and that he must always draw upon processes within the individual psyche and the cultural psyche that are prior to him and that lie beyond what he can fully understand. As he put it in the early "Portrait" sketch, the artist must always draw upon and attempt to simulate "some process of the mind as yet untabulated" (*Workshop,* p. 60), and in his second "James Clarence Mangan" lecture, Joyce said that poetry "speaks of that which seems unreal and fantastic to those who have lost the simple intuitions which are the tests of reality" (*CW,* p. 185). Joyce, that is, came to see that a writer does not have to comprehend the philosophical issues that are involved in his writing; that he does not require complete self-understanding; that as a writer he does not have to create his fictive world ex nihilo or from logically impeccable axioms; that he does not even have to re-present his fictive world exhaustively, if he can discern and re-present those aspects that evoke the meaning, the gist, of what he is depicting. Though he is the god of his particular literary creation, the writer need not assume Urizenic responsibility for generating everything; he can become a vehicle of things deeper and richer than he can understand, provided he has sufficient faith in himself and in certain givens of reality.[17]

I infer that Joyce did not feel the need of extensive philosophic theorizing partly from the cessation of his "expository" writing and his theoretical notebooks in 1904 (i.e., the Paris and Pola notebooks), and from the tone in which Joyce presents Stephen's theorizing in *Portrait* and *Ulysses*. One noteworthy aspect of Joyce's literary development is how early in his career he *stopped* writing material that was intended to clarify or amplify his "philosophical" ideas, and how completely he channeled his energies into his creative literary works. Joyce obviously did not feel the need for expository elaboration of his ideas that was felt by so many of his contemporaries who wrote a large volume of such work—e.g., Yeats, Eliot, Pound, Woolf, or Lawrence. The few non-literary writings that Joyce did after November of 1903 (his last review for the *Daily Express*) were ad hoc and occasional—the lectures on Blake and Defoe and on Irish politics, the Paduan essays. Quite clearly, Joyce did not write them in order to develop a philosophy. It is noteworthy as well that the "Trieste Notebook" (1909?) is very different in kind and in purpose from the earlier Paris and Pola "Aesthetic Notebooks."[18] This is a writer's notebook, not a theoretician's. In the "Trieste Notebook," "Esthetic" has become simply one category among a host of others, and it is clear that the notes Joyce has under that category are designed for use in his fictive works (e.g., "An enchantment of the heart" and "The rite is the poet's rest") not for forging an aesthetic philosophy (see *Workshop*, pp. 96–97). In a statement that testifies both to his lack of interest in doctrine and to his sense of personal entelechy, Joyce told Stanislaus in a letter of March 1, 1907 [?], "yet I have certain ideas I would like to give form to: not as a doctrine but as the continuation of the expression of myself which I now see I began in *Chamber Music*" (*Letters*, II, 217).

This very question of the degree of analytical self-understanding necessary to an artist is one of the main psychological issues that Joyce explores through Stephen Dedalus both in *Portrait of the Artist* and in *Ulysses*.[19] One of the most basic, persistent themes of *Portrait* is Stephen's struggle for self-understanding and self-determination, but Joyce, while sympathetic with this struggle, shows that it is in some respects mistaken, in that Stephen will never achieve the total self-awareness and self-determination that he aspires to—nor should he, for if he were to achieve total self-awareness, his life would become deracinated and trivialized. Furthermore, by the time of *Ulysses*, Stephen has begun to sense this himself, and his realization that he has much to learn becomes a motif of *Ulysses*. This question of how much the writer can or should understand is the central theme that Stephen is exploring in his interpretation of Shakespeare in the Scylla and Charybdis episode of *Ulysses*. There Stephen is struggling with the questions of how a writer's work can be meaningfully related to his life without being physicalistically "caused" by it, and how the work can convey insights the writer himself may not be able to draw upon in his own life. Stephen has come to see that artistic creation is far more complex and mysterious than the writer himself can consciously realize.[20]

श

From early in his career Joyce understood that the presumed distinction between mind and matter had penetrated deep into the modernist perception of reality, and he saw that one major task that fell to the aspiring twentieth century writer was to dramatize in his works the pernicious effects of this dichotomy and to help us get beyond the Cartesian dilemma. More specifically, Joyce saw this dichotomy manifested in the nineteenth-century literary modes of symbolism and naturalism (or realism), and he felt that the great twentieth-century artist would have to comprehend and draw upon both of these modes in order to effect their reconciliation. That is, Joyce saw the symbolist writing of Rimbaud and Mallarmé as exemplifying a subjectivist withdrawal into the psyche, in retreat from an external world that was increasingly being construed in mechanical, materialistic terms. Similarly, he saw naturalism, as exemplified by the brothers Goncourt and by Émile Zola, as aspiring to an objectivist literature that tried to conform to the dictates of the empirical method and to devote itself to the objective world.[21] Consequently, one of Joyce's most fundamental literary aims was to comprehend and to reconcile these two literary modes in his own writing.

Joyce's concern to reconcile naturalism and symbolism has been recognized and reiterated by critics from Edmund Wilson on.[22] What is less clear is how early in his career Joyce sensed the insufficiencies of these modes and reflected this in his works. Everyone recognizes that by the time of *Ulysses,* Joyce was concerned to present a work that is both symbolist and naturalist, both surface and symbol—but how much earlier in his career he had seen through these modes, and where *Chamber Music, Dubliners* and *A Portrait* stand in this process remains a matter of debate. In the view of some critics the fusion is not fully achieved until *Ulysses*. H. O. Brown for example says "in *Dubliners,* Joyce had attempted an objective, external picture of the city. *A Portrait* is the inner life of a young boy growing up in Dublin. *Ulysses* brings these two poles and their methods together in a way that is only implicit in the ending of 'The Dead' and in *A Portrait*" (*Biography of a Form,* pp. 130–31). This implies that *Dubliners* was essentially naturalistic, that *Portrait*, devoted to the "inner life" of its character, involves a swing of the pendulum toward symbolism, and that not until *Ulysses* does Joyce merge the inner and the outer. Whether *Portrait* is symbolist OR naturalist has been debated ever since the reviews of the novel, and a number of critics have presumed that *Dubliners* is quite simply in the naturalistic mode, and *Chamber Music* entirely symbolist.

My view is that his recognition of the partiality, the incompleteness, of these modes informed Joyce's works from his earliest years, and that even *Chamber Music* and *Dubliners* were in part explorations of these respective modes in an attempt to prepare himself for the greater, more comprehensive work that lay ahead. These earliest works play a role in Joyce's career comparable to that of the *Eclogues* in Virgil's, or the *Shepherd's Calendar* in Spenser's, or *Il Penseroso* and *L'Allegro* in Milton's: they are the études done in preparation for the more ambitious symphonies or oratorios to come.[23] Though indubitably more, these works are Joyce's studies in these complementary modes, to assure himself that he could understand the perspective upon reality that they involve, and could call on them as needed. Furthermore, the wholistic perspective reconciling these two modes is achieved in *Portrait*—not in the conscious mind of the character, but in the perspective of the author, and in the structures and techniques of the novel.[24]

There is no question that the young Joyce was interested in the French symbolists, and that *Chamber Music* reflects that interest. Philip Herring says "many studies have shown their [Joyce's and Stephen's] debt to symbolist poets," and he says that "It is common knowledge that Joyce could recite Verlaine and Baudelaire by the hour, that he derived much from the symbolist aesthetic, and that the mind of Stephen Dedalus in *Ulysses* is steeped in French culture" (*Uncertainty Principle,* pp. 140–41).[25] Similarly William York Tindall's edition of *Chamber Music* speaks repeatedly of Joyce's interest in the symbolists and of the symbolist aspects of the poems (e.g., pp. 54, 66). But for all Joyce's interest in the movement, he seems from the first to have seen its limitations, and rather than having been a devotee, wished to assure himself that he could, when necessary, invoke its ambience.[26]

Precisely how he felt while composing them about the poems he wrote as a young man we cannot say, but we do know Joyce composed a great many poems he did not care to preserve. Stanislaus tells us of a volume of some fifty or sixty lyric poems under the title *Moods,* and of another collection entitled *Shine and Dark* (*MBK*, p. 85). Further, Stanislaus tells us that "not all Jim's personality or even the most distinctive part of it found expression in verse, but only the emotive side, which in one respect was fictitious" (*MBK*, p. 143).[27] We do know that Stephen Daedalus in *Stephen Hero* burns his poems because "they were romantic" (*SH,* p. 226), and we know Joyce himself came to regard his *Chamber Music* poems quite negatively, losing interest in them to the extent that he abandoned the arrangement and editing of them to Stanislaus, and threatened to withdraw them even after they had been accepted for publication.[28]

An interesting case is provided by the villanelle Joyce uses in *Portrait.* We know Joyce wrote the poem at an earlier age (*MBK*, pp. 85–86 and 151), and while we cannot be certain about the attitude in which it was originally composed, we can confidently say that in *Portrait* it functions to epitomize the languorous, self-indulgent attitude of the symbolists; a strong hint in this direction is provided by the characterization in *Stephen Hero* of the "Vilanelle of the Temptress" as "some ardent verses" that Stephen composed from a "trivial incident" (*SH*, p. 211).[29]

Just as his early poetry is to some extent an exercise in the symbolist mode, permitting Joyce to assume for a time the perspective of Rimbaud or Mallarmé, *Dubliners* enabled the young Joyce to experiment with the perspective of naturalism, without devoting himself entirely to that mode. Many of the scenes and situations have about them a distinctively naturalistic ring—for example, the scene in "A Painful Case" of Mr. James Duffy reading the newspaper account of Mrs. Sinico's death while "the cabbage began to deposit a cold white grease on his plate" (*D,* p. 113), or the workmen's "spitting often on the floor and sometimes dragging the sawdust over their spits with their heavy boots" (*D,* p. 116).[30] And some of Joyce's comments in his letters seem to put the stories into the naturalistic mold. For instance he refers to the "special odour of corruption which . . . floats over my stories"; he says that he has written the volume "for the most part in a style of scrupulous meanness and with the conviction that he is a very bold man who dares to alter in the presentment, still more to deform, whatever he has seen and heard"; and he says that it is not his fault "that the odour of ashpits and old weeds and offal hangs round my stories."[31]

It is not, then, surprising that some early reviewers and more recent critics have seen the collection as expressing Joyce's own naturalism.[32] For example, H. O. Brown claims that "the realism of the *Dubliners* stories implies a dualistic split between observer and observed, spirit and matter, mind and body. The world, inert and despiritualized—'out there'—imprisons a bodyless spirit, a way of seeing."[33] But the worldview implicit within a work of literature—especially one so subtle and tonally complex as *Dubliners*—is not simply a matter of unsavory details and unhappy endings. The "worldview" of the work involves as well the hopes and frustrations the writer depicts in his characters and evokes in his audience, and the closer we look at the attitudes Joyce evokes in us toward these characters and their situations, the less we find that *Dubliners* involves a naturalistic worldview.

There is evidence both internal and external that *Dubliners* is not naturalistic. The internal evidence lies mainly in Joyce's repeated evocation of a sense of what might have been, or of the possibilities that these characters *should* avail themselves of. The persistent stumbling block to a naturalistic reading of *Dubliners*, as Kenner indicated in the quote above concerning "potency and act," is Joyce's sense of his characters' potentiality, and the consequent sense of hope, of expectation (even if frustrated), he evokes in his readers. The point of these stories is not that life is meaningless or even that the individual's situation is hopeless; it is rather that these people have permitted themselves to be deprived of life opportunities by various factors within their environment and within themselves.

As to the external evidence—various comments Joyce made in his letters show that he saw these stories as *epicleiti* (i.e., invocations of the Holy Spirit to confer meaning on what he was doing; see my "James Joyce and the Power of the Word" for explication of this); that he saw the theme of the volume as paralysis—which implies a healthy organism that has lost some of its potential; and that he felt reading his stories could be of great value to his Irish audience. He told Grant Richards "I seriously believe that you will retard the course of civilization in Ireland by preventing the Irish people from having one good look at themselves in my nicely polished looking-glass" (June 23, 1906; *Letters*, I, 64; note that this statement was made long before the writing of "The Dead," which several critics have presumed to signal a turnaround in Joyce's attitudes). None of these sentiments is compatible with the naturalistic assumption that we are all helpless victims within a mechanical system, differing only in degrees of awareness of our entrapment. Those who see these stories as naturalistic fail to appreciate the great concern Joyce had for frustrated human potential, and his belief in the capacities of the human psyche. His hope for what the reading of his volume could accomplish among his countrymen not only testifies to Joyce's faith in his art, but reflects as well his frustration with his fellow Irishmen for permitting themselves to be so victimized.[34]

Before leaving this topic of Joyce's early works as forays into symbolism and naturalism, we might ask why Joyce would bother to write works epitomizing perspectives that he had already disavowed. Joyce, in his aspiration to be the great twentieth century writer, felt the need to comprehend every significant literary genre or mode, every significant contemporary perspective on human nature. This temperamental compulsion is the reason Joyce's works contain so much "adventitious" material, whether it be newspaperese ("A Painful Case"), or Jesuit sermon rhetoric (Chapter III of *Portrait*), or sentimental mawkish fiction (Nausicaa), or psychoanalysis (Circe), or scientistic objectivity (Ithaca), or scholarly pedantry (Chapter I.v of *Finnegans Wake*). For Joyce, every style involved a perspective upon reality, and he wished to be sure he could draw upon and incorporate these perspectives, partial as they are. If it is true as Huge Kenner says that "Joyce eludes altogether the party politics of 'symbolism' and 'naturalism' " (note 22 above), it is because he assimilated them to his own distinctive purposes.[35]

In *A Portrait of the Artist as a Young Man* Joyce deals comprehensively with the subjective/objective division, presented here within the sharply controlled focus of the development of a single individual. It depicts with great fidelity the perspective of a sensitive and intelligent young man who is in many respects a product, or at least a reflection, of his time. Thus Stephen sees his experience as partitioned into inner and outer, subjective and objective, the private world and the real world. But at the same time Joyce shows Stephen categorizing his experience into these oppositions, he reveals by a variety of tactics—structural, stylistic, and tonal—that Stephen's dichotomous view is superficial. He shows, that is, that inner and outer interpenetrate and are inextricably interrelated, and that the distinction between subject and object, between mind and nature, is superficial and is not supported by a full view of human experience.[36] H. O. Brown is correct when he says that in this novel we have "a form which at once presents Stephen's experience as an alienated observer of the world around him and at the same time denies that separation, since *we see the world in that novel as it is present in Stephen's mind*" (p. 7; my emphasis). Brown here is referring to Stephen's sense of himself as socially alienated, but it is equally true that the novel presents—and undercuts—Stephen's deep-rooted tendency to dichotomize his experience.[37]

An important part of Joyce's purpose in this novel is to expose the paltriness of the modernist view of the self. This view of the self derives ultimately from Descartes' presumption of a schism between mind and matter, but its more immediate sources are the so-called empiricism of Locke and Hume, and the shallow rationalism of the Enlightenment philosophes. Humean "empiricism" is so fundamentally anti-experiential (as we saw in the preceding chapter) that it depletes and undermines our view of the self by presuming the psyche to be a *tabula rasa,* a blank tablet that has no inherent nature and no depth, and by presuming our experiences (more precisely, our sensations) to be discrete and disconnected. Enlightenment rationalism renders the self superficial by identifying the whole self with what we can rationally understand, and by the consequent presumption that we can and should articulate and criticize all of our ideas and assumptions. These are the ideas that lie behind modernist atomic individualism and sanction its main assumptions—first, the assumption that the self is a discrete and self-contained entity (in Satan's words, "The mind is its own place, and in itself / Can make a Heav'n of Hell, a Hell of Heav'n" [*Paradise Lost,* I, 254–55]); second, the assumption that it is feasible and desirable to be entirely self-aware and self-determining.

Predictably, the modernist view of the self as discrete and two-dimensional has been carried to its (il)logical conclusion by the postmodern idea that the self is simply a fiction or "a locus where various signifying systems intersect" (see the quotation from Silvio Gaggi on page 85). But I disagree with critics such as Hugh Kenner or Colin MacCabe or Cheryl Herr who would read into Joyce their own skepticism or confusion about the continuity and entelechy of the self.[38] Joyce's criticism of the insufficiency of the Humean view of the self does not mean that he disavows the idea of a self, but rather that he wishes to lead us to a more wholistic and sufficient view. The complex nature of the unity and entelechy of the self remained one of Joyce's central themes.

Stephen Dedalus, good modernist that he is, is sufficiently enamored of this empiricist/Enlightenment view of the self that he does (at least in *Portrait*) aspire to conscious control of all of the various forces at work within him. But we shall see in subsequent chapters how Joyce shows the insufficiency of Stephen's view of the self in this novel structurally, stylistically, and tonally. By structurally I mean that he permits certain structures of the novel to reflect Stephen's implicit view of reality, which he then reveals to us (partly through other structural patterns) to be simplistic and insufficient, and that he incorporates into the novel's structure "mythic" narratives and situations more comprehensive than Stephen can realize. By stylistically, I mean that he develops various techniques of psychological presentation that enable us to appreciate the depth and complexity of Stephen's psyche and to understand more of it than he himself understands. By tonally, I mean that the whole depiction of Stephen, including the structural and stylistic aspects noted above, is presented through a sympathetic irony, enabling us to see how limited, how constricting, Stephen's view of the world is, but at the same time to sense the wonderful depth and potential of Stephen's psyche, if he could shake himself free from the constraints of his modernist view.

Having in *Portrait* carried out this critique of the Modernist Syndrome on the level of the individual personality, Joyce was ready, thematically and technically, to attend to his fundamental subject on a broader social and cultural scale. More ambitious and more complex than *Portrait* in a variety of ways, *Ulysses* merges naturalism and symbolism on a grand scale. Set in the city of Dublin in one day and absolutely permeated with the details of that city, *Ulysses* is the most fully documented, the most *naturalistic,* work ever written. In its sheer detail, it easily out-Zolas Zola. But at the same time, its distinctive title calls attention to the hundreds of historical and literary allusions and schemata undergirding the novel—in other words to the *symbolist* dimension of the work. And no work has even been written that has so rich and pervasive a texture of psychological and mythic structures—of structures that evoke and represent the so-called inner world that the symbolist writers were exploring.

Furthermore, *Ulysses* shows even more fully than *Portrait* the insufficiency of the Cartesian dichotomization of reality and of the simplistic modernist view of the psyche.[39] For our purposes the main difference between *Portrait* and *Ulysses* is that while the former focuses upon the complexity of a single mind, the latter shows us how wonderfully interrelated are our so-called individual minds and evokes much more fully the public collective consciousness that we all participate in. *Portrait* does of course have a *cultural* aspect—Stephen is shown to be very much a part of his

milieu—but *Ulysses* does far more to invoke and develop the richly envel-
oping culture in which Stephen, Bloom, Molly, and all of their fellow-
Dubliners exist. This is done by attending to characters and places and
events beyond those involving the "main characters" (which he did not do
in *Portrait*), but it is done also through Joyce's incorporating into the novel
a far larger number of "mythic" situations and narratives. *Ulysses* involves as
well a refinement and extension of Joyce's techniques of psychological
presentation, still with the underlying aim of enabling us to understand
more than the character does. Through these devices Joyce can show how
much more complex, affective, and multilayered the psyche is than Descartes
(in his presumption that he could clear his mind of all presuppositions) or
Hume (in his analysis of experience into discrete aspects) would have us
believe, and he can show us as well the constant intercourse between inner
and outer, individual psyche and public world. His distinctive techniques of
psychological presentation suggest to us how indistinguishably our psychic
awareness shades off into affective and physical rapport with tangible objects and places (what D. H. Lawrence calls "the circumambient universe");
how constantly our psychic states are colored by memories that provide
touchstones or reverberating chambers for our "present" experience; how
much of our psychological merging with the world around us is affective or
imagistic rather than merely cognitive; and how fully our "individual" psychic worlds are interrelated.[40] Undergirding this is an array of "mythic" parallels that Joyce incorporates into the novel, all working to show us how
deeply our individual psyches are rooted in perennial modes of human
experience, how fully the schema of each individual's life is subsumed into
the many culturally transmitted schemata that we constantly draw upon,
knowingly and unknowingly. In doing all of this, Joyce illustrates on the
level of social intercourse and cultural reality the inextricability of subject
and object, private and public.[41] As Joyce told Arthur Power, "our [i.e., "we
moderns' "] object is to create a new fusion between the exterior world and
our contemporary selves . . . " (*Conversations*, p. 74). While *Portrait of the
Artist* deals with these themes on the level of a single individual, *Ulysses*,
the modern epic work that Joyce so long prepared himself to write, deals
with them on the level of many interrelating individuals, of the city, and of
modern culture generally.

Joyce probably foresaw from early in his career the writing of something
like *Ulysses*.[42] But in his youthful pre-visioning of himself as the prototypical
twentieth-century writer, Joyce probably did not foresee the need for any-

thing quite like *Finnegans Wake;* more likely, this anomalous book came as something of a surprise to Joyce himself. This is not to deny *Finnegans Wake* an integral part in Joyce's career; but it involves a different and a far more radical (i.e., more deep-rooted) response to the dilemmas and insufficiencies of the modern Western mind than Joyce had presented in his preceding works. Some time during his work on *Ulysses,* Joyce came to understand that the Cartesian dichotomy of subject and object was grounded in and reinforced by certain fundamental temperamental biases of the Western psyche, and it was these biases he attempted to address, and to redress, in *Finnegans Wake.*

In his *Psychology of the Unconscious,* Carl Jung made a fundamental distinction between two modes of thought, directed thinking, and undirected or fantasy thinking. The former mode of thinking is systematic and problem oriented and it provides us with a sense of directedness; it is a means to an end. Nondirected thinking on the other hand proceeds analogically and metaphorically rather than discursively, it seems to have little pragmatic purpose, and it is an end in itself. Jung says that for many centuries the Western mind has acted as if only the first mode of thought, directed thinking, is real thinking.[43] The essence, if not the most salient feature, of directed thinking is the denigration of metaphorical or analogical thinking in favor of linear, presumably progressive, discursive thinking. A large part of the reorientation toward reality the Western mind underwent in the Renaissance involved the abandonment of an analogical view of reality for a linear or discursive view. Though its roots can be traced back much earlier, this view emerged quickly and forcefully in the seventeenth century, manifesting itself in the criticism of natural language (denigrated because of its uncontrollable connotations and "accidental" analogies) and the search for a universal calculus, in a replacement of a Pythagorean understanding of the nature of mathematics with a pragmatic, Newtonian understanding, and in the ascendancy of a skeptical, reductionistic attitude over an imaginative and wholistic one.

This major shift of thought and attitude ushered in the modernism that Joyce seeks to redress in *Finnegans Wake.* Reading that novel requires the constant exercise of precisely those faculties that the Western mind has so persistently denigrated over the past several centuries. It invokes aspects of language that are "accidental" and physicalistic and synchronic (i.e., homophones, puns, rhyme, rhythm) rather than logical and diachronic (i.e., those that carry us toward some presumed goal of our mental activity). As Joyce himself several times said, *Finnegans Wake* explores the night-time side of the mind, the associative, metaphoric, analogic mode of thought that to the modernist mentality seems at best merely decorative and at worst distortive of reality.[44]

In *Finnegans Wake* Joyce takes us into what he called his "experiment in interpreting the 'dark night of the soul.' "[45] As he explained to Harriet Shaw Weaver, "one great part of every human existence is passed in a state which cannot be rendered sensible by the use of wideawake language, cutandry grammar and, goahead plot" (*Letters,* III, 146; Nov. 24, 1926).[46] What we have here is not another book offering counsel about how to temper the ego with the self or how to ground individualism in archetypal roots. It is rather a book devoted to the radically a-personal elements, generic elements, perhaps even pre-human elements, in human experience. And in order to lead us into these dimensions of experience, the book requires that we re-cultivate that metaphoric, non-directed play of mind Jung says we have for so long denigrated. *Finnegans Wake* enables us to experience that mode of thought to a degree unparalleled by any work I know, and in so doing it offers us a much-needed respite from the "single-mindedness" of mere rationality or of traditional individualism.[47] But this should not be taken as an indication of Joyce's loss of belief in the value of the individual or of consciousness, any more than one's willingness to sleep, to dream, to fantasize, should imply disdain of the waking state or of the process of individuation. This novel simply offers a healthy, if radical, balance or complement to these more respected modes of thought. Here again, that is, I disagree with those critics who would read into *Finnegans Wake* an attempt on Joyce's part to subvert the Western mind, or an attack upon the whole of Western "logocentrism." For all its apparent radicalness, *Finnegans Wake* is nonetheless a Western book. It calls upon us not to disavow or abandon our Western modes of thought, but to recultivate certain neglected or denigrated aspects of our tradition—aspects that involve metaphor and analogy and metamorphosis and process.

In light of Joyce's concern in his earlier works with "individualism," one of the most striking things about *Finnegans Wake* is the absence in it of anything like individualized characters. Though we can identify some of the "personages" of the novel and can talk with some specificity about the "family" that forms the nucleus of *Finnegans Wake,* discriminating in it a father, mother, two sons and a daughter, it would be foolish to claim that these personages exist in anything like the individualized form that characters have in all other novels, including Joyce's earlier works. In *Finnegans Wake* we are dealing not with individuals, but with types or conglomerates. But putting it this way may suggest that Joyce has here simply carried a few steps further his implicit criticism of the narrowly modernist sense of the self, the wrongly-based "integrity of the individual," that are dramatized in *Portrait* and *Ulysses*. In the past I myself thought this, mainly because I wished to give *Finnegans Wake* a place in some rather straightforward continuum from "individual" to "generic" in Joyce's thinking about the self. But *Finnegans Wake* is not best understood as the next logical step in a critique of atomic individualism. Rather, this book is fundamentally different from *Ulysses* not simply in its handling of individualism, but in the nature of the underlying issues that it addresses and consequently in the aspects of the psyche and of reality that it evokes and represents.

In *Ulysses* we are emotionally involved in the personal crises of the characters, and while we are often made aware that these very crises are in part the result of a narrow egoism or a misconstrued individualism on the character's part, we nevertheless continue to take these personal problems seriously and to hope for their resolution. Even in *Ulysses* there are voices that counsel an "objective" or "impersonal" or "eternal" perspective on the crises of Stephen and Bloom: in the Ithaca episode the narrator suggests scientistic equanimity as Bloom's proper response to Molly's adultery with Boylan (*U*, 17.2155 ff.). But that narrator cannot be identified with the underlying values of the novel.[48] In *Ulysses,* then, for all its qualifications of modern egoism, the individual is still center stage and his hopes, needs, and problems form the emotional substance of the novel. Furthermore, *Ulysses* is in some degree paradigmatic of how Joyce feels we should respond to our own life-crises—namely, by tempering our sense of ego and of our separateness from one another, but not by abandoning the conscious self and the values that it brings into being. Not so in *Finnegans Wake,* and it would be a mistake to conclude that Joyce offers us here an example of what we should aspire to. *Finnegans Wake* no more represents a dramatization of how we are to live in the world than do our dreams or fantasies, but we should not go to it for that, any more than we would turn to our dreams to tell us how to meet the deadlines or mundane crises of tomorrow. But this is not to say that *Finnegans Wake* is valueless, any more than to say that our dreams and fantasies are valueless. It is simply to acknowledge that the aim of *Finnegans Wake* is radically different from that of the earlier novels.

4

The Antimodernist Implications
of the *Bildungsroman*

*I*t will be clarifying to consider Joyce's *Portrait* within the context of the
genre it so well exemplifies—the *Bildungsroman*—since this genre is
inherently conducive to an antimodernist perspective. In attending to the
Bildungsroman I have no intention of broaching complex issues of literary
taxonomy or nomenclature. I invoke the form because I agree with Alastair
Fowler that "we identify the genre to interpret the exemplar."[1] But in the
case of Joyce's *Portrait* it is particularly needful that we consider its genre,
both because the origin and development of the *Bildungsroman* can clarify
certain relevant "antimodern" themes of modern literature, and because
Portrait so wonderfully fulfills certain potentialities of the genre.

The integrity of genres (or kinds, or types) varies considerably; some
of them represent arbitrary, ad hoc categorizations, while others have
their roots deep in some psychological/spiritual process, or in some perennial human need, or in some cultural structure. The genre of Aristotelian tragedy has considerable psychological/cultural integrity, and so
Aristotle appropriately speaks of tragedy's having taken some time "to
arrive at its natural form." Similarly, Aristotle's normative statements about
this genre are grounded in his assumption that certain techniques and
characters are more effective, and thus better, in "arousing pity and fear,
wherewith to accomplish [the] catharsis of such emotions" that is the
distinctive function of this genre.[2] But relatively few genres have such a
degree of integrity. It is much harder to offer firmly grounded, meaningful, generalizations about something so broad and amorphous as a lyric,

65

or so formally distinctive as a villanelle—both of which might be re-garded as "types."[3]

On a more practical level, genre criticism is potentially valuable because it can direct our attention toward relevant issues and facilitate our asking appropriate questions about the individual works that exemplify the genre. Further, as Fowler points out, comparing various examples of the genre may help us to realize and appreciate the importance of the different inter-ests, emphases, etc., that different authors have (Fowler, p. 38). On the other hand, one danger in genre criticism is that we may presume a work is intended as an example of a certain genre when it is not; another is that even when dealing with a work that is a valid example of a genre, the critic may misconstrue which traits of the genre are essential or normative and which are not, or may not be sufficiently open and responsive to meaning-ful variations on the form effected by an individual writer. For all of these reasons we should be cautious about invoking generic traits to argue that any writer should have done other than she did—since we may misunder-stand precisely what she intended to do or may fail to appreciate the implications of her variations on the form. When misapplied, the genre approach easily becomes procrustean.[4]

The *Bildungsroman* possesses a substantial degree of generic integrity, arising from certain currents in the intellectual/cultural milieu—in the En-lightenment *episteme*—that the genre came into being to explore and to counter. The *Bildungsroman* evolved out of its earlier cognate (or countergenre) the picaresque, to enable writers to explore certain issues about the individual psyche and its relationship to physical and cultural reality—issues raised by the superficial view of the psyche propounded by the British empiricists and the Enlightenment rationalists. Not that this pur-pose existed consciously for any of the early practitioners of the genre—or the later ones, for that matter—but nevertheless it was one of the most important things that these writers were doing with the genre. The *Bildungsroman* provided a means for exploring and combatting the super-ficial empiricist/rationalist ideas about the psyche and about a presumed subject/object split that were gaining authority in the late eighteenth cen-tury.[5] The emergence of the genre was facilitated by the cognate form already in existence—the picaresque—and the similarities and differences between these two can clarify the underlying purposes of the *Bildungsroman* and reveal what the nineteenth and early twentieth century practioners of the form were doing.[6]

My characterization of the *Bildungsroman* in the following pages does not give equal weight to each example of the form or to each of its traits. This is because the genre was called into being to serve certain broad cultural/psychological purposes that are illustrated more fully by some examples and some traits of the genre than by others. Furthermore, the earliest examples of the form do not present the themes the genre characteristically evokes and addresses as saliently as do examples from the early twentieth century. The contours of the genre emerged gradually during the nineteenth century in such a way that the "natural form" of the genre was most fully manifested in the early decades of the twentieth century.[7] Insofar, then, as my characterization is "normative," or I speak of the "nature" of the form, it reflects my belief in these cultural functions and in this evolution of the form. The implication behind such statements, again, is not that some Platonic genre-Idea was fully incarnated at one point in time, but that the particular cultural, psychological, and spiritual needs the genre came into being to express were most cogently felt at that time. One manifestation of this is the large number of quite coherent examples of the genre that were written during the second and third decades of this century. The cultural relevance of the genre at that time is suggested by William York Tindall's comments about the "novel of adolescence": "This form, which had flourished throughout the nineteenth century, producing *Wilhelm Meister, David Copperfield,* and *Richard Feverel,* received new life toward the end of the century from the science of biology and later from psychology. . . . The popularity of this form may be traced in part to the philosophy of determinism and in part to the growing revolt against it. . . . From 1903 onwards almost every first novel by a serious novelist was a novel of adolescence. . . . it produced some of the best novels of the early twentieth century" (*Forces in Modern British Literature 1885–1956* [1956], pp. 145–46).

My understanding of the *Bildungsroman* genre has been strongly influenced by certain paradigmatic early twentieth century examples of the form—examples that manifest clearly the cultural and philosophical issues that the genre so effectively dramatizes. Consequently I do not regard the prototype novel—Goethe's *Wilhelm Meisters Lehrjahre*—as the normative example of the form. On the contrary, while Goethe's novel possesses many characteristic traits of the genre, it also bears the impress of its having come out of another tradition, and thus certain traits that later emerged as important are lacking or obscured.[8]

꒜

It is a commonplace that Romanticism involved an increase of awareness of and interest in the self, the "inner world" of the psyche. In some
respects the literary exploration of the self had to await the support of late
nineteenth and early twentieth century philosophy and psychology before
it could fully develop. Certainly the work of Freud, Frazer, William James,
and Henri Bergson gave a grounding, an impetus, even a vocabulary and a
stock of metaphors, to the writers' continuing wish to explore and describe
the inner world. But the interest in the self emerges with clarity and force
more than a hundred years before, in the *Confessions* of Rousseau, in
Goethe's *Wilhelm Meister*, in Wordsworth's *Prelude*, the subtitle of which is
The Growth of a Poet's Mind. One expression of this interest in the self is
the emergence of the *Bildungsroman* or Apprenticeship Novel, its gradually replacing its earlier cognate the picaresque, and its full flowering in the
early decades of the twentieth century.

My eventual focus will be on Joyce's *Portrait of the Artist*, which I regard
as the finest example of the *Bildungsroman* or Apprenticeship Novel. I
agree, that is, with Maurice Beebe that "Joyce succeeded in giving definitive
treatment to an archetype that was firmly established long before the twentieth century."[9] In its structure, its style, certain of its themes, even its sympathetic irony, *Portrait* carries various "antimodernist" implications of the genre
to their fullest development. But in order to demonstrate this effectively, I
must begin with a comparison/contrast of the *Bildungsroman* and its pre-
decessor and complement, the picaresque, so as to demonstrate how certain characteristically modern themes are embedded in the
Bildungsroman—so as to show, that is, how a writer's turning to the genre
is itself an implicit engagement of the issues raised by the Cartesian mind/
matter dichotomy and by the Enlightenment view of the self. My compari-
son/contrast of these two forms is intended to illustrate two points: first,
that these forms are, in a variety of thematic and technical ways, complementary; second, that the *Bildungsroman* is a Romantic form—an anti-
Enlightenment form—brought into being by certain interests and needs of
the Romantic period, needs which persisted throughout the nineteenth
century and emerged with greater cogency in the early twentieth century.

Historically the picaresque is, of course, the earlier form, the earliest
instance being the anonymous sixteenth-century Spanish novel *Lazarillo
de Tormes* (1554). The term *picaresque* derives from the novel's focusing

on a picaro or rogue, who, though not an outright criminal, is always at outs with society. The genre occurs frequently in Spanish, French, and English literature from the sixteenth to the eighteenth centuries, in such novels as Thomas Nash's *Jacke, Wilton* (1594), Cervantes' *Don Quixote* (1605, 1615), Le Sage's *Gil Blas* (1615), Defoe's *Moll Flanders* (1722), Fielding's *Jonathan Wild* (1743) and *Joseph Andrews* (1741), and Smollett's *Roderick Random* (1748).

The *Bildungsroman* makes its appearance with the coming of the Romantic Period, Goethe's *Wilhelm Meisters Lehrjahre* (1795–96) generally being regarded as the prototype (though not the earliest instance) of the form.[10] Other works only a few years later that reflect these same concerns are the autobiographical poems of Byron and Wordsworth's *The Prelude*. During the nineteenth century we find a large number of "young man" or "young artist" novels, most of them interesting blends of the techniques and the concerns of the picaresque and the *Bildungsroman*. Carlyle's *Sartor Resartus* (1833–34), Dickens's *Great Expectations* (1860–61), Samuel Butler's *The Way of All Flesh* (1903, written 1873–1885) are examples of nascent *Bildungsromane* that retain many picaresque traits. But the *Bildungsroman* doesn't emerge full blown until the twentieth century, especially the period from 1910–1930. Then we find such clear, characteristic examples of it as Lawrence's *Sons and Lovers* (1913), Maugham's *Of Human Bondage* (1915), Joyce's *Portrait of the Artist* (1916), and Thomas Wolfe's *Look Homeward, Angel* (1929). In more recent decades, since World War II, interest in the *Bildungsroman* has waned, suggesting that the relationship between the individual and culture that brought the genre into being has somehow changed.

Comparison and contrast of these two forms shows that they serve similar and yet quite distinct purposes for their authors and for the culture that produces them. First, some broad similarities between the two forms, followed by attention to their more numerous and more interesting differences.[11]

Both the picaresque and the *Bildungsroman* involve a single major character; both, that is, are structured around a division, a tension, between one individual and the rest of the world. Furthermore, the two genres have a similar time span and narrative line, in that they typically begin with the birth or early childhood of the individual, pursue him through a variety of trials and vicissitudes, and end when the protagonist has reached what he regards as some relatively stable end point or distinctive juncture, usually in late adolescence or "young maturity." A third fundamental similarity is that both forms depict their protagonist as engaging in some search for a "father."

But even within these similarities there are significant differences. For example, while both genres are built around a division between the individual and the rest of the world, in the picaresque this division is social—i.e., the protagonist is separated from his society by virtue of his poverty or his class or his anti-social acts—while in the *Bildungsroman* it becomes metaphysical as well—i.e., it is rooted in a division between "inner" and "outer," between a private, subjective domain and a public, objective one. Similarly, while both genres chronicle the early years of one individual, the picaresque presents us merely with a series of discrete events, while the *Bildungsroman* tries to capture (in Joyce's fine phrase in his 1904 "Portrait of the Artist" sketch) the "individuating rhythm" of the character's psyche. Finally, the general rubric of a search for the father elides an important difference, for whereas in the picaresque the search for the father is literal (i.e., the boy is orphaned or separated from his family) or financial (i.e., the boy seeks a mentor who can provide wealth or social respectability), in the *Bildungsroman* the father the protagonist seeks is not an actual person, but a principle by which he can live. If this principle is manifested in some person, it is likely not to be the boy's physical father—very often father and son are at odds in the *Bildungsroman*—but someone who plays the role of his spiritual guide or mentor.

These, then, are the fundamental similarities that invite comparison between the picaresque and the *Bildungsroman:* both focus persistently upon a single protagonist who is at odds with his world; both follow the progress of this individual from birth or early childhood to "young maturity"; and both depict their protagonist as involved in some kind of search for the father. There are of course variations upon these characteristics in individual examples of the picaresque or the *Bildungsroman*. But even such variations can have important implications—i.e., they can reveal noteworthy differences in the writer's interests from the more typical aims of the genre.

To set the context for specific contrasts between the two forms, consider certain broad traits that express underlying differences between them. The picaresque is essentially a social novel—a novel about society—and its basic theme is the individual and society. The presentation of the main character is largely external—that is, there is little reflection on the protagonist's part, and there is virtually no "development" or growth by the protagonist—and the book ends with the hero's reconciling himself or adapting himself to society. The *Bildungsroman* by contrast is essentially a psychological and metaphysical novel, and its basic theme is the nature of the individual and of reality, manifested in the vicissitudes of a protagonist who is trying to align himself with whatever is most *real* in his own experience. The presentation of the main character is internal—i.e., we have immediate access to the protagonist's thoughts and feelings—and he or she undergoes real development, so that the book ends with the individual's having partly reconciled himself to reality, and partly reconciled reality to himself. Society does of course enter into the *Bildungsroman,* but only as one aspect of a larger reality the protagonist is struggling with.

We turn now to specific differences between the two genres—differences that have important implications, psychological and metaphysical. Though the practitioners of the *Bildungsroman* may not have been aware of this, most of these differences reflect the novelist's attempt to show the insufficiencies of the view of the mind (and of reality) implicit in empiricism and in Enlightenment rationalism—a view that the picaresque in some ways epitomized. Insofar as the *Bildungsroman* genre involves these issues, it has "antimodernist" implications.

First Person/Third Person Point of View

One interesting and perhaps surprising difference between the two forms is in terms of narrative point of view. The unreflective picaresque is almost always presented in first person point of view, while the more interior *Bildungsroman* is typically in third person. The first person perspective is used, for example, in *Lazarillo de Tormes;* in *The Unfortunate Traveller, or The Life of Jacke Wilton;* in *Moll Flanders;* and in *Roderick Random.* In contrast, the presentation is third person in *Sons and Lovers* and *The Rainbow,* in *Of Human Bondage,* in *Portrait of the Artist,* and in *Look Homeward, Angel.* Nineteenth-century examples of the form are often in the first person—e.g., *David Copperfield* and *Great Expectations*—though they tend increasingly toward an introspective presentation, and they often rely heavily upon the informed perspective of a mature narrator who can tell us more about his younger self than he understood at the time—which approaches a third person presentation. An interesting "transition" novel is Butler's *The*

Way of All Flesh, which is told in first-person, not by the focal character, Ernest Pontifex, but by the observer Edward Overton, who presumably understands Ernest better than Ernest understands himself.

The reason for this difference in point of view is that the third person presentation enables a fuller and deeper presentation of the character's psyche than does first person—a point that we shall explore more fully in regard to *Portrait* in chapter 6. In a first person narration, all that the protagonist can tell us is what he thinks—or more precisely, what he is *aware* of thinking. By contrast, use of third-person presentation enables the writer to suggest levels of the psyche far beyond what the protagonist himself is aware of. Insofar as it is true that the third-person enables a fuller, deeper presentation of the psyche, the third-person presentation of the *Bildungsroman* is itself antithetical to the *tabula rasa* view of the mind. If, that is, the mind were no more than a tablet, or if consciousness comprised the whole of the mind, then first-person presentation could tell all that is to be told—as is presumed by Enlightenment rationalists. The third person presentation in the *Bildungsroman* is necessary both because the writer has a more complex view of the mind than the *tabula rasa* image suggests, and because he wishes to take us deeper into the character's psyche than he himself can take us. Both Lawrence and Joyce are especially skillful at this exploration, though the feel of their respective styles and the specific means by which they convey the deeper levels of the psyche is very different.

Episodic vs. Developmental Structure

Another important difference between the two forms is that the typical picaresque consists of a series of discrete episodes, whereas the *Bildungsroman* is developmental, presenting stages in the process of the main character's growth. Since the picaresque is relatively uninterested in the protagonist's mind or soul, it depicts little or no growth on his part as the novel proceeds. If the picaro learns anything, it is simply how to avoid confrontation with society, or how to achieve financial security. As a result, the structure of the picaresque is episodic, the various escapades the picaro goes through being like beads on a string, with virtually no causal interrelation. The element of growth is so lacking that the episodes might easily be shuffled about without violence to the intention of the novel. Also, the ending of the picaresque novel is often arbitrary and precipitate, and does not reflect any fulfilled development of the protagonist. Rather, the hero suddenly, by some turn of chance or fate, comes into a fortune, or finds his father, and the novel ends. In *Roderick Random,* for example, it would do the novel no violence to rearrange the order of Roderick's various adventures, because there is nothing cumulative or progressive about them. And the novel ends when Roderick happens to find his long-lost father and thus comes into financial stability and social respectability.

In the *Bildungsroman*—as the name of the genre implies—the emphasis is decidedly upon the growth or *Bildung* of the hero, which necessarily implies a *process* of development.[12] Furthermore—and this is a distinctive trait of the genre—the very structures of the novel arise from and reflect the patterns, the rhythms, of the protagonist's growth. The episodes of the novel could not be shuffled, because each grows out of the preceding one, and taken together they convey the distinctive individuating rhythm of the character's psyche. The novel ends when the hero has reached a certain stage of development—usually, when he is, in his own estimation, "free." Of course the young protagonist's sense of freedom is often at odds with that of the author, which is one basis of the ironic handling of the protagonist typical of this genre.

In Joyce's *Portrait of the Artist,* each of Stephen's experiences involves what he regards as a progressive rejection of false possibilities and a progressively clearer realization of his true calling, or of what is most compelling, most "real" in his experience. Each of Stephen's experiences builds upon—largely by reacting against—the preceding ones. Obvious as this may seem, it is worth attending to, because this difference between episodic and progressive structure reflects not simply a difference in interest between Smollett and Joyce, but a difference in the conception of the psyche. For Joyce—and presumably for other writers who cast their material in the form of a *Bildungsroman*—the individual psyche involves an entelechy, an underlying developmental movement. The sequence of events in the hero's experience is not merely random, but developmental, and the aim of the writer is to discover within the "personalized lumps of matter" that constitute our bodies at various instants of time "their individuating rhythm, the first or formal relation of their parts" (phrases from Joyce's 1904 "A Portrait of the Artist"). In other words, the episodic structure of the picaresque comports well with Hume's view of the self as discrete and lacking continuity, whereas the developmental structure of the *Bildungsroman* rejects Humes's view in favor of a conception of the self as a unified and developing entity.[13]

The structures of the *Bildungsroman,* then, persistently reflect or embody the growth of the protagonist; to an impressive degree, the structures of the novel coincide with structures of the developing psyche. More specifically, the author of the *Bildungsroman* often presents the character's growth as a pattern of oscillation between two modes or two poles of experience. Though the nature of these poles necessarily varies from one novel to another, such growth by oscillation (or as Jung might say, by enantiodromic reaction) is a regular, recurrent feature of the *Bildungsroman,* presumably mirroring one of the most fundamental generic patterns of development of the psyche. In Lawrence's *The Rainbow,* Ursula Brangwen's oscillation is largely between self-assertion and self-abnegation—between trying to *achieve* meaning in her life by virtue of self-assertive acts, and trying to find something valid to *yield* herself to; in Maugham's *Of Human Bondage* the polarity Philip Carey swings between is similar to Ursula's, but is perhaps better described as involving sadism and masochism. In Eugene Gant in Thomas Wolfe's first two novels, the oscillation is largely between the needs of the "individual" on the one hand, and the claims of the family and of the community on the other. In Joyce's *Portrait,* the oscillation that Stephen experiences is more exactly described by my earlier terms, subjective and objective, internal and external, private and public. But in virtually every case, the psyche of the *Bildungsroman* protagonist develops through some such oscillation, and the structure of the novel reflects this. This is not, however, to imply that any *Bildungsroman* involves only one structural pattern; on the contrary, examples of the genre necessarily involve a number of intersecting, overlapping, mutually qualifying patterns, in reflection of the complexity of the evolving self. Joyce's *Portrait of the Artist* is the "archetypal" *Bildungsroman* largely by virtue of the amazing number of structural patterns—which are simultaneously patterns of Stephen's development—that ramify through the novel.

One interesting issue that this trait of the genre raises is the status within the protagonist's psyche of these various structural/developmental patterns. To what extent, that is, do the structural patterns of the *Bildungsroman* reflect the character's own imposition of pattern upon his experience, or to what extent do they reflect rhythms of the evolving psyche that lie beneath his conscious awareness? The answer is that the *Bildungsroman* typically involves both conscious and unconscious patterns, and that, generally speaking, the deeper and more profound the patterns, the less the protagonist is aware of them. In Dickens *Great Expectations,* for example, there is an important difference between the schema of his life that Pip is consciously trying to work out (including a successful relationship with Estella and the achievement of wealth and self-sufficiency), and the deeper, less conscious patterns that are working themselves out through him (involving Magwitch and Joe Gargery and a variety of things that Pip regards as "coarse and common" and would prefer to escape). Dickens goes to great lengths to develop both of these patterns throughout the novel, showing us finally that the less-conscious patterns better reflect Pip's own best interests than do his more conscious aspirations. In every *Bildungsroman* there are a number of structures, each of them reflective of different levels or strands (and degrees of awareness) of the evolving psyche of the protagonist.[14]

Similarly, we must recognize that patterns arising from beneath the character's awareness may have various sources—may arise for example from deeply implicit cultural patterns that he has internalized, or from the distinctive nature of his own psyche. We should never lose sight of this latter possibility, for the *Bildungsroman* does not present the character's psyche as naturalistically determined by environment; it typically presents the character as having a distinctive nature and as capable of a degree of self-determination.[15]

This claim that the structure of the *Bildungsroman* reflects the complex rhythms of the developing psyche suggests that many novels often loosely labeled *Bildungsromane* do not well exemplify the genre. To manifest the distinctive qualities of a *Bildungsroman,* a novel must depict an early and lengthy development span, so that it can display the emergent patterns that are characteristic of this individual psyche in its original forays into the world. Furthermore, the developing psyche should be presented not simply in response to a single crisis, but over a sufficiently long period of time that the "individuating rhythm" of the psyche emerges. We should, then, discriminate, between a novel of initiation (such as Hemingway's *A Farewell to Arms*), in which the structure reflects the response of an adult protagonist to one main life-crisis, and a *Bildungsroman,* in which the young psyche faces a series of crises, enabling the distinctive rhythms of the self to emerge.

Chance vs. Destiny or Calling

Another expression of the external focus of the picaresque is the large role fate, chance, or coincidence plays in novels of this genre. Very often in the picaresque an important turning point in the character's life is the result simply of a chance meeting. Smollett calls attention to the randomness of the influence on Roderick Random, both through the hero's surname and through his mother's dream of her unborn child as a tennis ball in the opening chapter of the novel. In Butler's *The Way of All Flesh,* important junctures in Ernest's life are determined largely by sheer chance or coincidence. One such example is Ernest's chance meeting with his mother's former housemaid Ellen (which Butler/Overton ascribes to "the fates"), which results in his disastrous marriage to her; another is his equally fortuitous running into his father's old coachman, John, from whom he learns that his marriage to Ellen is in fact invalid (chapters seventy-one and seventy-six, respectively).

The author of the *Bildungsroman,* on the other hand, disdains such coincidence, just as the typical *Bildungsroman* hero would disdain the idea that mere chance plays any part in his life-trajectory. The *Bildungsroman* hero has a sense of inner determination, of building his own life. If "fate" enters the *Bildungsroman* at all, it does so in the form of a sense of destiny, of calling, on the protagonist's part—a sense that reality may be seeking him out just as he is seeking it.

In many instances the *Bildungsroman* character's sense of autonomy and self-determination rises to such heights that it misconstrues and misrepresents the complex relationship between the psyche and the world. The character becomes so enamoured of his own self-determination that he refuses to acknowledge that his development could admit anything random or fortuitous—anything beyond his own control. Such an attitude is generally handled ironically by the author of the *Bildungsroman* and is likely to result in disappointment and chagrin for the character, perhaps in the sequel that often follows the *Bildungsroman.*

The Role of Satire

Another difference that reflects the essentially social nature of the picaresque, the "metaphysical" concern of the *Bildungsroman,* is that satire is a common, even integral, part of the picaresque, whereas it plays a much smaller role in the *Bildungsroman*. The various episodes the picaro goes through provide the author opportunity for satirical depiction of various social strata or institutions. In Fielding's *Joseph Andrews,* for example, a large part of Fielding's intention (as he tells us in his Preface) is to satirize the affectations that arise from vanity and hypocrisy, as we see in the pretension and pseudo-learning of medical doctors and lawyers, and in the lack of charity of the clergymen. In *Roderick Random,* Smollett explicitly acknowledges his satirical purpose in the opening words of his Preface—"Of all kinds of satire, there is none so entertaining and universally improving, as that which is introduced, as it were, occasionally, in the course of an interesting story"—and in the course of the novel he satirizes various groups, including the medical profession, the legal profession, and the military.

Satire in the picaresque is the author's acknowledgment of the importance of society and of his intention to reform it. In the *Bildungsroman,* especially in its twentieth-century examples, there is very little satirical element. The reason for this once again is the author's fidelity to the perspective of the protagonist, whose disengaged attitude toward the problems of his society reflects no concern for their remediation but simply a wish to fly by the restraints they would impose. And since he is so concerned with faithfully depicting the state of his character's psyche, the *Bildungsroman* author will not blur the focus by dragging into the novel a social concern that the character does not feel. In *Portrait of the Artist,* for example, the Roman Catholic Church is virtually omnipresent, and since Stephen regards it as one of the stumbling blocks to his development, it certainly is not depicted positively or sympathetically. But the novel involves little satirical depiction of the church, because Stephen—our viewpoint character—has no wish to reform this institution, only to escape it. In the *Bildungsroman,* society is only one aspect of the external reality the hero must come to terms with, and so the novel manifests little interest in social issues per se. The emphasis is rather on the inevitable conflicts between the internal and external, subjective and objective, private and public demands that the hero faces. The focus in the typical *Bildungsroman* is so completely on the evolving protagonist, and he takes himself so seriously, that there is little room in the novel for satire.

The Theme of Freedom

Another interesting difference between the picaresque and the *Bildungsroman* involves the protagonist's conception of freedom. There is a sense in which the protagonists of both forms are seeking freedom, but what that means varies significantly between the two forms. For the picaresque hero, freedom consists of financial security or independence or an acceptable place in society. For the *Bildungsroman* hero, freedom is a more complex psychological and spiritual matter. The typical *Bildungsroman* hero wishes to be free not simply of poverty or social ostracism, but of being dictated to by the ideas and ideals of others—of his family, his church, his social class, or his state. At the end of the picaresque, the hero accommodates himself to his society; at the end of the *Bildungsroman,* the hero undertakes what he presumes will be a personally fulfilling flight from the constraints of his milieu. In his view, in order to be himself, he must free himself from the various constraints that his culture imposes upon him; he must be self-aware and self-determining.

There is, however, more to the conception of freedom in the *Bildungsroman* that this account suggests. For within the *Bildungsroman* itself there is usually a significant disparity about the conception of freedom—a disparity between the view of the main character and that of the author, resulting in an inevitable irony in regard to this theme. While the view of freedom held by the protagonist of the *Bildungsroman* is more complex than that of the picaro, it is still callow and insufficient. For the typical *Bildungsroman* protagonist construes freedom in terms of escape or release from various constraining elements in his environment; he construes it, that is, in terms of an "atomic individualism" that presumes the self to be discrete and self-contained. The author of the *Bildungsroman,* however (some ten or twelve years older than his protagonist) has come to realize that such a view of freedom as escape and the self as autonomous is superficial and even self-defeating. The more mature author has seen that unless the protagonist arrives at some understanding of freedom in other than reactionary terms, his worldview will be very shallow indeed. The two senses of freedom at work in the *Bildungsroman,* then, produce a tension, an irony, that pervades the themes and structures of the novel but becomes especially pronounced at the end of the book. John Blades's criticism of Stephen in *Portrait* focuses specifically on this theme, and Blades pointedly says that "although Stephen strives for freedom the emphasis is on freedom *from* (family, Church, etc.) rather than freedom *to* (create, embrace, etc.)" (*James Joyce: "A Portrait of the Artist,"* p. 75; his emphasis).

The Inherent Irony of the *Bildungsroman*

While the picaresque is compounded of satire, it has virtually no irony, if by that we mean a dual perspective in which the protagonist is held by the author. This is because there is no significant difference between the picaro's "view of himself"—this seems too grandiose a conception to invoke for the picaro—and the author's view of him, whereas in the *Bildungsroman* this difference between the character's self-perception and the author's understanding is crucial to the genre and becomes the foundation of its characteristic irony. The *Bildungsroman* typically depicts a character whose view of the self, of individualism, of freedom, is at odds with that of the author. On certain levels—e.g., the level of immediate psychological presentation—the novel conveys the protagonist's perspective; but on other levels it reveals to us the simplifications and deficiencies of that perspective. The result is an inherently ironic mode of presentation. But this is not to say that the character is undercut or demeaned; on the contrary, the irony in the *Bildungsroman* is almost always a tempered, even sympathetic, irony—which is understandable, since the protagonist's career typically involves errors and misconceptions that the author himself has earlier suffered through. Critics often presume that an ironic presentation necessarily undercuts the character, but this is an unwarranted assumption. All that literary (or dramatic) irony necessarily involves is a dual perspective—in most cases that of the character, and that of the author. The tonal range of ironic presentation can run from scathing satire to wry humor to profound sympathy, and in Joyce's works it almost always veers toward the latter end of this scale; virtually all of Joyce's irony is sympathetic rather than coruscating.[16] The ironic perspective of the *Bildungsroman,* then, arises mainly from a discrepancy between the shallow, individualistic view of the self on the part of the protagonist, and the more complex view of the self held by the author and manifested in various ways in the text. In later chapters we shall examine specific ways that the irony in *Portrait of the Artist* conveys the insufficiency of Stephen's understanding of the self.

ॐ

From the preceding characterization of the *Bildungsroman* it may appear that I regard it as a more "profound" genre than the picaresque. But while the *Bildungsroman* does concern itself more fully with the development of the individual's psyche, and this is a matter of great concern to our culture, I do not presume that the *Bildungsroman* is inherently superior to or more profound than the picaresque; undoubtedly there are individual examples of the picaresque that are in virtually every respect superior as novels to certain individual *Bildungsromane*. Moreover, I do not presume that the view of the relationship between the psyche and the world that is dramatized within most examples of the *Bildungsroman* is inherently valid. On the contrary, because its mode of presentation is often so fully subsumed into the protagonist's worldview, the *Bildungsroman* is likely to involve various distortions—e.g., to exaggerate the degree to which the individual is self-determining. As far as veridicality or "wisdom" is concerned, Dickens' *Great Expectations* is probably "truer to life" than more recent, "purer" examples of the *Bildungsroman*. In *Great Expectations,* Pip's life-course is the result both of factors beyond his control (chance, coincidence, prescribed circumstances) and of his own capacity to learn and to grow; in purer examples of the *Bildungsroman* the hero appears to be virtually self-creating—which is less veridical than a depiction that acknowledges the role that factors beyond our control do inevitably play in our lives.

The *Bildungsroman* came into being in the late eighteenth century as a vehicle for the full-scale exploration of the development of the individual psyche. This is not to say that the genre is inherently "individualistic"; quite the contrary, those who have used the form have typically shown through it the insufficiency and superficiality of the underlying empiricist and Enlightenment ideas that fostered the idea of "atomic individualism." What modern readers can easily fail to appreciate about the form, however, is that it often depicts a protagonist who is enamoured of such individualism and of the Enlightenment idea that it is both feasible and desirable to be totally self-aware and self-determining. As a result the author regards his character ironically, depicting his quest for freedom—i.e., self-determination—and at the same time revealing to us in various ways how much of the protagonist's self lies beyond the purview of his own understanding. This implicit criticism of the simplistic view of the self fostered by empiricism and the Enlightenment does not, however, mean that the *Bildungsroman* involves a "parody" of the quest, or that it thus intends to undermine or deconstruct the underlying idea of a coherent self or of individual development. Quite the contrary, the novel vindicates on a deeper level than merely conscious awareness the idea that the psyche does have an entelechy that is not simply a result of the protagonist's conscious choice and self-determination, but also of cultural forces that may or may not be in the best interests of the individual, and of those deeper forces within his own psyche that are guiding him toward his own distinctive individuation.[17]

Part Two

❦

A Portrait of the Artist

5

The Structures

*W*e turn now to Joyce's novel, illustrating the distance between Stephen's modernist view of the world and of his psyche, and Joyce's fuller and richer antimodernist perspective. This chapter explains how indistinguishable the structures of the novel are from those of Stephen's psyche, and focuses on certain structural features that reveal how deep into Stephen's mind the Cartesian subject/object dichotomy has penetrated.

Joyce's *Portrait* depicts the development of Stephen Dedalus from early childhood to his more or less self-confident late-adolescent flight from Dublin in pursuit of his calling as an artist. Stephen is a typical *Bildungsroman* hero—sensitive, intelligent, continually trying to discover what life holds for him. Every experience is for him a potential gateway to life's meaning, a possible revelation of "the end he had been born to serve" (*P,* p. 169). He is typical also in that his development is a true *Bildung,* a process of individuation arising both from distinctive, innate traits of his psyche and from the influences of his milieu.

In the face of structuralist and poststructuralist claims that the individual is no more than a nexus of cultural patterns and structures—"a locus where various signifying systems intersect" in Sylvio Gaggi's apt characterization of this view—I must emphasize how *Portrait* testifies repeatedly to the distinctiveness of Stephen's "individuating rhythm," to how different he is from others in his cohort who have been subject to very similar cultural forces.[1] I agree with H. M. Daleski and Stanislaus Joyce that Stephen's development involves the realization of potentialities inherent in his psyche, rather than simply a response to his environment. Daleski says "in *A Portrait*

85

of the Artist, unlike *Mansfield Park* or *The History of Henry Esmond,* for instance, it is not so much the child's circumstances as his consciousness that determines the sort of adult he becomes and colors his whole personality. The child's consciousness is the 'embryo' of character that Joyce starts with and then sets into dynamic relation with circumstance" (*Unities,* p. 175). Daleski goes on to quote Stanislaus' remark that when Joyce set to work on the novel, "the idea he had in mind was that a man's character, like his body, develops from an embryo with constant traits. The accentuation of those traits, their reactions to hereditary influences and environment, were the main psychological lines he intended to follow, and, in fact, the purpose of the novel as originally planned" (*MBK,* p. 17).[2] Stanislaus' specification of both "hereditary influences and environment" as factors the embryo of character *reacts to* shows that he does not identify the psyche with either of these contributory influences.

Baruch Hochman's fine essay "Joyce's *Portrait* as Portrait" (*The Literary Review* 22 [Fall 1978]: 25–55) also addresses these issues. Emphasizing Stephen's development throughout the novel, Hochman points out that "Joyce does not render a merely passive process. Stephen, to be sure, does incorporate elements of his environment. . . . But the internalization is not passive. It is an appropriation, a taking and a making his own" (p. 30). Hochman stresses as well the self-identity that persists throughout the novel, saying "*Portrait* renders the disparate 'Stephens' of the successive moments of his experience. Yet it renders the same Stephen, who is identical with himself even as he undergoes the sea-change of biological, emotional, sociological and intellectual development" (p. 27). He also speaks intelligently to the complex question of the relationships between self and culture, pointing to a paradox that the novel keeps before us:

> One of the novel's governing themes is the primacy of culture—of all the words and images and ideas in which man is so entangled, that his "nature" cannot be discerned in its bare primordiality. Yet there is an important sense in which the thesis reverses itself. It can be said, if I am right about the priorities governing this novel, that the entire mass of cultural material has no vibrancy, hardly any meaning, except in Stephen as constituted: from his muscles and his guts, as we are asked to envision them, up through his rational and imaginative faculties. What animates culture and its images is, if not perceivable "nature," then knowable personality. (p. 51)

In the preceding chapter I proposed that the structures of the *Bildungsroman* reflect the *Bildung,* the development, of its protagonist. Essentially this same point about *Portrait*—that its structure is a function of Stephen's development—has been made by a number of critics; Thomas F. Staley, in a review of studies of the novel's structure, points out that "all of the studies agree that the central structural principle in the novel is informed and even controlled by Stephen's own spiritual growth and development."[3] This means that virtually every study of Stephen's psychological development simultaneously involves claims about structural elements, structural patterns, in the novel. While some of the patterns critics have proposed seem contrived or imposed, most of them are plausible: the number and variety of patterns that have been brought to light both testify to Joyce's genius and suggest how large an array of structural elements can enter into the "individuating rhythm" of one individual's psyche.[4]

I would make two general points about the novel's structures. First, so fully is this characteristic of the *Bildungsroman* realized in *Portrait* that it is questionable whether we can discover any feature of the book's structure that is not simultaneously a feature of Stephen's psyche. Certainly every motif (or complex) that we trace through the novel (e.g., birds, hands, rose, cow, red/green) is not simply a strand in an aesthetic fabric, but a component of the young man's gestating psyche, and analogously, each of the various structural patterns that we detect in the novel is simultaneously an aspect of Stephen's individuating rhythm.[5]

The second point is that virtually all such structural/psychic patterns exist as subconscious elements of Stephen's psyche, since Stephen is not consciously imposing—or even aware of—these patterns. That is, when we trace these patterns and motifs we render explicit something that necessarily exists implicitly in Stephen's psyche. Thus any such analysis of structural patterns inherently refutes the *tabula rasa* image of the mind and the Enlightenment ideal of total self-awareness.[6] The subconscious nature of the patterns is more likely to be insisted on in Freudian or avant garde psychoanalytical readings of the novel—which suggests an "antimodernist" conception of the psyche in such readings—but it is equally the case with all readings that propose underlying structures or patterns within Stephen's development.[7] Compared to the extensive subconscious dynamics of his psyche revealed by these studies of structural patterns, the degree of self-awareness and conscious control of his psyche that Stephen can achieve is relatively small, though not trivial.

While every structural pattern within Stephen's psyche thus involves implicit elements, the pattern or rhythm that I wish to focus on here is very deeply implicit. This pattern derives from his having internalized the Cartesian dichotomy between *res extensa* and *res cogitans,* and is reflected in his construing his experience as oscillating between poles that can best be described as inner/outer, subjective/objective, private/public. This implicit orientation on Stephen's part results in an underlying oscillatory pattern that manifests itself through successive chapters of the novel—and to a lesser extent among episodes within the chapters—and that undergirds most of the other structural patterns described by earlier critics.

᷒ঌৎ

Joyce's *Portrait* dramatizes Stephen's struggle to discover some principle by which to live. In each of the first four chapters Stephen responds to some call, some impulsion, which seems to manifest the life-principle that he is seeking. Consequently, each chapter involves a pattern of rising action or intensification, ending in a climactic scene that dramatically exemplifies his current sense of what is most real and most compelling in his experience. In the first chapter, this climactic scene is his appeal to Father Conmee; in the second, his visit to the prostitute; in the third, his confession to the priest; in the fourth his vision of the wading girl. Each of these scenes epitomizes for Stephen some newly-realized sense of what is most real in his experience and consequently of how he is to approach life. The fifth chapter significantly modifies the pattern of the first four, for two reasons. First, Stephen's discovery of his artistic calling at the end of chapter IV is valid, so that no more must he undergo dramatic rediscoveries of his life-course. Secondly, simultaneously with his discovering his calling as an artist, Stephen asserts a qualitatively greater degree of self-awareness and self-determination—this is what he construes his soul's "aris[ing] from the grave of boyhood" (p. 170) to involve—and this new attitude toward himself is the basis of a significant shift in his demeanor, and consequently in our attitude toward him, in chapter V. In this final chapter Stephen faces the less dramatic but more complex problem of coming to understand what his artistic calling involves—a problem that he has not solved by the end of the novel.

Let me briefly label the life-approaches that Stephen pursues in the first four chapters, offer a generalization about them, and then elaborate. In chapter I, Stephen undertakes a *social* approach to life; in chapter II this social approach collapses and is replaced by the *sensuous* approach; in chapter III this proves unsubstantial, and Stephen engages in a *religious* approach to life; in chapter IV, he finds the religious approach to life unacceptable, sees his true calling as that of artist, and embarks on the *aesthetic* approach to life.

My generalization about these successive life-approaches derives from my earlier observation that the *Bildungsroman* often depicts the protagonist involved in an oscillatory movement between poles of experience. Stephen exemplifies several types of oscillation, but the most fundamental is between modes of experience he construes as inner or subjective, and those he senses as outer or objective, thus reflecting his implicit division of his experience into outer and inner. That is, in Chapter I Stephen's social life-response is to forces that he senses as coming from *without* him. In contrast, the approach that he assumes in Chapter II, is a response to forces that he feels to come from *within* him. And as the schema indicates, there is a regular oscillation back to *outer* orientation in Chapter III, and once again to *inner* orientation in Chapter IV. But while this dichotomization of reality into subject and object, private and public, reveals how deeply into Stephen's psyche the Cartesian split has penetrated, Joyce by various means shows this dichotomization to be simplistic and un-veridical. It is by no means always easy for Stephen to construe his experience in these terms, since all human experience implicitly involves a fusion of "inner" and "outer." But this pattern of oscillation is necessary to Joyce's dramatization of the coming of age of an intelligent young man in a modernist, post-Cartesian intellectual milieu.[8] Nor is it accidental or trivial that Stephen's artistic calling (in chapter IV) comes to him on an inward (i.e., subjectivist) phase of his orientation. As we shall see, this reflects his innate predisposition toward an inner-oriented, symbolist view of art, and it consequently sets the terms of his reading of his problem of artistic identity and the relationship of the artist to society in chapter V.

The pattern I have just outlined is represented in the accompanying Figure. The schema shows that each of the first four chapters involves the surfacing of a distinctive approach to life on Stephen's part—an approach that is suggested by the rising line for each of the chapters and is epitomized by a climactic event just prior to the end of each chapter.[9] The descending lines in chapters II, III, and IV represent the subsequent collapse of the life-approach or orientation climaxed in the preceding chapter. Chapters II, III, and IV, then, have a chiastic structure, since they involve

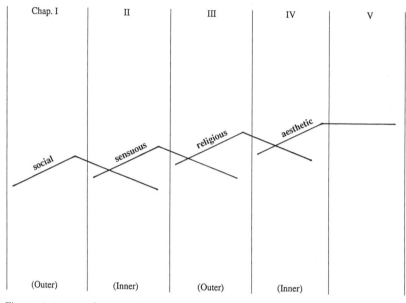

Figure. A structural pattern in Joyce's *Portrait of the Artist*.

both the erosion of the preceding approach, and the emergence of a new one, accompanied by an enantiodromic swing between the Cartesian inner/outer poles.[10] Each of the successive climactic peaks is higher than the preceding one, to indicate that for Stephen each successive view of life supersedes what he now regards as an insufficient or mistaken earlier view. That is, in chapter IV, he does not see his aesthetic calling as simply one other possible alternative, but as more profound and fundamental than the preceding life-orientations, which he feels he is now transcending. Each of these middle chapters, then, involves the falling away of one approach to life, accompanied by the coming into being of a "more comprehensive" view. As the diagram suggests, the climax of chapter IV is the true climax of the novel—the highest peak—in the sense that the calling that Stephen discovers there is his true calling: he is by his nature intended to be an artist, not a priest (chapter III), nor a devotee of sensuous experience (chapter II), nor one of "the fellows" (chapter I).

The agenda of chapter V is quite different from that of the earlier chapters: Stephen is intended to be an artist, and so there are no more roller-coaster rises and falls of life-orientation; what remains is the tougher and less dramatic problem of Stephen's coming to understand what an artistic vocation requires of him. But as I have suggested, the terms in which he construes his artistic calling are established by his having come to his artistic vision on an inward swing of his psyche, reflecting his commitment to the symbolist, aestheticist conception of the artist. While this view is challenged by several experiences in chapter V, it is not replaced by any new counter vision, leaving Stephen still entrammeled in a subjectivist view of art and the artist at the end of the novel. And while the Stephen that we see in *Ulysses* has been forcibly reoriented toward the material world by the trauma of his mother's death, and he has begun to cultivate a more realistic view of art (epitomized by his Parable of the Plums that stands in such contrast to his villanelle in *Portrait of the Artist*), he has not yet achieved the reconciliation of these presumed opposites that will enable his emergence as an artist.

Let me now clarify how Stephen's various life-approaches in the first four chapters of the novel manifest an oscillation between Cartesian poles. Once he gets beyond his infancy (pp. 7–8), Stephen's life-approach in chapter I is essentially social—i.e., it is a reaction to public, "objective" demands that he experiences as coming from *outside* himself. The primary forces impinging on Stephen during the Clongowes experience are from the society of his school, and during the Christmas dinner scene the young boy is subjected to forces arising from the public elements of politics, religion, and family. Though he does already have a distinctive, characterizable psyche quite different from that of his fellows at Clongowes, Stephen does not yet have any clear sense of his own self, and so he is continually buffeted by various influences and demands from a variety of directions— all sensed by him as arising from somewhere beyond or outside him. Perhaps the most constant note of this chapter is Stephen's puzzlement as to what is going on around him, and how to respond to it. This is epitomized by the questions put to him by Wells about whether he kisses his mother before bed; Stephen finds that either answer is wrong, and finds himself ridiculed by "the other fellows." His bafflement is manifested on a deeper and more traumatic scale by the terrible argument at the Christmas dinner table, and finally by the pandybatting. When he is pandybatted by Father Dolan for something that seems thrust upon him for no fault of his own, he is puzzled and disturbed over what the appropriate response to this injustice should be. Finally, at the urging of the other boys, he decides to pursue the regular social-hierarchical channels available to him, and to take his complaint to the rector. A passage late in chapter I shows how

strongly Stephen's coming to this decision is influenced by the importuni-
ties of his (older) fellow students:

> —I wouldn't stand it, Fleming repeated, from Baldyhead or any other
> Baldyhead. It's a stinking mean low trick, that's what it is. I'd go straight up
> to the rector and tell him about it after dinner.
> —Yes, do. Yes, do, said Cecil Thunder.
> —Yes, do. Yes, go up and tell the rector on him, Dedalus, said Nasty
> Roche, because he said that he'd come in tomorrow again to pandy you.
> —Yes, yes. Tell the rector, all said.
> And there were some fellows out of second of grammar listening and
> one of them said:
> —The senate and the Roman people declared that Dedalus had been
> wrongly punished.

• • •

> Yes, he would do what the fellows had told him. He would go up and tell
> the rector that he had been wrongly punished. A thing like that
> had been done before by somebody in history, by some great person whose
> head was in the books of history. And the rector would declare that he had
> been wrongly punished because the senate and the Roman people always
> declared that the men who did that had been wrongly punished. (pp. 52–53)

This passage suggests how fully Stephen's response to this crisis is socially formed and generated, and it involves a verbal motif that epitomizes
the social nature of the forces at work on Stephen—the motif of "the
fellows." This apparently bland, general term occurs frequently and at important intervals in this chapter. For example, section I.iv (pp. 40–59) opens
with "The fellows," and over the next two pages, six paragraphs have the
phrase either as their opening words or in their first sentence, and the last
paragraph of the chapter begins with the phrase.[11] Young Stephen's punishment and even his crime have been pressed upon him from without—he
feels no real sense of guilt—and now he pursues the socially-instituted
mode of appeal because his schoolmates urge it upon him ("Yes, he would
do what the fellows had told him"—p. 53.21), and because there is a public
pattern for it in history (the senate and the Roman people—pp. 53.10,
53.26, 54.9), which seems to Stephen to involve a reality far more substantial than his fledgling soul. As a result of this urging by his peers, Stephen,
in fear and trembling, makes his way through the corridors of the school to

Father Conmee's office and tells him of the injustice. The rector listens sympathetically to the trembling boy, tells him that he will look into the incident, and Stephen returns to the playing fields, to be cheered and acclaimed by "the fellows" (pp. 58.16, 58.20, 58.28, and 59.18)—the social reward for his social act.

In his response to this early crisis, Stephen is pursuing a social approach to life and its problems, both in the sense that the actions he takes are strongly influenced by his school mates, and in that he is responding through the channels that the society of his school makes available to him, rather than through wiles of his own devising. Though his fledgling psyche has not yet fully developed the categories of inner and outer, both the source of the crisis and the means of solution are presented as basically *external* to the boy, brought to bear upon him from the outside.

In chapter II (as in every subsequent chapter) there is a marked increase in Stephen's self-awareness, and given his post-Cartesian orientation, he inevitably experiences his self, his psyche, as existing "within" him. Consequently this chapter is marked by more explicit reading on Stephen's part of his experience in terms of inner and outer than was chapter I. Appropriately, John Blades says that "whereas in Chapter I his progress was often the result of his response to *external* stimuli, here it is usually the result of both maturation and obscure *internal* promptings" (*James Joyce: "A Portrait of the Artist,"* p. 33; my emphasis). As a part of his larger individuation process, two important complementary developments occur in this chapter. The first is the gradual but clear erosion of Stephen's attempts to live his life as a social creature, to maintain that unity with the community (including the familial community) that characterized the end of chapter I and the opening of chapter II. The other is his growing awareness of sensuality and sexuality, which he construes as arising *within* him. The public world of relationships with family and friends comes to seem to him less real, less substantial, and the inner world of imagination, especially of sensual and sexual imagination, elaborates itself more fully and more forcibly to him. These two processes are experienced by Stephen as antithetical, and his susceptibility to inner influences is no doubt enhanced and given impetus by his withdrawal from those outer forces that have been so baffling and so hurtful to him in his earlier phase.

Each chapter opens with a carry-over of the life approach that emerged so dramatically in the preceding one, and so here we find Stephen still pursuing, in his relationship with Uncle Charles and with the old trainer

Mike Flynn, though passively and perfunctorily, the social role that he had taken on. But we are told that Stephen "often glanced with mistrust" at the trainer's face, and, somewhat surprisingly, that he "respect[ed], though he did not share" his Uncle Charles' piety (pp. 61, 62). During this same period we are told that "his evenings were his own," and that they were spent in his poring over *The Count of Monte Cristo*. When Stephen comes to have a vague sense of his father's financial troubles—doubtless reminiscent for him of the threats he encountered at Clongowes—his response is to brood upon the image of Mercedes, and we are told that "sometimes a fever gathered within him and led him to rove alone in the evening along the quiet avenue" (p. 64). This is the first use in the novel of *within*, a word that occurs frequently as Stephen develops a fuller sense of a world "within" himself. Soon we are told of Stephen's growing sense that "he was different from others," and as a result, "he did not want to play. He wanted to meet in the *real* world the unsubstantial image which his soul so constantly beheld" (p. 65; my emphasis). This passage reveals his growing disdain for the society of his fellows, and the phrasing of the last sentence shows both that the inner world of his imagination (or his soul) is growing in authority for Stephen, and that he is coming to make a distinction between that interior realm and what he still regards as the "real world"—i.e., the public world. His experiences among his fellows and his teachers at Belvedere show Stephen to be much less susceptible to their appeals and accusations than when he was at Clongowes. His trip to Cork with his father only increases his alienation from his family and intensifies his sense of how utterly different he is from every one else, feeling that "an abyss of fortune or of temperament sundered him from [his father and his cronies]" (p. 95).

   The crisis of this chapter occurs when Stephen wins the essay prize money and spends it in one last futile attempt to re-cement his familial relations. The erosion of his social ties and the triumph of sensuosity are clearly indicated in several paragraphs late in this chapter, paragraphs that show Stephen's sense of being under the influence of forces that he experiences as "external" and "internal," and the triumph in this phase of his life of the latter:

> How foolish his aim had been! He had tried to build a breakwater of
> order and elegance against the sordid tide of life *without him* and to dam
> up, by rules of conduct and active interests and new filial relations, the

powerful recurrence of the tides *within him*. Useless. From *without* as from *within* the water had flowed over his barriers: their tides began once more to jostle fiercely above the crumbled mole.

He saw clearly too his own futile isolation. He had not gone one step nearer the lives he had sought to approach nor bridged the restless shame and rancour that divided him from mother and brother and sister. He felt that he was hardly of the one blood with them but stood to them rather in the mystical kinship of fosterage, fosterchild and fosterbrother.

He burned to appease the fierce longings of his heart before which everything else was idle and alien. He cared little that he was in mortal sin, that his life had grown to be a tissue of subterfuge and falsehood. Beside the savage desire *within him* to realize the enormities which he brooded on nothing was sacred. He bore cynically with the shameful details of his secret riots in which he exulted to defile with patience whatever image had attracted his eyes. By day and by night he moved among distorted images of the *outer world*. A figure that had seemed to him by day demure and innocent came towards him by night through the winding darkness of sleep, her face transfigured by a lecherous cunning, her eyes bright with brutish joy. Only the morning pained him with its dim memory of dark orgiastic riot, its keen and humiliating sense of transgression. (pp. 98–99; my emphasis)

While the experience that this passage describes obviously involves so subtle a blending of "inner" and "outer" elements that it is hard to discriminate them, it nevertheless shows that Stephen is construing his experience more and more in such dichotomous terms. The words that I have emphasized show explicitly Stephen's emerging sense of inner and outer, at the same time that other words or metaphors in this passage testify to the inner/outer distinction more subtly. Note the uses here of the images of *heart* and of *blood,* which are felt by Stephen to be inner, and the association of the public world with day and the private world with night. *cf U & FW*

But while this passage reveals Stephen's inclination to construe his experience in inner/outer terms, it simultaneously invokes more implicit elements of his experience that resist such reading. The term *image,* for example, used twice in this passage, is particularly interesting (and problematic) in terms of Stephen's attempts to distinguish his experiences into inner and outer, since every "image" necessarily involves an interface between subject and object, inner and outer. Probably in this inner-oriented phase of his life, Stephen regards images as something that spring up from within him, owing little or nothing to his public experience of the "outer world"; but we can see even in this passage that Stephen's images inevitably involve an inextricable blend of public and private aspects of his experience. This chapter ends with Stephen rejecting the call of family and society and, driven by lust and lured by the images his mind elaborates, winding his way through the streets of Dublin to his meeting with the prostitute, certain that, in giving himself over to what he feels rising within him, he is responding to the most real powers of life.

Chapter III also has a chiastic structure, depicting the falling away of Stephen's sensuous approach to life, and the rise of the religious approach. The chapter begins with a carryover of Stephen's sensuous phase—"stuff it into you, his belly counseled him" (p. 102)—but it quickly appears that this will be short-lived.[12] Reared and influenced by the Catholic Church—more precisely, by the Jesuits—as he has been, Stephen's sensuous/sensual experiences have always had the taint and the attraction of sin, and now that sense of sin comes to the fore. Under the searing effect of the retreat sermons, Stephen feels that in indulging his sensuality he has been building his life on shifting sands, and he must now turn to the firm rock of the Church. He sees that religion is the only true foundation upon which to build one's life. No doubt this decision is enforced by the sermons' being delivered by Father Arnall; we are explicitly told "the figure of his old master, so strangely rearisen, brought back to Stephen's mind his life at Clongowes. . . . His soul, as these memories came back to him, became again a child's soul" (pp. 108–109). The idea of Stephen as a vulnerable child is also played upon by the preacher's repeatedly addressing his hearers as "my dear little brothers in Christ," or as "my dear (little) boys." (The priest to whom he confesses also repeatedly calls him "my child.")

The effect of this on Stephen is shown in several ways. One is the sentimental little scene that Stephen imagines between himself and Emma in which both of them are seen as "children that had erred" (p. 116); another is the great access of fellow-feeling that Stephen has: "at last he had understood: and human life lay around him, a plain of peace whereon antlike men laboured in brotherhood, their dead sleeping under quiet mounds. The elbow of his companion touched him and his heart was touched . . . ," and a bit later, "in utter abjection of spirit he craved forgiveness mutely of the boyish hearts about him" (p. 126). This motif of social companionship is reiterated after Stephen's confession when he feels the beauty of living "a life of peace and virtue and forbearance with others" and we are told "the boys were all there, kneeling in their places. He knelt

among them, happy and shy. . . . He knelt before the altar with his class-
mates, holding the altar cloth with them over a living rail of hands" (pp.
145–146).[13] Once again the chapter ends dramatically with an act that expresses Stephen's complete acceptance of his new-found religious way of
life. Once again trembling with emotion, the boy makes his way through a
labyrinth of streets (in order to avoid making his confession at his college),
and the chapter ends in the dramatic scene of his pouring out his sins to the
old priest.

In terms of the schema proposed above, this chapter involves a swing
back on Stephen's part from influences that he experiences as subjective
and private, to influences that are public and "social." This may seem an
inappropriate characterization of something so emotionally powerful, so
intense and personal, as the religious experiences that he undergoes in this
chapter. But we are dealing here not with a Protestant fundamentalist or
"inner light" tradition in which religious experience is construed as inherently personal, but with Irish Roman Catholicism, in which the institutional
element is very strong, as are the ties between the church and other social
institutions. To a large extent for Stephen (and for Joyce) religion is a
public, social, "external" force, one that, especially in a Jesuit college, inescapably seeks one out and obtrudes itself upon one. Furthermore, there is
textual evidence of various sorts that Stephen regards what he is responding to in this phase of his life as an outer (i.e., social) rather than an inner
demand. There is, of course a sense in which the images and ideas of the
Church get into Stephen's soul so fully that they do become integral to his
self, and this is one device by which Joyce makes us realize the impossibility of categorizing modes of experience or influence into inner and outer.[14]
But the demands of religion, the possibility of a religious vocation, come to
Stephen primarily as external influences. It seems doubtful whether, left
entirely to himself and without the pressures of his mentors, Stephen would
seriously have considered a vocation in the priesthood, or even have developed on his own so deeply troubling a conviction of his own sin. It is the
skillful, subtle voice of the preacher that reawakens his childhood feelings
of vulnerability and guilt and sends him wandering once more through the
labyrinth of Dublin's streets, again trembling with emotion, this time in
search of a priest to confess to.

Chapter IV begins, as have the preceding ones, with a temporary continuation of the way of life dramatically expressed in the climax of the
preceding chapter. Stephen has given himself over to the religious life as

completely as possible—has laid his life out in devotional areas, etc. But once again the chapter depicts a falling away of one influence—the religious—and its replacement by another—the aesthetic—which Stephen once more presumes to be more substantial, more real, than the life-approach that he is turning his back upon. By this time, the reader may have sensed the pattern of the roller-coaster-like rise and fall of feelings that this young boy has already three times experienced, and so perhaps anticipates another such jaunt. We should not, then, be surprised to find that Stephen's religious approach to life soon begins to dissolve. What rises to take its place again involves a pendulum swing from the external to the internal, for Stephen's calling to art comes, he feels, from within the depths of his soul. Though we can see this most clearly in the ecstatic passages at the end of chapter IV, it is implied by a paragraph earlier in the chapter, when the true course of Stephen's destiny begins to become clear to him:

> He was passing at that moment before the Jesuit house in Gardiner Street, and wondered vaguely which window would be his if he ever joined the order. Then he wondered at the vagueness of his wonder, at the remoteness of his soul from what he had hitherto imagined her sanctuary, at the frail hold which so many years of order and obedience had of him when once a definite and irrevocable act of his threatened to end for ever, in time and in eternity, his freedom. The voice of the director urging upon him the proud claims of the church and the mystery and power of the priestly office repeated itself idly in his memory. His soul was not there to hear and greet it and he knew now the the exhortation he had listened to had already fallen into an idle formal tale. He would never swing the thurible before the tabernacle as priest. His destiny was to be elusive of social or religious orders. The wisdom of the priest's appeal did not touch him to the quick. He was destined to learn his own wisdom apart from others or to learn the wisdom of others himself wandering among the snares of the world. (pp. 161–62)

Several aspects of this passage deserve attention. We should mark especially the statement that "his destiny was to be elusive of *social or religious* orders," further supporting the claim that in Stephen's mind the religious perspective is paired with the social as representing external forces (my terms *social* and *religious* for chapters I and III derive from this sentence). Also, the passage testifies in various ways to the "externality" of the priest's exhortation: Stephen's soul is not there to hear or greet it; the appeal does not "touch [Stephen] to the quick"; and he contrasts that ineffectual call with "his own wisdom."

The climax of the chapter—the scene on the beach when Stephen sees the wading girl and realizes that his true calling, his destiny, is to be an artist—is also the climax of the novel. That is, the calling to art that Stephen feels in this lyrical, ecstatic passage is his valid calling. While it does require the whole of this famous passage to convey Stephen's ecstasy, I quote only those aspects that show how fully the experience derives from within Stephen's psyche, Stephen's soul, with relatively little provocation from the "external world."

> A girl stood before him in midstream, alone and still, gazing out to sea. She seemed like one whom magic had changed into the likeness of a strange and beautiful seabird.
>
> . . . when she felt his presence and the worship of his eyes her eyes turned to him in quiet sufferance of his gaze, without shame or wanton-ness. . . .
>
> —Heavenly God! cried Stephen's soul, in an outburst of profane joy.
>
> • • •
>
> Her image had passed into his soul for ever and no word had broken the holy silence of his ecstasy. Her eyes had called him and his soul had leaped at the call. . . . A wild angel had appeared to him, the angel of mortal youth and beauty, an envoy from the fair courts of life, to throw open before him in an instant of ecstasy the gates of all the ways of error and glory. (pp. 171–72)

The passage expresses the depth and completeness of Stephen's feeling that he has now found his true life's calling, and clearly Stephen is express-ing something that he senses as coming from within himself, not something foisted upon him from the public, external world. The cry that Stephen utters comes straight from his soul, and his communion with the wading girl has nothing of the social or the institutional about it. Undoubtedly Stephen's ignorance of who the girl is facilitates her serving as an objectifi-cation of what is welling forth from within him.

Stephen arrives at his artistic calling on an inward swing of his psychic pendulum. What this implies, and what is borne out by various aspects of chapter V, is that Stephen's conception of art and the artist arises from an inward, subjectivist orientation and thus implicitly expresses his commitment to a "symbolist" (rather than a "naturalist") understanding of art. This is not to say that his view of art is "caused by" his inner orientation; rather, it is characteristic of something deep in his psyche that he would come to a sense of this calling on an inner swing of the pendulum, rather than an outer (as Zola presumably would have). This subjective orientation reveals Stephen's symbolist/aestheticist conception of the artist—which is very much a function of his milieu. Granted, not every artist who emerged around the turn of the century necessarily construed his calling in symbolist/aesthetic terms. But it is important that (as Marguerite Harkness has pointed out in the passage quoted above in chapter 3, footnote 22), most of them did construe the artist's calling in terms either of symbolism/aestheticism OR naturalism/realism, both of which Joyce regards as partial and incomplete. Precisely what predisposed Stephen toward the aestheticist approach to art rather than the naturalistic—i.e., why he implicitly feels art to be an expression of his soul rather than a documentation of the world around him—we cannot fully explain. Doubtless the Dublin milieu depicted in *Dubliners*, which drives all sensitive persons into inward retreat (see "Araby" and "A Painful Case"), had something to do with it, as did the powerful examples of Pater, Wilde, and Yeats (though we should not forget that other young writers sought out the pattern of Zola and the brothers Goncourt). But Stephen's own distinctive temperament plays a large role in his construing the nature of the artist as he does. In any event, the fact that he discovers his artistic calling on an inward phase of his oscillating orientation enables us better to understand the biases and deficiencies of his view of the artist, and to appreciate what Stephen must begin to do in this novel and in *Ulysses* to redress that imbalance.[15] His problem in chapter V is to understand the meaning of this new-found calling.

Several elements in this scene on the beach suggest that this fourth realization is more substantial than those in the first three chapters. In the first three scenes Stephen makes his way to his climactic meeting by wandering through a maze or labyrinth—first in the school corridors, and then in chapters two and three, through the streets of Dublin. This motif invokes the treacherous maze that Daedalus made for King Minos of Crete, and suggests that in these scenes Stephen is wandering blindly. The climactic scene of the fourth chapter occurs on an open beach with a feeling of breadth and expansiveness, suggesting that this affirmation is qualitatively different from the others, and that the calling of artist is Stephen's true calling. Appropriately, the subject of chapter V, then, is not another violent rise and fall or orientation on Stephen's part, but the more mundane, less dramatic, question of Stephen's attempts to work out what his vocation as artist involves.

One interesting pattern among the four climactic scenes that undergirds the oscillation between external and internal influences is the sex of the other person involved in each of the scenes. In chapters I and III—those designated as the social and religious phases and manifesting an external claim—the climactic scene presents Stephen with a male figure of considerable authority (Father Conmee, and the priest), whereas in chapters II and IV, sensuous and aesthetic, involving an internal orientation, the other figure is a woman (the prostitute, and the wading girl). This is in keeping with Joyce's inclination throughout his canon to associate the male with some mode of external or social authority and the woman with the inner self or the soul. Though Jung had not yet articulated his ideas of the anima and the animus when *Portrait* was published, it seems clear that Joyce is here thinking in such terms. In chapters I and III, Stephen is responding to some "external," authoritative behest, represented in each case by a male figure (more specifically by a priest). In chapters II and IV, Stephen is responding to some deeply personal and internal call, in both cases epitomized in a female figure who objectifies this latent part of his psyche.[16]

In true *Bildungsroman* form, then, the very structure of the novel derives from and expresses the patterns and rhythms of Stephen's development—its rises and falls, its swings from outer to inner. Each chapter climaxes with a new and presumably fuller understanding on Stephen's part of how to live life, and each succeeding chapter shows this orientation dissolve under the influence of other more compelling demands.

I agree with the consensus that the end of chapter IV is the climax of the novel.[17] The validity of Stephen's aesthetic calling is borne out not only by the remainder of this novel, but by *Ulysses* as well. That Stephen has not yet become a successful or full-fledged artist even by the time we leave him in *Ulysses* does not disprove that art is his calling; rather, it simply reflects his not yet having found an orientation, a life-grounding, out of which to write. Such a *point d'appui* must, among other things, involve Stephen's getting beyond the dualism that now holds him in thrall—i.e., his coming to understand that matter is not the enemy of spirit, but is the indispensable means of its manifestation.

But Stephen's discovery of his artistic calling is not the only thing that happens at this crucial point in the novel, and from the perspective of the themes that we are tracing, perhaps not the most important. The fundamental theme that emerges here is that of Stephen's self-awareness and self-determination, rendering this scene the novel's climax because Stephen sees himself as no longer the passive product of the forces acting upon him, but the arbiter of his own destiny. This is reflected, of course, in his discovering his artistic calling, but it is reflected even more profoundly in Stephen's remaking, redefining for himself, the meaning of various aspects of his experience. In Stephen's own view this episode is a crucial step toward his self-understanding and self-determination, toward his becoming captain of his fate and master of his soul. Now that he has realized the implications of his name—realized who he is—he is no longer a mere pawn, no longer the creature of forces acting upon him, but is actively creating his own self: "his soul had arisen from the grave of boyhood, spurning her graveclothes. Yes! Yes! Yes! He would create proudly out of the freedom and power of his soul, as the great artificer whose name he bore, a living thing, new and soaring and beautiful, impalpable, imperishable" (p. 170). But we shall see that this idea of self-creation, grounded as it is in Stephen's superficial modernist sense of the self, is naive and unfeasible.

Stephen's presumption of taking responsibility for his own destiny generates a change in tone from chapter IV to chapter V that has been noted by many critics.[18] But while Joyce does to some extent recede from his character, he does not lose sympathy with him. In the period that intervenes between chapters IV and V, Stephen as assumed the mantle and the mannerisms of self-determination. He has become more circumspect, more defensive. Like Lucifer, he has made claims to self-sufficiency, and he must assume the burdens of that claim. Gone is the naive young boy who was so vulnerable to forces sweeping over him from within or without. And as a result of this defensiveness and presumptuousness, Stephen is less appealing than he was in the preceding chapters. But this too is a necessary phase of his overall development, a phase that has not yet been completed even in *Ulysses,* though there are promising signs in that novel.

We can trace in chapter V various effects of Stephen's aspirations to self-knowledge and self-determination, and of his construing his artistic calling subjectively. One of these is his implicit view of freedom as escape, which exemplifies my earlier claims about the way that theme often works in the *Bildungsroman*. As we have seen, the character and the author of the novel often conceive of freedom differently, which provides the thematic basis for irony. This may seem surprising, since we think of the *Bildungsroman* as an autobiographical form, and often identify the author and his character. For many readers, Stephen Dedalus is Joyce, Eugene Gant is Thomas Wolfe, Paul Morel is D. H. Lawrence. But scrutiny of most *Bildungsromane* will confirm the distance between author and protagonist—a distance that usually manifests itself (among other ways) in two contrasting conceptions of freedom. The young hero, in his late 'teens or early twenties, sees freedom as escape, lack of restraint, as utter self-determination; the author, writing from the perspective of his late twenties or early thirties, sees this view as simplistic and escapistic, and is more likely to regard freedom as a realization of one's potentialities, necessarily involving a degree of social relatedness—or at least the acknowledgment of the social nature of one's own self—that the young protagonist finds intolerable. In this situation the writer must find a way to convey this ironic distance between his character's views and his own. *what is this silly thing about 'control'? Totally irrelevant.*

Stephen's elaboration of his aesthetic theory is another effect of his aspiration to self-knowledge and self-control. In this chapter it becomes clear that Stephen is more adept at aesthetic theorizing than he is at writing works of art. He develops a subtle and overwrought theory of art which he derives from Aristotle and Aquinas. But his only artistic creation is his effete, narcissistic villanelle.[19] Perhaps some modicum of theorizing about life and art is necessary to the growth of the artist, but Stephen is in danger of taking refuge in theorizing, rather than engaging life and art. Apparently Stephen feels that he cannot become an artist until he has fully formulated an aesthetic theory, which he sees as simply a part of his being totally self-aware. But I argued earlier that an important turning point came for Joyce when he understood that his being an artist did not require his developing a full-fledged theory of art (see above, pp. 50–52).

This aesthetic theory has been the subject of a great deal of critical commentary, dealing with the nature of the theory itself, and its relationship to Joyce's own ideas and to his works. For the purposes of my present argument the specific philosophic claims of the theory, or its autobiographical status, are not so important as are the manner and the motives of Stephen's presentation of it, and his devoting so much of his energy to theoretical issues. That is, we should recognize that the primary function of this theorizing in *Portrait* is not to present Joyce's ideas on art, but further to characterize Stephen.[20] Joyce's distancing from Stephen here manifests itself not in regard to the theory itself—which I find not only coherent but very close to what Joyce himself believed—but in the tenor and the purposes of its presentation, and in Stephen's resort to it to maintain some control over his experience. This theorizing on Stephen's part, then, involves one of the most fundamental questions that Joyce is exploring here and in *Ulysses*— the question of how much abstract, theoretical knowledge one must have in order to be an artist.

Stephen's subjectivist orientation toward art and the artist also puts him in danger of what Joyce considers an even worse failing—the use of his art, or his role as an artist, as a refuge from unpleasant aspects of life. Joyce was keenly aware that for some artists art becomes not a means of engaging reality, but of escaping from it. While such an attitude may not be a logical corollary of a subjectivist conception of art, the inward turn of the aestheticist does easily involve his regarding the "exterior world" as something to be retreated from. Perhaps the classic text here is Wilde's statement (through the persona of Gilbert in "The Critic as Artist") that "it is through Art, and through Art only, that we can realize our perfection; through Art, and through Art only, that we can shield ourselves from the sordid perils of actual existence" (*Oscar Wilde*, p. 274).

But attractive as this view may be to Stephen, Joyce himself did not see things this way. Quite the contrary, Joyce felt that the artist had an obligation far beyond that of the "ordinary person" to face up to every aspect of life, including those that might seem coarse or sordid. The story is told that, soon after the publication of *Ulysses*, Joyce met his cousin Kathleen, daughter of his favorite aunt, Josephine Murray, in London, and he asked her how her mother had responded to *Ulysses*. Kathleen replied, with embarrassment, that her mother had said the book was not fit to read. "If *Ulysses* isn't fit to read," Joyce replied, "life isn't fit to live" (*JJ II*, p. 537). Joyce's reply conveys his belief that the artist must face up to life squarely, that he cannot use his art as a crutch or an escape.[21]

That Stephen has not yet learned this is shown by several passages reflecting his attempts to use his art as a means of distancing or protecting himself from life's less appealing aspects. Consider this passage describing his morning walk to the university through one of the lower sections of Dublin:

His morning walk across the city had begun, and he foreknew that as he
passed the sloblands of Fairview he would think of the cloistral silverveined
prose of Newman, that as he walked along the North Strand Road, glancing
idly at the windows of the provision shops, he would recall the dark humor
of Guido Cavalcanti and smile, that as he went by Baird's stonecutting works
in Talbot Place the spirit of Ibsen would blow through him like a keen wind,
a spirit of wayward boyish beauty, and that passing a grimy marinedealer's
shop beyond the Liffey he would repeat the song by Ben Jonson which
begins:
I was not wearier where I lay. (p. 176)

Stephen's inclination to use the realm of art as a retreat from the sordid
reality of the external world is clear here, and is one sign that he has not
come to terms with the implications and responsibilities of his calling.[22]

While on one level Stephen is sincerely striving to see what it means to
be an artist, on another he is merely playing out the current stereotype of
the artist that derives from Walter Pater and Oscar Wilde and other fin de
siècle aesthetes whose names are now obscurity.[23] It involves seeing the
artist as sensitive, almost too sensitive for life, as inherently misunderstood
by the Philistines around him, and as therefore necessarily alienated and
outcast. Such an attitude shows through in several of Stephen's characteristic comments and stances toward his fellow students, and in certain of the
diary entries that close the novel (e.g., 20 March; 21 March, night; 3 April).
But if we look closely, we will see as well some of those deeper and better
qualities in Stephen that remind us Joyce's ironic perspective on Stephen is
essentially sympathetic and even admiring. (I referred briefly to some of
Stephen's more appealing, self-effacing qualities in footnote 18 above.)

Consider the April 15 diary entry, on the next-to-last page of the novel:

Met her today pointblank in Grafton Street. The crowd brought us together. We both stopped. She asked me why I never came, said she had
heard all sorts of stories about me. This was only to gain time. Asked me,
was I writing poems? About whom? I asked her. This confused her more and
I felt sorry and mean. Turned off that valve at once and opened the spiritual-
heroic refrigerating apparatus, invented and patented in all countries by
Dante Alighieri. Talked rapidly of myself and my plans. In the midst of it
unluckily I made a sudden gesture of a revolutionary nature. I must have
looked like a fellow throwing a handful of peas into the air. People began to

look at us. She shook hands a moment after and, in going away, said she
hoped I would do what I said.

Now I call that friendly, don't you?

Yes, I liked her today. A little or much? Don't know. I liked her and it
seems a new feeling to me. Then, in that case, all the rest, all that I thought I
thought and all that I felt I felt, all the rest before now, in fact . . . O, give it
up, old chap! Sleep it off! (p. 252)

This interesting and complex passage focuses the problem of Stephen's
inadequate personal relationships, especially with women. He is snide and
sarcastic to Emma, then feels sorry and mean, then attempts to retreat into a
Platonic relationship by turning off the valve of human sympathy and turning on the spiritual-heroic refrigerating apparatus that Western culture has
learned from Dante. But most important is his statement in the last paragraph, which suggests that this liking—not passion, not adoration, but *liking*—might be the doorway to fuller and more meaningful personal
relationships for Stephen. But if that is the case (he asks himself), what
about all the supposed isolation of the artist, all that Stephen had thought
he thought and felt he felt? But he opts to sleep it off. Apparently he is not
yet ready to pursue the difficult, tangled path of relationships with others;
he still prefers the heady heights of aesthetic isolation. But the seed of
social relatedness is there, and will germinate.[24]

The last two diary entries also contain interesting implications in regard
to Stephen's autonomy:

26 *April:* Mother is putting my new secondhand clothes in order. She
prays now, she says, that I may learn in my own life and away from home
and friends what the heart is and what it feels. Amen. So be it. Welcome, O
life! I go to encounter for the millionth time the reality of experience and to
forge in the smithy of my soul the uncreated conscience of my race.

27 *April:* Old father, old artificer, stand me now and ever in good stead.
(pp. 252–53)

Stephen here seems to take a softer attitude toward his mother, acknowledging her love and sympathy for him, and sensing that her love may well
be—as Cranly has told him (pp. 241–42)—the most real thing in life. Later
Stephen himself wonders whether a mother's love may not be the "only
true thing in life" (*U,* 2.143 and 9.843). But he cannot pause now to consider that—he is about to set out to create the conscience of his race.

   The image he uses in the final diary entry recalls Stephen's earlier thought of the fabulous artificer, Daedalus, and the story of Daedalus and Icarus, who attempted to fly from their island of Crete to the mainland. But if we reflect on this, we realize that Stephen, wittingly or unwittingly, calls upon the father, Daedalus, thus casting himself as the naive and exuberant son. Does he realize this? Probably not, but Joyce does, and wants us to. (For fuller discussion of this passage, see pp. 144–45, below.) In this, too, the novel is typical of the *Bildungsroman,* in that Stephen is regarded by his creator with sympathetic irony. Stephen will eventually find the meaning of his calling as an artist, and will accept its challenges and responsibilities. For now, though, he remains naive and romantic. Joyce is willing to have us see this and understand that this promising young man yet has some way to go.

6

The Verbal Simulation
of Stephen's Psychic Milieu

①My analysis of *Portrait* in this chapter develops three points. The first is
that Joyce reveals Stephen's psyche to be far deeper and more complex than he himself can comprehend or articulate, thus illustrating the
insufficiency of the empiricist/Enlightenment view of the self ②The second is
that Joyce's distinctive mode of third-person presentation undermines the
subject-object distinction that Stephen would read into his experience, thus
showing the superficiality of the Cartesian division between mind and
matter, inner and outer ③The third is that the authorial voice in the novel,
rather than expressing either a traditional "omniscient author" or a distinct
persona/character, simulates the social or collective psyche that Stephen
constantly, implicitly participates in, thus illustrating the inextricable interrelatedness of "individual" and "social," conscious and unconscious. My
claim, then, is that virtually everything in this novel simulates a dimension
of Stephen's psychic milieu—either his individual psyche, or the
circumambient social psyche. But while these techniques testify to the
pervasiveness of the social psyche, Joyce's aim throughout is not to subvert
or parody the idea of the coherent self; quite the contrary, it is to show that
the continuity and entelechy of Stephen's self has sources deeper than the
conscious, individual mind.[1] (U.) ps. appn.

Perhaps the most distinctive feature of Joyce's presentation of his characters' psyches both in *Portrait* and in *Ulysses* is the persistent merging of
figural consciousness and exposition, of character's voice and author's voice,
of individual psyche and collective psyche. This merging results from a

carefully wrought third-person mode of presentation by which Joyce can convey the inextricability of these entities. It distinguishes Joyce's practice sharply from that of Edouard Dujardin's totally *interior* monologue in *Le Lauriers sont Coupés* on the one hand,[2] or from the reified personas of Henry James or Thomas Mann on the other. Dorrit Cohn recognizes this quality in Joyce's presentation when she says that "in sharpest contrast to Mann's narrator, Joyce's cannot be grasped as a separate entity within the text. His most striking characteristic is, in fact, that he is ungraspably chameleonic" (*Transparent Minds,* p. 30). Joyce intentionally sought this quality in order to evoke, to simulate, the social psyche that we all participate in but none of us can consciously articulate.[3]

Language Chez Joyce

The theme of language in Joyce's works—or simply in *Portrait of the Artist*—is so complex that no brief discussion can do justice to it, yet I cannot discuss how the novel presents Stephen's psychic milieu without some prior observations on Joyce's ideas about language. For our present purposes the underlying point is that language by its very nature undercuts any would-be division of reality into inner and outer.[2] Our every utterance is simultaneously "mental" and "physical," "private" and "public," and in this respect language mysteriously solves the mind/matter dilemma of Descartes. Each human utterance, that is, consists simultaneously of a physical articulation of *sounds* that are traceable on a sound spectrograph, and of a *meaning* that directly expresses our psyche. Similarly, language inherently bridges the categories of private and public, for while every spoken utterance is individual, it must at the same time be public. This is true both in the sense that the language precedes the individual, who does not make up the words that he or she uses, and in the sense that the functions language serves are necessarily social, whether they involve explicit communication among persons, or accommodation of the world to the self (and vice versa) via reflection. And so in spite of Stephen's penchant for partitioning his world into inner and outer, public and private, his every utterance testifies to the inextricability of matter and mind. Not surprisingly, we find the kernel of this idea in Joyce's Paris Notebook, in a statement he copied from Aristotle: "A voice is a sound which expresses something."[4]

language

It is not easy to think clearly about the relationships among language, mind, culture, and nature—broadly speaking, the relationship between language and reality. These interrelationships are so immediate to our experience that we can never find a removed, Archimedean locus from which to analyze them, which makes it hard to articulate what is involved in the most ordinary linguistic phenomena. As Anthony Burgess says, "It is one thing to use language; it is quite another to understand how it works" (*Joysprick,* p. 11).[5] Furthermore, in ascertaining Joyce's views on language we must either rely on the relatively few explicit comments that he made in notebooks, reviews, letters, or reported conversations, or we must infer his views from his literary works. While the works comprise our most cogent evidence, it requires tact and subtlety to infer from them, and some critics have badly misconstrued the implications of the works in this regard. They have argued, that is, that Joyce's earlier works involve a naive realism in regard to language and reality, while the later ones present language as co-extensive and identical with consciousness, with culture, even with reality.[6] But such a view simplifies the many subtle ways in which language reifies and mediates among the mind and cultural and physical reality even in *Dubliners,* and it exaggerates the role of language vis a vis reality in *Finnegans Wake.*

Joyce never, even in his earliest days, had an "absolutist" or naively realistic view that would posit "reality"—especially cultural reality—existing fully fledged and intact, independent of human perception and not shaped by language. Certainly by the time of his earliest writings he shows an awareness of the immense role that human imagination and the medium of language play in bringing cultural realities into being, and even in modifying the more obdurate physical aspects of reality. Joyce arrived very early at an awareness of how intricately interrelated (though not identifiable) language, reality, and culture are, and I see no evidence of fundamental differences in his views on these issues from *Dubliners* to *Finnegans Wake.* From early on Joyce saw that, while language is not identical with reality, it does form an inextricable part of all cultural realities, and it remains our most subtle means not only of perceiving the world but of effecting changes in ourselves and in our milieu. But while the structures of language, mind, culture, and nature are *inseparable* in Joyce's works, they are not (as Owen Barfield would point out) *indistinguishable,* and it is useful to infer what we can about Joyce's views on their interrelationships.

The term "structures of language" indicates simply that every language involves patterns of grammar and syntax, which make it in effect a multiple substitution frame. In English, for example, we can without violating any rule of grammar or syntax link any adjective with any noun: we can speak of a red rose, or a green rose, or an opaque rose, or a hypothetical rose, or yellow ivy, or yellow ivory, or ivory ivy. Whether these locutions refer to anything that exists in the real world, we can construct them without violating any of the structures of our language. Such structures are present even in *Finnegans Wake,* where we can often feel the general forms of sentence syntax even when the elements within the sentence do not relate easily with one another.[7] Another less regularized aspect of the "structure of language" is that each language involves innumerable "arbitrary" relationships among words, created by homophones, by rhyme, by other sheerly phonetic qualities, and these too have their effects on the mental map of reality that each member of the language community constructs—effects deplored by logicians, exulted in by poets, and persistently drawn upon by Joyce. These qualities especially interest writers (and children), inviting them to play with juxtapositions involving various phonetic affinities and the possibilities of the real world. Stephen does this with his poem about the yellow ivy whining on the wall, of which he says "Did any one ever hear such drivel? Lord Almighty! Who ever heard of ivy whining on a wall? Yellow ivy: that was all right. [i.e., sanctioned by reality] Yellow ivory also. And what about ivory ivy?" (p. 179).

By the "structures of mind" (or structures of thought) I refer inclusively to the logical principles that underlie syllogistic thinking or Venn diagrams, or the principle of non-contradiction, or to other looser but still "structured" modes of mental procedure, such as valid modes of inference or even arguments from analogy. These structures of thought are often closely linked to the structures of language—we see the effects of linguistic structures and associations upon thought in any passage of stream of consciousness such as Proteus or Lestrygonians—but the two can be discriminated. That these two kinds of structure are not identical is shown by the fact that the rules of thought or logic transcend cultural and linguistic boundaries—i.e., languages with utterly different syntactic or phonetic structures do accommodate these principles of thinking, with the result that we can to an amazing degree translate logical statements—or recognize illogical ones—from one language to another. Such translation among utterly different languages would be impossible if the structures of thought were not potentially separable from those of language. (We shall consider the relationship between language and thought more fully later in this chapter.)

The structures of culture, while they must have language as their sine qua non, are not identical with the structures of language or of thought. Cultural "structures" include a wide variety of entities, ranging from tangible, material objects such as furniture or houses, to abstract ones such as institutions and ideals. Among the structures that distinguish one culture from another are physical structures brought into being by agriculture (i.e., modes and patterns of land use), or the physical structures involved in housing. Less concretely, a culture involves structural patterns of the disposition of labor, patterns of family and kinship, modes of worship, etc. While all of these (and many more) qualify as structures of the culture, and while they depend upon language for their existence, they are obviously quite different from the structures of grammar and syntax, or of logic. No writer has ever focused more fully, more minutely, on the inextricable interrelationships that exist between language and culture than has Joyce, and he does so from *Dubliners* through *Finnegans Wake,* but nowhere in Joyce's works do I detect a simple *identification* of the structures of language and those of culture.

The structures of nature include those intractable aspects of the physical world that are both our blessing and our bane—i.e., those regularities of nature that we constantly depend upon, but that prevent our bringing into being everything that we might imagine. These include the reliable physical properties of various materials (granite, cedar, silk, etc.) and the various laws of nature that govern their interactions (e.g., the acceleration of a falling body). Science, and for that matter every tangible human project, inevitably relies upon these structures of nature. But any one who has tried to carry out any such project, from cultivating a garden to building a house, has inevitably felt the resistance of the structures of reality. We may wish to raise orchids, or okra, but our climate or the nature of our soil may not permit it. M. C. Escher can draw a plausible-looking staircase that continually *ascends* from level to level ("Ascending and descending" he calls it), but a carpenter attempting to use Escher's drawing as a blueprint would find nature very recalcitrant indeed. The structures of nature are also manifested in such things as the characteristic, distinctive physical/spatial patterns that are formed by the bole, branches, and leaves of a white oak tree as contrasted with those of a sugar maple or a black locust; or less obviously, in the different "natures" of these types of trees, manifested in the very different uses to which we can put them. That such structures are not language-dependent is shown by the fact that the distinctive capacities of various trees and plants are responded to even by creatures without language. Birds, that is, do not require language to discriminate reliably between pine mast and thistle down, and to put them to different uses.

Joyce's works throughout his career persistently show how intimately, inextricably related these four things are—language, mind, culture, and nature. In the opening pages of *A Portrait*, we see for example how the structures of language serve as a medium by which the imagination plays over various as yet unrealized possibilities in the world. Stephen's "green rose" violates no rules of syntax, but it evokes something that nature does not sanction—or did not at the time the novel was written. (There is now, I understand, a rose that is green—a rose hybridized by someone who set out to bring into being in nature what had at first existed only in language and imagination. Perhaps the botanist got the idea from Joyce's *Portrait?*) Obviously, then, one of the ways that we extend the limits of reality—i.e., of culture or even of nature—is by playing over the possibilities that are implicit in language.

Another aspect of the complex interrelationship between language and reality that Joyce simply and skillfully evokes in these early pages of *Portrait* is that "arbitrary" links among words, such as those between homophones or rhyming words, do inevitably find their way into our cultural map of reality, forging in our minds connections among otherwise unrelated things that are the bane of logicians and that drive them to resort to symbolic logic. Because Stephen speaks English, his mind makes a connection between the *belt* that one wears around one's waist and the *belt* that one gives a fellow—a connection not sanctioned by logic or by nature and that presumably does not exist for a speaker of Chinese or Swahili. We come to realize as well, through Joyce's evocation of the child mind, that linguistic utterances can themselves become the object of value judgments, quite apart from the rightness or wrongness of the acts that they refer to. Thinking of Cantwell's saying "Give Cecil Thunder a belt. I'd like to see you. He'd give you a toe in the rump for yourself" (p. 9), Stephen says "That was not a nice expression," quite obviously judging not the act—the fellow might very well deserve a toe in the rump—but its verbal vesture.[9]

In these and many other ways, then, Joyce shows us how inextricably linked are mental and physical, psychological comprehension and phonetic accident, value and verbal vesture, through the medium of the language we speak. The very existence of this medium, constantly blending as it does these presumably disparate aspects of reality, shows the superficiality of the metaphysical categories of subject and object that we have inherited from early modernist philosophy.

While this theme of the inseparability of subject and object in language is (as we shall see) implicit throughout the novel, it comes into focus especially in a passage late in chapter IV. As Stephen is on his way to the Bull Island and his epiphanic vision of his artistic calling, his mind turns to a phrase that he especially values:

> He drew forth a phrase from his treasure and spoke it softly to himself:
> —A day of dappled seaborne clouds.
> The phrase and the day and the scene harmonized in a chord. Words. Was it their colours? He allowed them to glow and fade, hue after hue: sunrise gold, the russet and green of apple orchards, azure of waves, the greyfringed fleece of clouds. No, it was not their colours: it was the poise and balance of the period itself. Did he then love the rhythmic rise and fall of words better than their associations of legend and colour? Or was it that, being as weak of sight as he was shy of mind, he drew less pleasure from the reflection of the glowing sensible world through the prism of a language manycoloured and richly storied than from the contemplation of an inner world of individual emotions mirrored perfectly in a lucid supple periodic prose? (pp. 166–67)

This subtle passage deserves careful attention if we are to appreciate its implications.[10] What is most interesting about it for our purposes is that while the phrase evokes a wholistic impression, and though Stephen even thinks explicitly that "the phrase and the day and the scene harmonized in a chord"—harmonized within his *mind,* of course—he foists upon the phrase an analysis that pointedly reflects his penchant for discriminating "outer" from "inner." Pondering what it is that he finds most attractive and appealing about the words of the phrase, Stephen first attends to their "colors," but then decides that what appeals to him more is something else—"the poise and balance of the period itself." Then in the next two sentences he analytically divides the utterance into two aspects, one reflecting the outer, public world (colors, associations of legend), the other reflecting the inner world of the psyche (the rhythmic rise and fall of words; the poise and balance of the period itself; a supple periodic prose). His analysis involves separating the sheer meter or rhythm of the phrase (epitomized in his highly scannable phrase "it was the *poise* and *bal*ance of the *per*iod it*self*"), which he presumes reflect his psyche (the "inner world of individual emotions"), from all of its content of color and association, which he presumes represent the public world. And the question underlying this entire exercise in Stephen's mind is the essentially specious one of which of these two aspects he prefers. While we can of course analytically discriminate the rhythm of any utterance from its content, Joyce wants us to understand this exercise on Stephen's part as an extension of his penchant for dichotomization, and to recognize the arbitrariness and speciousness of Stephen's analytically separating the elements of his experience in this way. What we most value and enjoy about such phrases is precisely that they do harmonize phrase (i.e., language) and day (i.e., world) and "scene" (i.e., observer)—medium and world and mind.

Having read Joyce's works carefully with this question in mind, I find no evidence that he *identified* language with reality, or with culture, or with human consciousness or thought processes.[11] (Ironically, it is his unparalleled skill in using language to evoke and simulate various aspects of reality that causes some critics to make this unwarranted inference. Anthony Burgess makes precisely this point in regard to Joyce's presentation of his characters' psychic life; see below, footnote 14.) It is very hard even to know what such claims of the "identity" of language and reality *mean*, because they involve so fundamental a confusion of categories and fly so directly in the face of our experience. That is, not even the most abstruse theoretician can believe that pain or death or an earthquake are sheerly linguistic, and we should not attribute such metaphysical confusions to Joyce. He was not simply a word-crafter existing in a vacuum; he was a living person who struggled with a variety of experiences, from the death of his brother George and of his mother, to severe iritis, to the mental imbalance of his daughter, and he cannot have believed that these traumatic personal experiences were sheerly linguistic. He did of course communicate with his eye doctor through language, but that must have made it all the more obvious to this lord of language that the pain he suffered in his eyes was not a matter of grammar or syntax or assonance; if it had been, Joyce could have exorcised it far better than a medical doctor. While Joyce knew that language is the most subtle device we have for the apprehension and extension of reality, he never simply identified the two. He remained aware that there does exist some public proto-reality, prior to us and in some respects independent of us, which we apprehend, and modify, through language.[12]

I disagree as well with those who would see language as Joyce's sole theme or subject, or who would argue that language comprises the source and substance of his characters' problems and failures. This claim that Joyce's Dubliners are inescapably paralyzed by their language was proposed years ago by Hugh Kenner (see esp. the first chapter of his *Dublin's Joyce*, 1955), and more recently it often forms a part of structuralist approaches to Joyce's works. But while Joyce certainly shows in his works that language can become limiting and constricting, he also shows that language is the most subtle and comprehensive tool we have for freeing ourselves from convention or ordinariness. Joyce knew that it is simplistic and evasive to blame the medium, the tool, for either failures or successes of the human imagination. If we use language to achieve fresh perceptions of the world, or to find new means of self-understanding and self-realization, language itself should not be credited with the achievement; but neither should it be blamed if we are so unimaginative or passive that we permit ourselves to become inured to ordinariness and cliché.

That Joyce did not identify language and reality is made clear by a number of his own statements at various times during his career—statements that show he saw language as a means of conveying or engaging some entity, some aspect of reality, and that consistently involve a discrimination between language and the cultural reality it conveys. In "Ireland, Island of Saints and Sages" (1907), Joyce says "nationality . . . must find its reason for being rooted in something that surpasses and transcends and transforms changing things like blood and the human word" (*CW*, p. 166). In his 1907 essay on Mangan, he speaks of him as having " . . . expressed in a worthy form the sacred indignation of his soul" (*CW*, p. 186). In "The Home Rule Comet" (1910), Joyce says of Ireland, "She has abandoned her own language almost entirely and accepted the language of the conqueror without being able to assimilate the culture or adapt herself to the mentality of which this language is the vehicle" (*CW*, pp. 212–13). In his Trieste Notebook, s.v. Dedalus, Joyce wrote "He desired to be not a man of letters but a spirit expressing itself through language . . . " (Scholes and Kain, *The Workshop of Daedalus*, p. 96). And lest it be objected that all of these are early, naive statements that Joyce had "got beyond" by the time he came to *Finnegans Wake*, consider the following statements relating to that work:

to Ernst Robert Curtius, Joyce said "The night world can't be represented in the language of day" (*JJ II*, p. 590). Ellmann tells us of "Anna Livia Plurabelle" that "to a friend who complained that it was just dada, he said 'It is an attempt to subordinate words to the rhythm of water,'" and further that "he felt some misgivings about it the night he finished, and went down to the Seine to listen by one of its bridges to the waters. He came back content" (*JJ II*, p. 564, and footnote). And in an often-quoted letter to Harriet Shaw Weaver he said "One great part of every human existence is passed in a state which cannot be rendered sensible by the use of wideawake language, cutanddry grammar and goahead plot" (Nov. 24, 1926; *Letters*, III, 146). These comments show that Joyce did not *identify* language with various psychological, cultural, and natural entities.

ॐ

Analysis of Joyce's techniques of psychological presentation involves questions about whether such techniques attempt to *replicate* the activity of the psyche or to *simulate* it, and about the relationship between language and consciousness. I regard all such fictional modes of psychological presentation as literary techniques designed to give us the *impression* of being in touch with the character's psyche—i.e., as simulations, rather than attempts by the writer to reproduce or replicate the psyche. Since we are dealing with a written medium, these simulations are necessarily verbal, but that does not imply that the simulated psychic processes exist only in language or that the writer believes they do.[13]

I explained in the preceding section that I do not identify thought or consciousness with language, nor do I believe Joyce did. Joyce knew that psychic processes (including semi-coherent thought) have a mode of existence prior to and beyond the margins of language, and that these psychic processes, especially those that are pre-conscious or unconscious, affective and somatic, are not confined to language. While the psychic processes of a reflecting, remembering, experiencing, human consciousness rely heavily upon language, they are not co-terminous with it, and the full array of these processes is far too complex and multi-leveled ever to be fully replicated in language. Language (or one of its derivatives—e.g., mathematics) is necessary for extensive reflection or analysis. But consciousness precedes language both phylogenetically and ontogenetically and continues to run ahead of it in various ways. Writers of course are confined to words on the page, but a skillful writer can use those words to evoke imagistic, affective, even somatic, aspects of the psyche.[14]

Surely writers who present psychological processes in their novels know their aim is similitude, not replication, and the worth of their novelistic presentation does not depend upon its psychological veridicality. Faulkner would not have been surprised or disturbed if some psychologist had demonstrated that the mechanisms of insanity are not faithfully represented in the Benjy section of *The Sound and the Fury* (nor the inner speech of a dead person "accurately presented" by Addie's section of *As I Lay Dying!*), nor would we toss *Ulysses* aside if it were demonstrated that Proteus or Lestrygonians or Penelope is not a veridical replication of the workings of the mind—which means we acknowledge all such techniques are, finally, simulations and inherently involve literary conventions. Stuart Gilbert attributes to Joyce the claim that from his point of view, "it hardly matters whether the technique in question is 'veracious' or not; it has served him as a bridge over which to march his eighteen episodes, and, once he has got his troops across, the opposing forces can, for all he cares, blow the bridge sky-high" (*James Joyce's Ulysses: A Study* [Revised edition. New York: Vintage Books, 1955], p. 16). Conversely, we should not be troubled by objections that techniques such as stream of consciousness or interior monologue necessarily simplify or misrepresent the mind by their verbalization. *Every* literary technique verbalizes and thus simplifies whatever aspect of experience it deals with.[15]

While these ultra-linguistic aspects of the psyche can be conveyed even through first-person modes of presentation—i.e., in true interior monologue or stream of consciousness—they can be more readily and more richly evoked in a third-person mode such as that used by Joyce in *Portrait*. Interior monologue or stream of consciousness does (generally) involve a feel of greater immediacy by virtue of its first-person presentation, but what it gets us "closer to" is a fairly well articulated dimension of consciousness—especially in soliloquy or interior monologue, in which ordinary syntax is for the most part observed. (The highly conventional nature of interior monologue should be obvious, since we know that none of us in fact maintains so coherent a dialogue with himself or herself.) A skillful writer can, even in first-person stream of consciousness, suggest affective, preverbal, subconscious modes of psychic activity—e.g., associations involving images that are not explicitly stated—especially if the writer is willing, as Joyce is in *Ulysses,* to blend authorial exposition into the stream of consciousness. There are inherent limitations, though, on the degree to which any technique that confines itself to words, phrases, and sentences that are ostensibly verbalized by the character can get us very far beneath what the character could tell us explicitly.

While the various third-person modes sacrifice a degree of immediacy, they enable for both author and reader a fuller access to ultra-linguistic psychic processes beneath what the character could articulate. What is printed on the page may represent what she *would* say if her thoughts/ feelings were given some articulation, or it may involve affective dimensions and images that she could never articulate in language. This means that in third person presentation, what is on the page exists much more clearly for the reader than for the character. Thus while interior monologue or stream of consciousness provides more immediacy and accessibility, third person involves us in deeper, less conscious modes of psychic activity. Joyce, though, does achieve an impressive degree of immediacy through his third person presentation in *Portrait,* mainly because it mirrors so closely in diction and syntax the distinctive psychic processes of the character. As John Paul Riquelme has said, "One of Joyce's great achievements as a stylist is his development of third-person narrating strategies that create an effect of intimacy essentially similar to the effect of first-person techniques. By the end of 'The Dead,' his mastery of these strategies is evident" ("*Stephen Hero, Dubliners,* and *A Portrait of the Artist as a Young Man:* Styles of Realism and Fantasy," in Attridge, *The Cambridge Companion to James Joyce,* p. 126).[16]

We shall see, then, that Joyce's third-person presentation in *Portrait* facilitates his presenting dimensions of Stephen's psyche that Stephen is not himself aware of. We shall see as well that in this fully-realized *Bildungsroman,* there are no aspects of the novel's structure or style that are merely authorial or artifactual—i.e., that reflect simply the view of a "persona," or of "the structure of the novel," rather than the psyche of Stephen Dedalus. While the two claims that Joyce presents aspects of Stephen's psyche beneath his awareness, and that everything in the novel comprises or reflects some dimension of Stephen's psyche, individual or cultural, are not identical, I shall develop these claims simultaneously. I want, that is, to argue that while much of what Joyce presents to us through the print on the page lies beyond Stephen's conscious awareness and control, all of it should be regarded as forming a part of his psyche—either of his individual psyche, or of the cultural or social psyche that underlies it. We shall see that Joyce's carefully crafted third person presentation makes it virtually impossible for us to know how "conscious," how "individual," some of Stephen's psychic content is; or to draw a clear line between "exposition" and Stephen's psyche; or to know whether certain structures or images are "authorial" or "figural." While this mode of presentation may frustrate our critical wish to categorize, this merging of figural consciousness and exposition, of character's voice and author's voice, of individual psyche and cultural psyche, is an essential and distinctive feature of Joyce's presentation. It involves carefully developed devices on Joyce's part, and is an integral part of his intention to show how inseparable are inner and outer, psyche and world, individual mind and cultural mind.

꒰ꔛ꒱

Critics who discuss such techniques customarily speak of the representation of the character's "mental state" or "state of mind" or of the "flow of thought in the character's mind" (cf. T. Reinhart, p. 68, for example). But such terminology is inaccurate and misleading, implying that what is being represented is merely mental or cognitive, and imputing a strong vector quality to the activity of the psyche. What we are concerned with is the full psychic life of the character, not just its cognitive aspect: what Joyce aims to simulate is not the *flow* of *thought* in Stephen's *mind,* but the *flux* of *thought/feeling/sensation/mood* in Stephen's *psyche.* This flux, since it exists in time, necessarily has some vector quality, but not so much as the term *flow* implies; our psychic activity is meandering at best.

Critics concerned with the presentation of consciousness in literary texts have proposed various schemata for discriminating among types of such presentation, most of them grounded in grammatical and literary categories—i.e., first person or third person, subordinated or direct presentation, "consonant" or "dissonant" narration. But while these schemata can help clarify certain issues, none does justice to the subtlety and flexibility of Joyce's presentation, or to his distinctive aims, thus confirming Derek Attridge's statement that "our activities as readers are usually more complex than the terms in which we represent those activities to ourselves" ("Reading Joyce," p. 5).[17]

One of the more comprehensive and relevant such schemata is that of Dorrit Cohn, in her *Transparent Minds.* Since her schema helps to focus certain issues about third person presentation of figural consciousness, it is worth considering in some detail, even though it is finally insufficient to do justice to what is going on in *Portrait*. Cohn distinguishes three modes of third-person presentation: psycho-narration, quoted monologue, and narrated monologue. Cohn's first mode, psycho-narration (e.g., "He knew he was late," or "He wondered if he was late") involves the narrator's interpretive recounting of the character's psychic processes, not confined to the character's words, and thus enables the narrator to convey to the reader far more than the character understands or can articulate. This mode occurs commonly in *Portrait,* though it is not the most pervasive mode. This form of presentation often involves irresolvable ambiguity as to the level and the modality of the psychic content that is being conveyed—i.e., whether it is conscious or unconscious, and whether it is verbal, imagistic, somatic. This is especially true if the inquit phrase is affective rather than cognitive (e.g., "he felt" rather than "he thought" or "he understood") or when the narrator uses metaphors or images. This mode also facilitates a "dovetailing between the inner and outer realms of fictional reality" (p. 49), because the narration of sensations and perceptions can merge so readily with the psycho-narration that "there is no clear borderline between the external and the internal scene" (p. 49).

The second mode, quoted monologue (e.g., "([He thought:], I am late") involves a high degree of articulation by the character and thus confines itself to psychic contents that are verbalized and quite conscious. In this mode the distinction between expository/narrative and figural material is maintained by tense and person markers. This mode approaches stream of consciousness and can, when sustained and presented by an effaced narrator, achieve a feeling of immediacy. Cohn finds very few instances of this mode in *Portrait*.

The third mode of presentation, narrated monologue (e.g., "He was late"), Cohn describes as "rendering a character's thought in his own idiom while maintaining the third-person reference and the basic tense of narration" (p. 100; the examples in all three cases are Cohn's own). This mode— by far the most common in *Portrait*—is distinguished from quoted monologue by use of the third person and the past tense, and from psycho-narration by the absence of a relative clause marker or of verbs and nouns of consciousness, and by the vague criterion of the material's being in the character's "own idiom." While the psychic material presented via this mode is fairly conscious and articulate, the figural content is difficult to distinguish from ordinary narrative/expository elements. One interesting aspect of this mode for my purposes is that (in Cohn's words) it can provide a "seamless junction between narrated monologues and their narrative context," thus "fusing outer with inner reality" (p. 103).

While Cohn makes some perspicacious comments about the presentation of figural consciousness and frequently uses Joyce's texts to illustrate her points, her categories remain of limited use for analysis of *Portrait,* though the reasons for this are illuminating. First of all, only a very small part of Joyce's presentation of Stephen's psyche falls into Cohn's second category of quoted monologue,[18] so that almost the whole of the text is either psycho-narration or narrated monologue. Furthermore, Joyce is obviously not interested in maintaining the distinction that Cohn makes between these two categories, and many passages in the novel would have to be separated sentence by sentence if we were to try to employ them, while in other instances it is virtually impossible to know which of the two categories would be appropriate. Meanwhile, the focus upon discriminating the two modes deflects us from seeing what Joyce is really getting at. Cohn herself comments on how a passage from *Portrait* in which the "predominant technique" is psycho-narration involves a kind of "stylistic contagion," that "can serve to designate places where psycho-narration verges on the narrated monologue, marking a kind of mid-point between the two techniques where a reporting syntax is maintained, but where the idiom is strongly affected (or infected) with the mental idiom of the mind it renders" (pp. 32–33). Moreover, the mode of "narrated monologue" encompasses a wide range of very different-feeling effects because of the vague criterion of its being presented "in the character's idiom"; this could range from verbatim fidelity to the character's language (i.e., virtually interior monologue), to a slight coloring of the character's idiom.[19] Furthermore, there is a certain tension between Cohn's first and third categories, causing them to work at cross purposes in regard to the level of consciousness that they involve. This is true because the first mode, psychic narration, does involve verbs and nouns of consciousness ("he knew that . . . ") but is not confined to the character's own idiom or imagery. By contrast, the third mode, narrated monologue, makes no explicit assertion about the character's consciousness, but does employ the "character's own idiom." That *Portrait* virtually excludes one of her three categories and often hovers indeterminately between the other two shows that Joyce's purposes in the novel are not well served by this schema.

Another more significant way Joyce's presentation of Stephen's consciousness in *Portrait* eludes Cohn's schema—or for that matter any schema that confines itself strictly to presentation of figural consciousness—is that many sentences that would be exposition or "ordinary narrative" in most novels here take on a psychic aspect. As we have seen, Cohn points out that narrated monologue can provide a "seamless junction between narrated monologues and their narrative context," thus "fusing outer with inner reality" (p. 103), but the degree to which Joyce does this in *Portrait* carries us beyond ordinary figural presentation. When Cohn quotes from *Portrait* to illustrate narrated monologue (p. 102), the distinction that she tries to maintain between narrated monologue and "ordinary narrative passages" is not feasible. To maintain the integrity of her category of narrated monologue she must confine herself to sentences that could easily be translated into interior monologue, but the other sentences in that same context that reflect Stephen's *sensations,* and even in the sentences of what would be sheer exposition in other novels—all have a figural content in *Portrait of the Artist* that Cohn's categories simply do not accommodate.

In the following paragraph, for example, some of the sentences seem sheer exposition, and others hover indeterminately between ordinary narrative and figural presentation; yet each of the sentences leads us progressively deeper into Stephen's psyche.[20]

> The wide playgrounds were swarming with boys. All were shouting and the prefects urged them on with strong cries. The evening air was pale and chilly and after every charge and thud of the footballers the greasy leather orb flew like a heavy bird through the grey light. He kept on the fringe of his line, feigning to run now and then. He felt his body small and weak amid the throng of players and his eyes were weak and watery. Rody Kickham was not like that: he would be captain of the third line all the fellows said. (p. 8)

The first sentence seems to provide exposition or "ordinary narration" with virtually no coloring of affect—all the more so because it occurs at the beginning of a new section and in mature language that contrasts with the childlike language of the preceding section. In most novels, the sentence would be sheer exposition. The second sentence, still expository and in a mature syntax and vocabulary, does involve affective terms, but they are not grounded in Stephen's individual psyche—*urged, strong.* The third, still apparently expository, still syntactically mature and not yet invoking any individual consciousness, does involve specific sensations (pale, chilly) and even a distinctive image of the ball as a bird—though we do not yet obviously have a consciousness for these sensations to reflect. The fourth sentence, beginning "He," invokes a personal psyche, but the sentence (still mature) seems expository and the perspective exterior to Stephen—though "feigning" involves a distinctive intent. The fifth sentence, beginning "He felt," specifically invokes the boy's sensations and feelings, and the syntax is simpler, but it does not very fully simulate the feel of the boy's psyche. Only in the sixth sentence do we move "into" the boy's psyche, with the syntax and diction distinctively reflecting his perspective—though even here the presentation is third person and past tense. The succeeding paragraph picks up where this last sentence has arrived, consisting of simple diction and syntax and conveying the boy's perspective very fully, though still technically narrated monologue:

> Rody Kickham was a decent fellow but Nasty Roche was a stink. Rody Kickham had greaves in his number and a hamper in the refectory. Nasty Roche had big hands. He called the Friday pudding dog-in-the-blanket.

In terms of any schema that focuses specifically on the presentation of figural consciousness, very few of the sentences in the first paragraph above would qualify, but in fact every one of them involves either Stephen's personal perspective, or the larger "psychic context" or social consciousness that it inheres in. Any schema whose categories cannot acknowledge the presentation of figural consciousness involved in each of these six sentences and that does not help us to appreciate the overall effect of unifying public and private that they achieve, is of relatively little use in getting at what is most distinctive about Joyce's *Portrait*.

A similar inextricable blending of objective and subjective, of public percept and private images, appears in a paragraph describing Stephen's observation of the dean of studies lighting the fire. The paragraph begins with straightforward exposition: "He [the dean] produced four candlebutts from the sidepockets of his soutane and placed them deftly among the coals and twisted papers" (p. 185). The rest of this paragraph, all of it presented in third person, takes us into Stephen's private reflections on the man before him. But the images of Stephen's evaluation of the dean are reflexes of the public scene that he is observing but that is not explicitly described to us—the striking of the match, the lighting of the fire, the spreading of the flame and of the odor of the burning candlebutts and sticks.

Consider how subtly Stephen's "inner" psychic processes reflect his sensations and his perceptions of the outer world—or to put it in artifactual terms, how the "external" aspects of the scene that come through the third person authorial voice blend inextricably with the consciousness, the imagery, of the character. In the following passage I have italicized those images and metaphors that are engendered in Stephen's mind by the public objects and events of the scene before him: "His very body had *waxed* old in lowly service of the Lord—in *tending the fire* upon the altar, in bearing tidings secretly, in waiting upon worldlings, in *striking* swiftly when bidden—and it had remained ungraced by aught of saintly or of prelatic beauty. Nay his very soul had *waxed* old in that service without *growing towards light* and beauty or *spreading abroad a sweet odour* of her sanctity" (p. 185). Interestingly, Joyce is quite explicit about the inextricability of outer and inner in a passage very shortly afterwards, while the fire is still burning and after Stephen and the dean have explicitly used the image of Epictetus' lamp in their conversation: "A smell of molten tallow came up from the dean's candlebutts and *fused itself in Stephen's consciousness* with the jingle of the words, bucket and lamp and lamp and bucket. The priest's voice too had a hard jingling tone. Stephen's mind halted by instinct, checked by the strange tone and the imagery and by the priest's face *which seemed like an unlit lamp* or a reflector hung in a false focus" (p. 187; my emphasis). Here, as Joyce tells us, Stephen's inner thoughts derive directly from the fusion within his consciousness of sensations—visual, olfactory, and auditory—producing, among other things, the strange image of the priest's face as an "unlit lamp."[21]

There are many passages in *Portrait* where I cannot demonstrate so neatly that Stephen's "inner thoughts" are intimately linked with his perceptions of public events (many of those events are left unnarrated—as was the striking of the match in the preceding scene), or that an image or simile that seems to be authorial is in fact figural. But there are enough instances where we can show that Joyce does merge outer and inner, authorial voice and figural perspective, object and psychic image, so as to make symbiosis between such categories a likelihood in other cases. Scrutiny of *Portrait* and *Ulysses* with this issue in mind would doubtless bring to light many other passages where the fusion of inner/outer and narrator/character is demonstrable.[22]

Given how totally this novel is devoted to the evocation of Stephen's psyche in its fullest context, we find ourselves regarding from Stephen's perspective even those few scenes that do not specifically evoke his consciousness. During the Christmas dinner episode, for example, we presume that Stephen senses and perceives all that goes on, and that it forms an integral part of his psychic milieu, even though from p. 31.1 to p. 39.33, Joyce provides no direct representation of Stephen's consciousness. Clearly this scene is included in the novel because of its impact upon Stephen— because of its contribution to and reflection of the social consciousness in which Stephen's "individual conscious" subsists—and so we presume that all of this forms a part of his psychic substance, though we are not justified in concluding (in the absence of direct presentation of his psyche) which emotions or images are "consciousness" and which are "subconcious."

While all of the passages in *Portrait* come down to print upon the page, we readers project from those printed words a full panoply of psychic states and affects, some of which are clearer and more accessible to Stephen than others. The verbal fabric of *Portrait* involves contents that are presumably quite clear and conscious to Stephen, and others that are far beneath the surface of his psyche, existing almost viscerally or somatically. My working hypothesis is that all of these contents are elements within Stephen's psyche, even though we cannot say precisely what is conscious, what subconscious, or (to evoke less accustomed categories) what is individual and what is social or collective.

To illustrate by brief reference to a motif that we shall discuss more fully later—the bird motif—when Stephen hears the phrase "The eagles will come and pull out his eyes," he pictures to himself, presumably consciously, the image of an eagle. But what are we to say about the status of a corresponding bird image in passages where there is no word that explicitly evokes the image—for example in the description of Father Dolan on p. 50 or the phrase "swish of a soutane" on p. 154? Is there any basis for arguing that Stephen's psychic processes in those instances involve a *subconscious* bird image? Such a claim can, I believe, be substantiated by reference to the surrounding context, or to other passages in the novel where these same words or phrases are more explicitly accompanied by explicit avine imagery. Furthermore, if we do not project such "subsconsious" dimensions of Stephen's psyche, presuming images and associations that are not explicitly given in the language of the text, we miss an important part of the richness of texture of this novel, and of Joyce's purpose.

This is even more true of *Ulysses,* where (to use Dorrit Cohn's categories) Joyce relies less upon narrated monologue and more on quoted monologue—in spite of Cohn's claim that this mode of presentation shows that in *Ulysses* Joyce identifies language with thought. On the contrary, the highly elliptical nature of the monologues in *Ulysses* forces us to ask what holds the mental/psychic process together beneath the language presented on the page, and the answer—as careful analysis of any passage in *Ulysses* will show—is subliminal non-linguistic or pre-verbal associations, images, sensations, memories, perceptions—very few of which are directly represented in the words of the character's monologues. Rather than being the whole of the characters' thought in *Ulysses,* their explicitly given language is little more than its surface.[23]

There are in *Portrait* several kinds of passages that illustrate how limited and incomplete Stephen's self-awareness is, how much richer his psyche is than he can consciously realize.

(1) In many instances the text explicitly tells us that Stephen's awareness was vague or incomplete. We are told that he "dimly apprehended" something (p. 62.24–25); that he "wondered vaguely" and even that "he wondered at the vagueness of his wonder" (p. 161.31–33); that "he heard a confused music within him as of memories and names which he was almost conscious of but could not capture even for an instant" (p. 167); and are often told that Stephen "felt" something (p. 65.33).[24] Similarly, during Stephen's intensely religious phase, Joyce tells us "Consciousness of place came ebbing back to him slowly over a vast tract of time unlit, unfelt, unlived" (p. 141.5–6), and later, "The clear certitude of his own immunity [from temptation] grew dim and to it succeeded a vague fear that his soul had really fallen unawares. It was with difficulty that he won back his old consciousness of his state of grace . . . " (p. 153.3–6). Immediately after one of the Dedalus family's removals we are told: "Stephen sat on a footstoll beside his father listening to a long and incoherent monologue. He understood little or nothing of it at first but he became slowly aware that his father had enemies and that some fight was going to take place. He felt too that he was being enlisted for the fight, that some duty was being laid upon his shoulders" (pp. 65–66). Each of these passages conveys to us a clearer understanding of Stephen's psychic states than he himself has.

As a more extended example of such a passage, consider:

In a vague way he understood that his father was in trouble and that this was the reason why he himself had not been sent back to Clongowes. For some time he had felt the slight changes in his house; and these changes in what he had deemed unchangeable were so many slight shocks to his boyish conception of the world. The ambition which he felt astir at times in the darkness of his soul sought no outlet. A dusk like that of the outer world obscured his mind as he heard the mare's hoofs clattering along the tramtrack on the Rock Road and the great can swaying and rattling behind him. (p. 64)

Given Stephen's youth—he is probably no more than nine or ten years old—and the nature of the changes that are taking place in his family, it is understandable that his awareness of what is going on is vague and is experienced by him as slight shocks or as an almost tangible dusk. While this passage represents the state of Stephen's psyche, the words are not spoken by Stephen himself, and so the thoughts and feelings do not rise to the level of articulation. The image here of a dusk of the mind *exists in* Stephen's psyche, even though he probably does not name it to himself. The sounds of hoofs and cans probably are conscious—i.e., Stephen would if asked acknowledge having heard them—but their association or connection with the dusk settling upon him almost certainly is not.

There are many other passages throughout the novel that refer explicitly to Stephen's vague, incomplete awareness, but in his wish to be autonomous, he manages for the most part to bury or deny any nascent sense that he is not self-aware and self-determining.

(2) At other times Joyce reports to us bodily states that Stephen could hardly be "aware of." Examples include: "Bodily unrest and chill and weariness beset him, routing his thoughts" (p. 136.27–28), and "At once from every part of his being unrest began to irradiate. A feverish quickening of his pulses followed and a din of meaningless words drove his reasoned thoughts hither and thither confusedly" (pp. 160–61). While Stephen's mind responds to these somatic effects, it is unlikely indeed that he tells himself that his thoughts are routed. Often Stephen's bodily states are conveyed by some physical metaphor that presumably has an unarticulated somatic/psychic counterpart. For example, we are told that "the sight of the filthy cowyard . . . sickened Stephen's heart" (p. 63.32), and shortly afterward, "the same foreknowledge which had sickened his heart and made his legs sag suddenly . . . dissipated any vision of the future" (p. 64.14); or "a faint sickness sighed in his heart" (p. 91.9). Precisely what the physical correlate

of such metaphors is we cannot say—presumably his legs may actually sag, but his heart does not literally sicken or sigh—but in any event Stephen has little cognitive awareness of the processes.

Closely related to this are passages involving moods or states of emotion that exist beneath Stephen's awareness. (I presume that we, and Stephen, can be happy, or apprehensive, without saying to ourselves "I am happy," or "I am apprehensive" and thus without explicit awareness of our state of being.) For example, Joyce tells us that "a vague dissatisfaction grew up within him as he looked on the quays and on the river" (p. 66.33); refers to "the incommunicable emotion which had been the cause of all his day's unrest" (p. 75.6); later tells us that "a dim antagonism gathered force within him and darkened his mind as a cloud" (p. 164.33); and subsequently that when he looks on the naked swimming boys, "he, apart from them and in silence, remembered in what dread he stood of the mystery of his own body" (p. 168).

Another passage suggests that Stephen's sensations effect an emotive state almost reflexively, virtually bypassing his mind: "When evening had fallen he left the house and the first touch of the damp dark air and the noise of the door as it closed behind him made ache his conscience, lulled by prayer and tears" (p. 139.11–14). The passage makes no reference to Stephen's thoughts, and the implication is that the tactile and auditory sensations impinged directly on his "conscience."

(3) In other passages of *Portrait*, the mental contents explicitly given by words on the page are organized by images or associations that are not explicitly stated and are presumably subconscious. Often we can confirm *[that's why dissassoc]* such implicit images or associations through links to other passages in which the images are explicit. Such subtle, ramifying associations can best be illustrated through recurrent motifs or complexes, which we shall explore in the next chapter.

(4) Several times the novel presents us with full and detailed psychic processes that must be virtually instantaneous and thus not susceptible to conscious control or articulation by Stephen. (Joyce uses this technique on a larger scale for the presentation of the characters' "subconscious" in Circe, as when we have a long fantasy of Bloom's occurring between two successive statements by Zoe—*Ulysses,* 15.1354–1956.) One such experience occurs during Stephen's interview with the Director of Belvedere. The priest has just referred critically to the dress of the capuchin—*les jupes* (the skirts, or petticoats); Stephen smiles in response and we are told a "tiny flame

kindl[ed] upon his cheek" (p. 155). After that we have six paragraphs—some 600 words—of reverie on Stephen's part, involving memories from his childhood and even remembered sentences spoken by a priest, before we are told "The tiny flame which the priest's allusion had kindled upon Stephen's cheek had sunk down again and his eyes were still fixed calmly on the colorless sky" (pp. 156–57). Then there follows another 120 words of reverie, involving remembered sights and sounds, and including the statement that "The echoes of certain expressions used in Clongowes sounded in remote caves of his mind," before we are told "His ears were listening to these distant echoes amid the silence of the parlour when he became aware that the priest was addressing him in a different voice." The time that has passed cannot have been more than several seconds, and yet on some level of his mind Stephen has engaged in a detailed and extensive reverie—a reverie that cannot have taken as long in Stephen's mind as it takes us to read it.

It is unlikely that everything that passes through Stephen's mind in this brief moment—a content so varied and so lengthy that it requires many paragraphs to present—is available to Stephen as conscious, reflective thought. We the readers can of course ponder it, reread it, analyze it, but for Stephen it passes quickly and with little articulation, consisting in large part of an array of feelings, memories, images. And Joyce tells us as much by one sentence in the midst of the passage: "Masked memories passed quickly before him: he recognized scenes and persons yet he was conscious that he had failed to perceive some vital circumstance in them."[25] Furthermore, whatever the organizing principle behind these reveries—and it seems largely to involve juxtaposition of Clongowes and Father Conmee, and Belvedere and the director—Stephen can hardly be said to be "in control" of it or to have intentionally called it up; more likely it presents itself to him as a given of his experience.

If these reveries and images are not conscious to Stephen, are the images perhaps better construed as those of the interpreting narrator, rather than as a part of Stephen's psychic experience? I think not. My view, stated earlier, is that such material exists on some level of Stephen's psyche—exists "subconsciously," exists as part of his "psychic milieu."[26] That Stephen's psyche does involve such material can often be shown by considering other related contexts. For example, we are told that "the echoes of certain expressions used at Clongowes sounded in remote caves of his mind" (p. 157). This sentence is particularly interesting and problematic, because it involves both the memory of certain phrases from the past, and the image of the "caves" and "echoes" in Stephen's mind. It is difficult in the first place to say how conscious the remembered phrases or expressions are, in this almost instantaneous reverie, but it is even harder to know the status of the image of the cave and echo in Stephen's mind. This metaphor of caves and echoes might in a more conventional text be purely authorial; that it has some figural status here is suggested by several factors. For one, the next sentence tells us that "His ears were listening to these distant echoes . . . when he became aware that the priest was addressing him in a different voice"— which attributes the "echoes" more directly to Stephen's mind. For another, images of caves and caverns and echoes do enter explicitly into Stephen's experience at other points in the novel, and to regard this current instance of the cave image as "sheerly authorial" would deprive us of seeing the image as part of a strand or motif of Stephen's psyche.[27]

This question of whether an image exists in the mind of the author or the character becomes even harder to adjudicate—at least in this novel— when the image in question is a common, natural, potentially archetypal one. That is, the image of a cave, or of a shadow, or of a rose, is so readily available to us as to be capable of being subliminally evoked in anyone by the most ordinary experiences. In such cases it is virtually impossible to deny the image to the character, because such images are so much a part of the material of our collection psyche that none of us can say whether they have been present or absent from our own ruminations. Interestingly, some of the more exotic images of the novel are clearly not "authorial," but are unambiguously ascribed to Stephen. These include the image of a spiritual cash register on p. 148, and another striking and unusual image later in the novel: "The heavy lumpish phrase sank slowly out of hearing like a stone through a quagmire. Stephen saw it sink, as he had seen many another, feeling its heaviness depress his heart" (p. 195).

Equally interesting for my purposes is the instantaneous reverie that occurs while Heron and Wallace taunt Stephen. In response to Heron's challenge and his striking Stephen with his cane, Stephen begins to recite the Confiteor, and as he is doing so, Joyce tells us, "The confession came only from Stephen's lips and, while they spoke the words, a sudden memory had carried him to another scene called up, as if by magic, at the moment when he had noted the faint cruel dimples at the corners of Heron's smiling lips and had felt the familiar stroke of the cane against his calf and had heard the familiar word of admonition" (p. 78). What makes this scene so interesting is that the magically-evoked memory is extensive and detailed, requiring some four pages to recount, though it all occurs during the very brief time Stephen's conscious mind is reciting the Confiteor—no more than a minute or two at most.[28] The implication is that, just as the material presented instantaneously in Circe is somehow a part of Bloom's psyche, this material presented in such detail over pp. 78–82 enters in some way into Stephen's—but not in the clarity and detail in which it is conveyed to us by the print on the page. Obviously Stephen's psyche has a vitality and richness of which he is not even aware.[29]

(5) Another interesting form of testimony to Stephen's incomplete self-awareness and self-determination is the spontaneous activity of his mind that occasionally takes him aback, leaving him the surprised, sometimes appalled, observer of his own psychic activity. One such instance occurs in the anatomy theatre in Cork, in response to the word *Foetus* that he finds cut into a desk:

> The sudden legend startled his blood: he seemed to feel the absent students of the college about him and to shrink from their company. A vision of their life, which his father's words had been powerless to evoke, sprang up before him out of the word cut in the desk. A broadshouldered student with a moustache was cutting in the letters with a jackknife, seriously. Other students stood or sat near him laughing at his handiwork. One jogged his elbow. The big student turned on him, frowning. He was dressed in loose grey clothes and had tan boots.

Stephen hurries after his father, to get away from the vision, and he ponders where such images and reveries come from:

> His recent monstrous reveries came thronging into his memory. They too had sprung up before him, suddenly and furiously, out of mere words. He had soon given in to them and allowed them to sweep across and abase his intellect, wondering always where they came from, from what den of monstrous images, and always weak and humble towards others, restless and sickened of himself when they had swept over him. (pp. 89–90)

Obviously, Stephen is puzzled and appalled by these actions of his own psyche, actions that he can neither control nor understand.

Another instance of Stephen's self-surprising mental activity occurs as he and his fellow students are standing on the Library portico, as Emma passes by. Thinking briefly of the phrase "Darkness falls from the air," Stephen then retreats to a darker part of the portico, to elaborate the revery inspired by Emma's passing. But after a paragraph of images involving loose women, we are told, "The images that he had summoned gave him no pleasure. They were secret and enflaming but her image was not entangled by them. That was not the way to think of her. It was not even the way in which he thought of her. Could his mind then not trust itself?" (p. 233) That he cannot in fact trust his mind is shown also by his realization just a few lines later:

> it was not darkness that fell from the air. It was brightness.
>   *Brightness falls from the air.*
>   He had not even remembered rightly Nash's line. All the images it had awakened were false. His mind bred vermin. His thoughts were lice born of the sweat of sloth. (p. 234; Stephen has in the interim between these two passages picked a louse from himself.)[30]

Stephen's inability to control the tonal, imagistic movements of his mind is shown even more pointedly by his inability to sustain his creative reverie while composing the villanelle. His poetic mood is rudely interrupted by the intrusion of the idea of "an ellipsoidal ball," from a student's gross remark earlier: "The earth was like a swinging smoking swaying censer, a ball of incense, an ellipsoidal ball. The rhythm died out at once; the cry of his heart was broken. His lips began to murmur the first verses over and over; then went on stumbling through half verses, stammering and baffled; then stopped. His heart's cry was broken" (p. 218).

Though Stephen does eventually recover his mood of poetic receptiveness, he sees from this experience how fragile that mood is, how little control he has over maintaining the poetic process and forcing it to continue and proceed. This episode helps by contrast to explain the importance of theory generally for Stephen, because it is through the conscious, rational development of theory that he can come closest to maintaining the illusion of self-control. The analytical process, unlike the creative, can be maintained by force of mind, even in the midst of interruptions; this clarifies Stephen's apparent pride in being able to maintain this structure of argument to an interlocutor so out of tune with his intellectual interests as Lynch, and perhaps even casts light on why he has chosen the unlikely Lynch as the audience of his theorizing. This clarifies as well the statement that Stephen's mind, "emptied of theory and courage, lapsed back into a listless peace" (p. 216); this linking of theory and courage grows out of Stephen's implicit identification of the analytical, ratiocinative process of his mind with his own autonomy. For a young man who needs to believe in this autonomy, theory is a much more compatible field than poetic creation, which involves processes that he knows he cannot fully manipulate or control. But not even while developing his abstract theory is Stephen confident of his own mental autonomy. As he and Lynch walk along the Grand Canal we are told that "a crude grey light, mirrored in the sluggish water, and a smell of wet branches over their heads seemed to war against the course of Stephen's thought" (p. 207.7).[31]

The passages that we have been looking at are simply the most striking examples of a principle that pervades the novel so completely that we are likely to overlook its presence and its implications, especially for Stephen's claims to autonomy. The fact is that very little of Stephen's mental/psychic activity is under his conscious, rational control. That his mind has "a life of its own" is shown repeatedly by its associations, by its responsiveness to bodily sensations, to associations triggered by scenes, odors, etc.[32]

(6) Michael Levenson has shown that this principle that Stephen is not aware of his own deepest mental/psychic processes is at work in a portion of the novel where we might least expect it—the articulate diary entries that conclude the novel. Through a careful analysis of the diary entries and of passages earlier in the novel, Levenson shows that in his diary Stephen is unwittingly reworking material from his earlier experiences. Stephen's psyche, that is, on a level presumably unavailable to his conscious mind, is using the diary as a means of reviewing, replaying, coming to terms with, earlier experiences, so that through the diary Joyce shows us that "an intimate account of the present could become an involuntary record of the past, and that the self could never know how much of its life history it might inadvertently disclose."[33] Levenson points out a number of passages that involve striking verbal similarities between a given diary entry and some earlier experience, one of the most interesting being the dream recorded in the March 25 entry and the earlier confession scene. As Levenson says "Stephen himself betrays no awareness of the connection between the dream and the earlier incident, but the startling method of the diary is to look past conscious recognitions in favor of subterranean relations established among words themselves. . . . His language knows what Stephen may not. . . . The diary abounds with such echoes of earlier passages. . . . Beneath the casual surface of Stephen's personal record, there is

an extraordinary linguistic density, and here, as elsewhere in Joyce, one might speak of a linguistic unconscious which carries meanings that do not depend on the intentions of the speaker" (pp. 1025–26).

This principle of unawares recapitulation of earlier motifs, images, etc., applies not only to the diary entries, but is increasingly a factor in the novel as Stephen's development progresses and becomes more complex. Erwin R. Steinberg, for example, discovers complex patterns of thesis-antithesis-synthesis among the climaxes of chapters II, III, and IV of the novel, including some twenty-three specific parallels of language, situation, theme, and motif; see "The Bird-Girl in *A Portrait* as Synthesis: The Sacred Assimilated to the Profane," *JJQ* 17 (Winter 1980): 149–63. Such interweavings of the text (and thus of Stephen's psyche) illustrate the amazing coherence and continuity of Stephen's development and reveal the superficiality of Colin MacCabe's claims of discontinuity of event and character among the chapters of the novel (*Joyce and the Revolution of the Word*, p. 66).

Stephen's lack of conscious, rational control over his psyche does not mean that it is therefore chaotic, or that it is simply a product of various linguistic or cultural factors. That there is a considerable degree of continuity and cohesion and even entelechy to Stephen's psychic processes, is shown by the innumerable strands, motifs, images, memories that twine so complexly through his psychic evolution, manifesting its considerable coherence and integrity. But the source of this coherence and integrity is not Stephen's conscious mind. If that were the case, his psyche would perhaps be better ordered, but it would be so thin and paltry as to be of no interest to anyone.

7

Motif/Complex/Allusion

*A*s any attentive reader knows, Joyce's *Portrait* is structured around many recurrent motifs. Among the most obvious such motifs are the bird, the cow, the rose, hands, eyes and blindness, various colors such as white, grey, red and green, such verbal motifs as "hither and thither," etc.[1] Because the very structure and texture of this *Bildungsroman* so fully simulate the psyche of its main character, these motifs are simultaneously artifact and complex. Regarded from the perspective of the artist-craftsman who wove the fabric of this book, they are intricate aesthetic leitmotifs; from that of the character Stephen Dedalus, they are the substance of his psyche. In other novels, especially those involving a number of characters, such recurrent elements are motifs of the novel, not complexes of one character's psyche. In *Portrait of the Artist,* to a degree that is perhaps unique, the structures of the novel and the complexes of Stephen's mind are so fully identified that every motif is simultaneously aesthetic/structural and psychological.[2]

The Bird Motif

The bird motif is appropriate for my purpose for several reasons. For one, the meanings the image takes on as the novel progresses involve a subtle blend of "inner" and "outer" factors—i.e., of Stephen's "inherent" attitude toward the image, and of negative associations surrounding his early experiences with the image. The motif first appears on the second

137

page of the novel (p. 8), in an ambiguous but fearful, emotion-charged context that dictates its meaning for Stephen for some time to come. There is evidence later in the novel that Stephen's innate disposition toward the image of the bird is positive, but so strongly negative is its original experiential context that the positive connotations the image has for him cannot manifest themselves in Stephen's psyche until much later. (That Stephen's psyche has such innate dispositions is suggested by certain notes in "The Trieste Notebook," s.v. "Dedalus": "He had an inborn distaste for fermented foods"; "He liked green"; "He disliked bottles" [*Workshop,* p. 95].) Another point of interest in the bird image is Stephen's attempt self-consciously to reconstitute the meaning of the image for himself at a crucial point in his life—the climactic scene on the beach in chapter IV. The motif also permits us to see how subtly various conscious and subconscious dimensions of the image ramify in Stephen's psyche. That is, while certain instances of the motif establish clear-cut meanings and associations, radiating from these are others in which the image exerts subconscious influence in Stephen's mind.

Let us consider the original context of this motif:

The Vances lived in number seven. They had a different father and mother. They were Eileen's father and mother. When they were grown up he was going to marry Eileen. He hid under the table. His mother said:

—O, Stephen will apologize.

Dante said:

—O, if not, the eagles will come and pull out his eyes.

> *Pull out his eyes,*
> *Apologize,*
> *Apologize,*
> *Pull out his eyes.*

> *Apologize,*
> *Pull out his eyes,*
> *Pull out his eyes,*
> *Apologize.* (p. 8)

The context here involves certain meanings and connotations that recur in subsequent occurrences of the motif—that become a complex, in the Jungian sense of the term. The main elements of this complex are 1) accusation and threat of punishment for something that Stephen does not fully understand or is not in fact guilty of; ② the involvement of his eyes; and ③ the presence of the bird image. The vagueness in this episode about what Stephen must apologize for is probably a reflection of his own puzzlement about his "crime." Since Eileen is a girl and there is reference to marriage, and since she is (as we learn later) a Protestant, his offense may involve nascent sexuality, or religion. But precisely what the offense is we do not know, nor does Stephen. What is crucial is that the bird is forcibly presented to him as an instrument of punishment for some vaguely understood offense, and that the threat involves his eyes.[3]

Throughout the first four chapters of the novel, this complex reoccurs with considerable integrity: the presence of certain elements of the complex is usually sufficient to trigger the whole. The next instance occurs on this same page, though separated from it in time by several years. Stephen is a very young boy at Clongowes, and we are told of his reluctance to take part in the rough sports that the others play:

> The wide playgrounds were swarming with boys. All were shouting and the prefects urged them on with strong cries. The evening air was pale and chilly and after every charge and thud of the footballers the greasy leather orb flew like a heavy bird through the grey light. He kept on the fringe of his line, out of sight of his prefect, out of the reach of the rude feet, feigning to run now and then. He felt his body small and weak amid the throng of players and his eyes were weak and watery. (p. 8)

This brief passage contains the elements of the complex—Stephen feels guilty about not taking part in the games, and so he feigns to run and tries to avoid the glance of the authority figure who would doubtless upbraid (perhaps even punish) him for his reluctance. Obviously he feels inadequate and vulnerable, and the reference to his bodily weakness focuses specifically on his "weak and watery eyes." The context here of Stephen's feelings of inadequacy and vague guilt make it appropriate that the ball should appear to Stephen as a bird—thus completing the complex and objectifying the nascent fear of punishment that he feels.[4]

The episode most fully manifesting this complex is the pandybatting scene. Once again certain elements of the complex are literally present and others are projected into the experience by Stephen. Stephen is accused of something of which he is not guilty, and the purported crime involves his eyes: he is accused of having broken his glasses so that he will not have to do his lessons. Moreover, the description of Father Dolan, the punisher, invokes the image of an avenging eagle:

> Stephen lifted his eyes in wonder and saw for a moment Father Dolan's whitegrey not young face, his baldy whitegrey head with fluff at the sides of it, the steel rims of his spectacles and his nocoloured eyes looking through the glasses. (p. 50)

Here again, Stephen views Father Dolan as a bald eagle because the other elements of the complex suggest such a perception. In this context of vaguely understood guilt and fear, once again involving his eyes, it is natural that the punisher be seen as a bird. But the words *bird* or *eagle* are not present in the text, suggesting that the image may not be "consciously" present in Stephen"s mind.[5]

Other contexts in the early chapters of the novel involve a bird (or bird imagery) associated with fear. Stephen's apprehension about the "bird here waiting for you" he finds in the center of the dining room table at Christmas cannot be fully assuaged by his reassuring himself that his father purchased the turkey in Dunns of D'Olier Street, in part because of the unhappy coincidence that Mr. Barrett at Clongowes calls the instrument of punishment a turkey—though he tries by thinking, "but Clongowes was far away" (pp. 29–30).

Another instance of the motif occurs in the episode with Heron, of whom Stephen "had often thought it strange that Vincent Heron had a bird's face as well as a bird's name" (p. 76). Appropriately the situation involves both accusation and punishment, in that Heron asks Stephen to "Admit" to having a girl friend (a dubious accusation of a noncrime) and strikes Stephen with a cane. And while this episode does not seriously disturb Stephen, it calls to his mind an earlier episode that he had found painful. In the wake of Mr. Tate's having accused Stephen of heresy (once again a "crime" of which he was not really guilty), Heron and others had taken the opportunity to attack the "heretic" and punish him over his refusal to disavow his admiration for Byron.

Other instances of the bird image or its associations seem not to rise fully to the surface in Stephen's mind—i.e., they are not explicit in the novel's language. Consider, for example, the sound associated with the flapping of the brothers' soutanes. The sound is first referred to on the day of Stephen's arrival at Clongowes; just as his parents are leaving, there is a reference to the rector's "soutane fluttering in the breeze" (p. 9). While this phrase offers no confirmation as to whether the fluttering of the winglike soutane evokes in the boy's mind an image of a bird, conditions conducive to the bird-complex are present: the young boy, just separating from his parents, is in a state of apprehension, perhaps even guilt, about his timidity and his wishing to be back at home, and the rector is for him a figure of awesome authority. Also, the sound of the soutane figures prominently in the pandybatting scene, where we are three times told that Stephen heard "the swish of the sleeve of the soutane as the pandybat was lifted to strike" (pp. 50, 50, 52). But even though the context provided by the description of Father Dolan would readily support it, no explicit association of this sound with a bird is made at this point. But in a later passage the association of the soutane with a bird's wings is explicit; we are told that "the excited prefect was hustling the boys through the vestry like a flock of geese, flapping the wings of his soutane" (p. 74)—which suggests that ornithic associations were unconsciously present in the earlier instances of this image.

Furthermore, Joyce very subtly draws upon the negative associations of the sound of the soutane in a later passage, but once again without explicit bird reference. As Stephen is waiting for the director at Belvedere, struggling to find the meaning of his message, we are told that as the director comes in Stephen hears "the swish of a soutane" (p. 154). Joyce tells us nothing about Stephen's reaction at this time, but the reader attuned to the associations of the motif understands that the sound of the priest's garment involves such negative emotions for Stephen that the director has in effect already lost his case. Not surprisingly, Stephen does during the priest's monologue recall two pandybattings at Clongowes and thinks specifically they "had been dealt him in the wrong" (p. 156), invoking the "unjustified punishment" aspect of the complex. And another possible echo of the pandying occurs when, parting from the priest, he "raised his eyes to the priest's face and . . . detached his hand slowly" (p. 160; compare the passage on pp. 50–51 where Stephen "lifted his eyes in wonder and saw for a moment Father Dolan's whitegrey not young face" and in which the priest's grasping and releasing Stephen's hand figures prominently). This shading off of the associations of the bird image from explicit to implicit, conscious to unconscious, shows that the image can exert influence even when not explicit in the novel's language; whether the swish of the soutane consciously evokes a bird image in Stephen's mind, it involves an array of negative feelings that persist from earlier bird-linked experiences.

In the early chapters of the novel, then, the bird image has consistently negative associations for Stephen—associations doubtless forced upon him by the original context of the image. The image can be evoked in Stephen's mind by situations involving an imputation of guilt, especially if his eyes are in some way involved. And in some situations the disturbing effect of the image seems to affect Stephen without ever rising fully to the surface of his mind. In any event, for much of his young life, Stephen is in thrall to the frightening connotations associated with the image of the bird.

The turning point in regard to this image comes at the end of the fourth chapter, when, as a part of his self-assertive redefinition of himself—his soul's arising from the grave of boyhood—Stephen reconstrues the image, in terms more appropriate to his own wishes. The result is that this image which always had connotations of fear and guilt is remade into an image of beauty and of his destiny.[6] This change is expressed both in his reflections on the figure of Daedalus, whose name he bears, and in his apprehension of the wading girl. During the scene on the strand, Stephen thinks explicitly of his strange name, and it seems to him "a prophecy" (p. 168). Of Daedalus, we are told,

> Now, at the name of the fabulous artificer, he seemed to hear the noise of dim waves and to see a winged form flying above the waves and slowly climbing the air. What did it mean? Was it a quaint device opening a page of some medieval book of prophecies and symbols, a hawklike man flying sunward above the sea, a prophecy of the end he had been born to serve and had been following through the mists of childhood and boyhood, a symbol of the artist forging anew in his workshop out of the sluggish matter of the earth a new soaring impalpable imperishable being?
>
> His heart trembled; his breath came faster and a wild spirit passed over his limbs as though he were soaring sunward. His heart trembled in an ecstasy of fear and his soul was in flight. His soul was soaring in an air beyond the world and the body he knew was purified in a breath and delivered of incertitude and made radiant and commingled with the element of the spirit. An ecstasy of flight made radiant his eyes and wild his breath and tremulous and wild and radiant his windswept limbs. (p. 169)

In this passage the winged form flying above the waves is not an image of punishment but of freedom and release; the image Stephen thinks of here—hawk rather than eagle—is not one foisted upon him by intimidating authority, but one of his own making, his own imagining. His "eyes" participate in the transformation, both in that he "sees" the winged form climbing the air, and that his once weak and vulnerable eyes are now "radiant."

The girl is described in a variety of avian terms, all of them connoting beauty rather than threat:

> She seemed like one whom magic had changed into the likeness of a strange and beautiful seabird. Her long slender bare legs were delicate as a crane's and pure save where an emerald trail of seaweed had fashioned itself as a sign upon the flesh. Her thighs, fuller and softhued as ivory, were bared almost to the hips where the white fringes of her drawers were like featherings of soft white down. Her slateblue skirts were kilted boldly about her waist and dovetailed behind her. Her bosom was as a bird's soft and slight, slight and soft as the breast of some darkplumaged dove. (p. 171)

Clearly the image of the bird is no longer associated with fear and guilt and punishment; Stephen has remade the meaning of the image for himself into something far more positive—into an image of the beauty of the natural world and a promise of flight and of release.

The change that takes place here in Stephen's apprehension of the bird image is simply one part of a larger metamorphosis at this climactic point of the novel, because in Stephen's mind this is the juncture in his life at which he ceases to be dictated to by circumstance and becomes self-defining. (See the earlier discussion of Stephen's re-definition of himself at the novel's climax, pp. 102 ff.) For the first four chapters of the novel, Stephen felt himself a passive victim of the meanings of the image that were branded into his psyche as a child. But at this climactic point of the novel, Stephen remakes the meaning of this image and of others. This confirms that this climactic event involves not simply his realization of his artistic calling, but his determination to take charge of his destiny, to become not the passive recipient of experience but the initiator.

This change in Stephen's sense of the bird image does carry over into chapter V, in that the bird images that occur there are associated with escape or release or with augury or destiny. When talking with Davin, Stephen makes the statement that "when the soul of a man is born in this country there are nets flung at it to hold it back from flight. You talk to me of nationality, language, religion. I shall try to fly by those nets" (p. 203). Here Stephen himself invokes the bird image (rather than having it pressed upon him by frightening circumstances) and presents it as an image of escape and freedom. Later, while standing on the steps of the library, he sees the birds flying around the house at the corner of Molesworth Street; he sees them as birds of augury, and he thinks again of "the hawklike man whose name he bore" (p. 225).

But even into these newly-projected images of the bird, there creeps an undertone of unease and fear. The birds of augury, for example, are said to sound "like the squeak of mice behind the wainscot: a shrill twofold note," and though he tells himself "but the notes were long and shrill and whirring, unlike the cry of vermin," we must wonder whether the sound does not recall to him an image evoked by the retreat sermon: "The wind of the last day blew through his mind; his sins, the jeweleyed harlots of his imagination, fled before the hurricane, squeaking like mice in their terror and huddled under a mane of hair" (p. 115—the only other mention of mice in the novel). Another note of unease in regard even to the image of the "hawklike man" is sounded a few paragraphs further on in the augury scene, when we are told "a sense of fear of the unknown moved in the heart of his weariness, a fear of symbols and portents, of the hawklike man whose name he bore soaring out of his captivity on osierwoven wings" (p. 225). Stephen may not have exorcised the fearful aspects of the bird image as fully as he thinks.

This same implication surfaces in the final instance of bird imagery in the novel—one of particular relevance to the theme of self-awareness and self-determination. The bird imagery of the closing paragraphs has implications Stephen himself seems unaware of and would probably be taken aback by. In the April 16 diary entry, Stephen thinks of certain enticing figures as "shaking the wings of their exultant and terrible youth," and then in the final sentence of the novel, he again invokes the figure of Daedalus, who was so important to his redefinition of the bird image. But here the invocation is significantly different, for in saying "old father, old artificer, stand me now and ever in good stead," Stephen is implicitly identifying himself with the son, Icarus. The image of flight, then, while still freed from the negative connotations that it had for the younger Stephen, is nonetheless more complex and more ominous than he realizes, for here at the very outset of his flight to freedom and self-realization, it forebodes a fall. Probably if Stephen were queried on this point—on why he has identified himself with the son rather than the father—he would deny any such implication, or certainly any such intention on his part. But the implication is there, and it has tonal and thematic appropriateness, in that it reveals how much more complex Stephen's psyche is than he himself realizes. Furthermore, as to whether this statement of Stephen's involves an (unwitting) Icarus allusion, we should note the passage in the Scylla and Charybdis episode of *Ulysses* where Stephen reflects on his departure from Dublin in the following terms: "Fabulous artificer. The hawklike man. You flew. Whereto? Newhaven-Dieppe, Steerage passenger. Paris and back. Lapwing. Icarus. *Pater, ait.* ["Father, he cries"—the cry of Icarus as he falls] Seabedabbled, fallen, weltering. Lapwing you are. Lapwing be" (*U*, 9.952). A chastened Stephen himself acknowledges the Icarian nature of his attempted escape from his island prison.[7]

I have focused on this motif because it illustrates that Stephen's psyche is more complex than he can realize, and that his sense of self-determination is exaggerated. This is shown first of all by the bird image entering into the psyche of the young Stephen in ways that he has virtually no awareness of, quite subconsciously. Also, the major change of meaning the image undergoes occurs at that climactic point when Stephen feels that he comes into control of his own destiny, redefining the bird image into one of Daedalian flight to freedom. But even this redefinition of the image is not completely within Stephen's conscious control, as the ironic implications of the final sentence of the novel show. Intending to cast himself as Daedalus, he unwittingly—perhaps under the influence of the negative connotations that the image so long held for him—casts himself as Icarus, expressing a subconscious sense that his flight to freedom is not so secure as he would like to believe. *Good*

"In Your Heart You Are an Irishman": Stephen's Irish Shadow

A second extended illustration of currents at work in Stephen's psyche beneath his awareness or control is provided by his "Irish shadow." Given the attention that has been paid to Stephen's relationships with his family, his church, and his state—all of them indubitably Irish—it may seem that nothing further remains to be said on the topic of his Irishness or his attitudes toward "the old sow that eats her farrow" (p. 203). But the aspect of Stephen's experience I wish to bring to focus here is not identifiable with church or family or nationalism; it is an aspect we may overlook because it *St George* is at once so pervasive, and so implicit. *& boring...*

God save England. and

What I am calling Stephen's Irish shadow consists of a complex of inter-related images, of attitudes, of fears, so deeply affective and so intimately a part of himself that while he can sense its importance for him and its influence over him, he can never fully bring it to the surface of his psyche.[8] Some of the motifs that make up this complex of Irishness are those of *race,* of *peasants,* of *darkness,* of *terror,* of the *Irish countryside,* of *cottages,* and of *dark country lanes.* Some aspects of the image of woman also enter into this complex, usually a peasant woman standing in a cottage doorway, and thought of as seductive or bat-like. Further, there is one character in the novel who is associated with this complex and who conse-quently has a distinctive and troubling effect on Stephen—the young peas-ant Davin. *cf. Wales & accents.*

Stephen's "Irishness" is particularly appropriate to the present argument because it represents a part of himself he senses to be important but *cannot* render fully conscious, and thus it frustrates his aspiration to be self-aware and self-determining. Stephen's grudging sense of his inability to come to terms with this aspect of his psyche gives it a different status from his feelings about his religion, his family, or from more abstract questions of Irish politics or nationalism, all of which he believes himself to have objecti-fied sufficiently to "fly by" them. The issue here is not whether Stephen is in fact "in control of" his relationships with church, family, or state (it is demonstrable that he is not), but whether he *feels* himself to be, and to a great degree he does—with the exception of this Irish shadow that contin-ues to trouble him. But while Stephen regards this gap in his self-awareness as a liability and a threat, Joyce does not, for he knows that were Stephen to become fully self-conscious, fully "freed from" the affective claims of his milieu, it would be disastrous for him as a person and as an artist.

Stephen's "Irish shadow," then, has a different status in his psyche than his more fully objectified ideas. Because of Stephen's own sense that this complex poses a threat to him, he feels unease and defensiveness when-ever the complex is evoked, and the words on the page then seem to represent something less coherent than thoughts in Stephen's mind—some-thing more like strongly connotative mental images that merge in and out of one another, affective tonalities that blend and fade, suggesting that this Irish complex has an ineluctably subliminal status in Stephen's conscious-ness. The elements of this complex exist for him like a shadow so close behind him that he cannot catch a view of it, or like a dream that he cannot fully recall, or a dream-antagonist or dark angel that he must struggle with.

Because he cannot bring this Irishness to light, he cannot gauge either its nature or its depth, nor can he say when or how it may make some claim on him, and so it remains necessarily in the penumbra of his experience, a source both of fascination and of fear.[9]

An important part of what Irishness involves for Stephen is reflected in his statement at the end of the novel that he will forge the "uncreated conscience" of his race. To be "Irish" seems to Stephen to involve a rudimentary state of conscience and even of consciousness, one not yet fully evolved and differentiated, one existing in an inchoate or twilight state, and always in danger of falling back into undifferentiated darkness. This helps to explain Stephen's association of Irishness with bat-like peasant women; to Stephen this image suggests something rudimentary or proto-human, something not yet fully evolved. The same quality is suggested by Stephen's viewing Tommy Moore (the national poet of Ireland) as a "Firbolg in the borrowed cloak of a Milesian," and by his shortly afterwards characterizing Davin too as a Firbolg. (The Firbolgs were a dark, dwarfish, primitive race in Irish protohistory.) There is a similar implication in Stephen's characterizing the early Irish myths as myths "upon which no *individual mind* had ever drawn out a line of beauty" (p. 181; my emphasis), attributing to that body of material a quality that is pre-individual and whose meaning is primitive and incipient. For Stephen, then, Irishness involves being insufficiently conscious and thus insufficiently self-determining. It means existing uneasily on the threshold of full humanness, full self-awareness, always in danger of being drawn back into some lemur-like, proto-mammalian state.

One of the earliest passages invoking this complex occurs when Stephen is a young boy praying in the chapel at Clongowes:

> There was a cold night smell in the chapel. But it was a holy smell. It was not like the smell of the old peasants who knelt at the back of the chapel at Sunday mass. That was a smell of air and rain and turf and corduroy. But they were very holy peasants. They breathed behind him on his neck and sighed as they prayed. They lived in Clane, a fellow said: there were little cottages there and he had seen a woman standing at the halfdoor of a cottage with a child in her arms, as the cars had come past from Sallins. It would be lovely to sleep for one night in that cottage before the fire of smoking turf, in the dark lit by the fire, in the warm dark, breathing the smell of the peasants, air and rain and turf and corduroy. But, O, the road there between the trees was dark! You would be lost in the dark. It made him afraid to think of how it was. (p. 18)

Young as he is, Stephen feels distinctly that the peasants are of some other class, some lower order of creatures, and a certain primitiveness and ominousness is suggested by their breathing behind him on his neck. The whole passage is rendered wonderfully sensuous and sub-cognitive both by the feelings aroused in Stephen and by the appeal to so many of the senses—the smells of rain and turf, the tactile quality invoked by the corduroy, the low but audible quality of the peasants' mixed prayers and sighs, their praying (preying?) behind him, the vivid visual images of the fire and of the woman at the half-door. And Stephen's ambivalence toward all of this is suggested by his feeling that it would be lovely to sleep for one night (only) among the peasants, along with his simultaneous fear of the darkness of the road between the trees. And even in this early passage we find the image of the woman at the cottage doorway—an image that will become crucial to this complex.

The elements of this complex have a primordial, archetypal quality for Stephen, causing them to coalesce and surface in his psyche especially in unguarded moments. As a small but significant example, consider the passage about Stephen's trip to Cork with his father, describing his responses when he awakes as the train moves across the dark Irish countryside. The setting and situation link this event in various ways with the one we have just considered—sleep, travelling across the countryside, even the motif of prayer—and provide several elements of the complex—the twilight, the "provinciality" of the country they are passing through. It is as if Stephen has got his wish that he might spend one night in the countryside among the peasants:

> When he awoke the train had passed out of Mallow and his father was stretched asleep on the other seat. The cold light of the dawn lay over the country, over the unpeopled fields and the closed cottages. The terror of sleep fascinated his mind as he watched the silent country or heard from time to time his father's deep breath or sudden sleepy movement. The neighborhood of unseen sleepers filled him with strange dread as though they could harm him; and he prayed that the day might come quickly. (p. 87)

That the experience this passage describes is so ordinary and undramatic is all the better for the point I am illustrating: such a passage suggests a complex of feelings, of fears, that exist in Stephen just beneath the surface, waiting to be triggered by certain images and conditions. In this case, Stephen's having just awakened to this scene doubtless makes him more vulnerable to the subliminal threats of this complex.

The image of the woman at the cottage door deserves particular attention. The most important subsequent occurrence of the image is in the story that Davin tells about his nighttime walk across the Irish countryside after a hurling match, and in Stephen's reflections on Davin's story. But before glancing at that we should recall certain traits of Davin himself and of Stephen's relationship with him. Of Stephen's three interlocutors in chapter V (the others being Lynch and Cranly), Davin is the most distinctively Irish. Nor is it that he represents abstract Irish nationalism. Certainly Davin does espouse the nationalist cause, and he does so with a directness that should offend Stephen but seems not to. But what interests him about Davin is a feeling, a quality of life, that Stephen finds simultaneously appealing and disturbing, as is shown by Stephen's first thoughts about him. It is noteworthy that Stephen refers to Davin as the "peasant student" and then thinks of how Davin's *cf. Wales*.

> rude Firbolg mind . . . had drawn his mind towards it and flung it back again, drawing it by a quiet inbred courtesy of attention or by a quaint turn of old English speech or by the force of its delight in rude bodily skill . . . repelling swiftly and suddenly by a grossness of intelligence or by a bluntness of feeling or by a dull stare of terror in the eyes, the terror of soul of a starving Irish village in which the curfew was still a nightly fear. (pp. 180–81)

too psych. This cluster of images inspired by Davin is not for Stephen simply some exercise in free association; somehow, however sub-rationally, Stephen feels that this native Irish fear of curfew (which etymologically means the covering of the fire, and hence darkness) still makes a claim on something deep in his own soul. The reason Davin fascinates Stephen and comes to have what is in some ways a more intimate relationship with him even than Cranly, is that through this Firbolg, Stephen senses the reality and the lurking power of the claim that the Irish race—i.e., his own Irishness—would make on him.

To return to the story Davin tells of the peasant woman at the cottage door—Davin tells Stephen of an experience he had one night while walking home from a hurling match, when a young woman invited him into her cottage for the night. Especially interesting is Stephen's response to the story:

> The last words of Davin's story sang in his memory and the figure of the woman in the story stood forth, reflected in other figures of the peasant women whom he had seen standing in the doorways at Clane as the college cars drove by, as a type of her race and his own, a batlike soul waking to the consciousness of itself in darkness and secrecy and loneliness. (p. 183)

Clearly, this set of images has its roots in the first passage that we looked at, where it was the peasants of Clane who first evoked this complex for Stephen.[10] But the crucial part of this passage, because it concentrates so much of Stephen's conception of Irishness and the threat it poses, is his seeing this woman "as a type of her race *and his own,* a batlike soul waking to the consciousness of itself in darkness and secrecy." The central meaning of Irishness for Stephen is incompleteness of consciousness, epitomized here by a "batlike soul [just] waking to consciousness," and what he most fears is the threat this poses to his quest for complete self-awareness and self-determination.

The degree to which Davin and what he represents has filtered down into Stephen's psyche is suggested by another noteworthy passage—another illustration of the spontaneous activity of Stephen's psyche that we examined above, pp. 133 ff. There is in the last chapter of the novel a minor character called the captain, a dwarfish, simian creature who is rumored to be the product of an incestuous union. At one point after he sees this captain, Stephen fantasizes to himself in some detail a scene of incestuous love. Consider the last few lines of that passage, and Stephen's reaction to his own fantasizing:

> [the lovers] embraced without joy or passion, his arm about his sister's neck. A grey woolen cloak was wrapped athwart her from her shoulder to her waist: and her fair head was bent in willing shame. He had loose redbrown hair and tender shapely strong freckled hands. Face. There was no face seen. The brother's face was bent upon her fair rainfragrant hair. The hand freckled and strong and shapely and caressing was Davin's hand.
>
> [Stephen] frowned angrily upon his thought and on the shrivelled mannikin who had called it forth. . . . Why were they not Cranly's hands? Had Davin's simplicity and innocence stung him more secretly? (p. 228)

Whether it is "innocence and simplicity" in Davin that have stung Stephen is questionable, but Stephen's self-surprising casting of Davin as the brother here does suggest how deep beneath Stephen's skin this young Firbolg has got. All that Stephen can do is wonder about what is going on beneath the surface of his own psyche.

That this complex continues to be a recurrent element in Stephen's psyche is shown by another passage late in the novel, just before Stephen's long talk with Cranly. Here Stephen's complex train of thoughts begins with the name of Maple's Hotel and moves from that to the "sleek lives of the patricians of Ireland," and thoughts of how "peasants greeted [these patricians] along the roads in the country." Then Stephen thinks:

> How could he hit their conscience or how cast his shadow over the imaginations of their daughters, before their squires begat upon them, that they might breed a race less ignoble than their own? And under the deep-ened dusk he felt the thoughts and desires of the race to which he belonged flitting like bats, across the dark country lanes, under trees by the edges of streams and near the poolmottled bogs. A woman had waited in the door-way as Davin had passed by at night and, offering him a cup of milk, had all but wooed him to her bed; for Davin had the mild eyes of one who could be secret. But him no woman's eyes had wooed. (p. 238)

Within the span of these few sentences are coalesced most of the images we have seen earlier—the word *race,* the dark country lanes, the peasants, the flitting bats, the woman in the doorway, the person of Davin—and most important, here again the central idea that holds the passage together is how to elevate the conscience and the mentality of the Irish race. Once again, when Stephen reflects on Irishness, he feels the threat of some primitive, unformed mode of being that he must struggle against.

That this is the case is shown by another passage late in the novel where Stephen reflects on the Irish speaker whom John Alphonsus Mulrennan met in a mountain cabin the in west of Ireland. Of this old man, who seems to epitomize much of what is Irish, Stephen records in his diary

> I fear him. I fear his redrimmed horny eyes. It is with him I must struggle all through this night till day come, till he or I lie dead, gripping him by the sinewy throat till . . . Till what? Till he yield to me? No. I mean him no harm. (p. 252)

The subconscious integrity of this complex is suggested by the tonal and verbal links between this passage and an earlier one we looked at. On his train ride across Ireland Stephen thinks "the neighborhood of unseen sleepers filled him with strange dread as though they could harm him; and he prayed that the day might come quickly" (p. 87), linking that passage with this by virtue of the night and the fear that Stephen feels, and specifically by his hoping that the day might soon come.[11] But the present passage seems to involve as well an allusion to Jacob's wrestling "until the breaking of the day" (Genesis 32:24) with the angel who eventually blessed him.

That Stephen is willing to carry out such a struggle is indicated by the next-to-last sentence of the novel, in which he, in terms that this complex enables us to appreciate more fully, describes the mission of his life: "Welcome, O life! I go to encounter for the millionth time the reality of experience and to forge in the smithy of my soul the *uncreated conscience* of *my race*" (pp. 252–53; my emphasis). The italicized words suggest again that for Stephen, to be Irish is to be only marginally self-aware, and that insofar as he does acknowledge the claim of the Irish upon him, his task is to create their conscience.[12]

Both the bird motif and the complex of the Irish shadow illustrate how much deeper and richer Stephen's psyche is than he himself realizes, and, especially in the Irish complex, we see how fearful Stephen is of those elements that confound his attempts to be totally self-aware and self-determining. In this we see that while Stephen aspires to the Enlightenment program of complete self-knowledge, Joyce wishes us to realize how specious that aim is, and how simple and superficial a view of the psyche it involves.

Allusive Contexts

We turn now to another device by which Joyce dramatizes a broader and deeper sense of the psyche than his characters themselves understand and shows how inextricably public and private are interwoven—one that he uses on a limited scale in *Portrait* and much more fully in *Ulysses*. The primary function of the literary and historic allusions and parallels that permeate *Portrait* and *Ulysses* is to deepen and to reverberate and (especially in *Ulysses*) to interrelate the personalities of the characters in these novels, in ways that they themselves cannot become fully aware of. The "mythic analogues" (which I use as a generic term to include *all* of the historical and literary parallels that Joyce evokes) beneath their presumably individual personalities provide Stephen and Bloom and Joyce's other characters with a significant respite from the "atomic" individualism that has become the modern world's most precious, and most expensive, commodity.

In *Portrait of the Artist* one of Stephen Dedalus' fundamental ways of coming to a sense of his own self is by identifying with various literary characters or historical figures. For example, on the first page of the novel, we see Stephen already identifying himself with a literary figure by responding to his father's story of baby tuckoo by saying, "He [i.e., Stephen himself] was baby tuckoo." Throughout the novel Stephen uses a variety of literary characters and historical personages as a means of exploring and understanding his own identity. These include Edmond Dantes from *The Count of Monte Cristo*, the poet Byron, Jesus Christ, and, of course, Daedalus, the fabulous Greek artificer whose name Stephen bears.

In each of these cases the young Stephen Dedalus rather naively assumes that there is a fairly simple, one-to-one identification between himself and the mythic figure—an identification that is entirely his own doing and that he quite fully understands. He seems also to presume that there is a highly individual, personal element in these identifications. That is, he feels that identification with these figures is something done by himself alone, and he would doubtless be surprised and chagrined to learn that the aspirations of innumerable late-nineteenth-century adolescents were shaped by their similarly identifying with Edmond Dantes—in other words, that there is something inherently public and generic about his individuation process.

For our purposes the most important "mythic" material that Stephen draws upon in the process of his development is his identification with the Greek craftsman Daedalus. Joyce goes to some lengths to make us aware of the public, cultural quality of this skein of allusions in ways that Stephen himself does not realize. Stephen does not consciously avow the implications of his surname until the climactic scene of the novel—the epiphany of the wading girl at the end of chapter IV.[13] At that time, Stephen feels a great access of self-awareness and self-determination. He realizes that his calling is to be an artist, and he proclaims an identification with Daedalus, "the fabulous artificer whose name he bore," thus attempting to use this mythic identification personally, just as he had earlier in the novel done with the story of baby tuckoo, with *The Count of Monte Cristo*, and even with the long retreat sermon, of which he naively thought "every word for him!" (p. 125).

But Joyce has already implicitly invoked and incorporated the Daedalian schema in a variety of ways earlier in the novel: we readers are apprised of this allusive context even before Stephen Dedalus appears on the scene, by virtue of the novel's epigraph from the *Metamorphoses,* which quotes Ovid's lines about Daedalus' setting his mind to unknown arts. This epigraph has an interesting, anomalous status in a novel that confines itself so scrupulously to Stephen's psychic processes. Through this epigraph—a device that he uses nowhere else in his canon—Joyce invokes, quite apart from the mind of Stephen Dedalus, the controlling allusive context of the novel. And so while Stephen comes into awareness of this material only relatively late in the novel, we readers have been aware of it as an inclusive cultural context all along—by virtue of the epigraph, by virtue of various subtle allusions to the Daedalus story, such as the several references to mazes, and of course by virtue of Stephen's very name, Dedalus.

There is, then, an inevitable irony in seeing Stephen at the end of chapter IV treat this mythic material so personally. Stephen sees the myth simply as a function of himself, a vehicle of his individual self-expression, realizing whatever meaning it has from his appropriation of it. We, from our privileged perspective, know that the myth has a public existence prior to Stephen and even that it has implicitly structured Stephen's development and influenced the direction his self-understanding will take. To vary a phrase of Robert Frost's, we see that Stephen was the myth's before the myth was Stephen's.

As one specific instance of how the myth is larger and more subtle than Stephen realizes, we should reflect again, from a different angle, on the allusion to the myth in the final sentence of *Portrait of the Artist,* written by Stephen into his diary as he prepares to leave Ireland for the European mainland: "Old father, old artificer, stand me now and ever in good stead." Stephen does not realize that in this last allusion to the myth he has taken so personally, he casts himself not as Daedalus, the father, but as Icarus, the son, unconsciously invoking another aspect of the myth, casting himself in a different role than he intends—the role not of the experienced father but of the naive son. As we have seen, such a reading of this sentence is confirmed in *Ulysses,* when Stephen himself, after his rather ignominious return from Paris to Dublin, recognizes that he was then Icarus rather than

Daedalus. In the Scylla and Charybdis episode a soberer and more self-aware Stephen acknowledges the naive unreflectiveness of his earlier relation to the myth.[14] But Joyce's aim in all of this is not to undermine his hero; the irony here and throughout *Portrait* and *Ulysses* is sympathetic, not corrosive.[15] Joyce's point is rather to suggest that Stephen's selfhood, and the various images and allusions he uses to construct it, is not nearly so private as he thinks it is, but has a public, cultural aspect deeper and more extensive than Stephen can realize. This claim about the "public" nature of the Daedalian allusions in *Portrait of the Artist* applies all the more fully to the dozens (or hundreds) of mythic schemata that pervade *Portrait* and *Ulysses.*

Joyce's incorporating so many such schemata into his novels suggests something about the nature of culture and about how individuals participate in their culture, as well as about the "individual psyche." Joyce wishes us to understand that every culture provides its members with a rich nexus of historical accounts, of stories, of schemata by means of which they come into self-awareness and self-understanding. But in spite of the modernist presumption that such schemata are given meaning by the individual—i.e., are purely subjective—Joyce shows that they have a public, "objective" quality about them, such that when we invoke them as a means of our own self-understanding, we necessarily invoke an array of structures and meanings that we do not fully comprehend or control. We think, that is, that our identification with, or invocation of, the myth is entirely personal, entirely under our control, whereas we may find ourselves under the control, or at least the influence, of the myth.[16]

To pursue this point we need briefly to follow Stephen's development into *Ulysses,* for there is an important difference between *Portrait* and *Ulysses* in terms of Stephen's stance toward and understanding of the allusive material, and consequently toward the very questions of self-knowledge and self-determination we have been tracing throughout this study. In *Portrait* Stephen remains to the end unaware of the irony of his position vis-à-vis the mythic material he uses. But in *Ulysses,* Stephen has achieved sufficient self-awareness to be able to twit himself about his unwitting Icarus identification as he left Dublin. He has realized that his selfhood is not as solipsistic as he had believed, and that the meanings and structures he finds in myths are not entirely of his own making—that as a matter of fact he can by dwelling on and exploring myths learn valuable things about *himself.* This is perhaps the main motive behind his discussion of Shakespeare—coming to understand himself more fully by developing a view of the relationships between Shakespeare's life and his works.

Stephen has also begun to realize that the categories of inner and outer are not so radically distinct as he had thought. Appropriately, Stephen's emergent understanding of inner and outer is expressed most explicitly in a claim he makes about Shakespeare, when, at the conclusion of his presentation, he says of the mature Shakespeare, "He found in the world without as actual what was in his world within as possible. Maeterlinck says: *If Socrates leave his house today he will find the sage seated on his doorstep. If Judas go forth tonight it is to Judas his steps will tend.* Every life is many days, day after day. We walk through ourselves, meeting robbers, ghosts, giants, old men, young men, wives, widows, brothers-in-love. But always meeting ourselves" (*U*, 9.1041). In other words, what we are capable of finding, even of experiencing, in the "public," "outer" world is a function of what exists in our "private," "inner" world. Not that Stephen yet knows fully and experientially whereof he speaks here, but he does at least know it in principle, and this is very promising.

Because Stephen in *Ulysses* has come to a new understanding of what can be learned from such schemata, he now approaches the material of the Shakespeare myth not brashly or egotistically, but respectfully. Also, he plays more fully over the various structures and perspectives that the myth provides, viewing it at times from the perspective of Shakespeare himself, at times from that of Hamlet, at times from of that of old King Hamlet, etc., in order to glean as much as he can. But to say that Stephen's understanding has progressed, is still not to say that he is capable of understanding all that the myth has to offer.[17]

Obviously the many parallels between Shakespeare's situation and those of the characters in *Ulysses* are of Joyce's own contriving; However complex all of this may appear, Joyce's point can be stated quite simply. The point is that the myths we consciously or unconsciously invoke to help structure our lives always remain larger and more comprehensive than we can ever realize. This is true because our response to any literary or historical or mythic schema always involves projections of hidden aspects of our own self. But it is true even more because such myths are preexisting public, cultural entities, linking us to others and to the world in ways we can never fully comprehend. Such myths constitute an important part of the fabric of our culture, providing for us the basis of an interrelatedness, an intersubjectivity, that goes far beyond what we can understand. In handling this allusive, mythic material in this way, Joyce shows us the paltriness and superficiality of the empirical/Enlightenment view of the self, and he shows as well that the division between inner and outer, subjective and objective, private and public is not nearly so deep or so clear cut as the modernist mentality is wont to think.

As one further means to articulating Joyce's purposes, I would call attention to a passage from Thomas Mann's lecture on "Freud and the Future," in which, drawing upon psychoanalysis and upon his own aims in *Joseph and His Brothers,* he discusses the relationship between the individual and the mythic in terms singularly appropriate to what Joyce is doing in *Portrait of the Artist* and *Ulysses.* Mann says,

> while in the life of the human race the mythical is an early and primitive stage, in the life of the individual it is a late and mature one. What is gained [as the individual develops] is a . . . knowledge of the schema in which and according to which the supposed individual lives, unaware, in his naive belief in himself as unique . . . of the extent to which his life is but formula and repetition and his path marked out for him by those who trod it before him. [The individual's] character is a mythical role which the actor just emerged from the depths to the light plays in the illusion that it is his own and unique, that he, as it were, has invented it all himself. . . . Actually, if [a person's] existence consisted merely in the unique and the present, he would not know how to conduct himself at all: he would be confused, helpless, unstable in his own self-regard, [he] would not know which foot to put foremost or what sort of face to put on. His dignity and security lie all unconsciously in the fact that with him something timeless has once more emerged into the light and become present; it is a mythical value added to the otherwise poor and valueless single character; it is native worth, because its origin lies in the unconscious.[18]

Contrary to the common assumption that James Joyce is a champion of "individualism," his works show that while some of his characters espouse a superficial, Enlightenment-based view of the self, Joyce himself does not share their view. On the contrary, he sees the self as far deeper and more complex than can be done justice to by any such view. One source of the richness of the self is the many historical, literary "schemata" that our culture consists of, by virtue of which we come to some degree of self understanding and are subtly interrelated to our fellow human beings. In his

Notes
Bibliography
Index

Notes

1. Introduction

1. Readings of *Portrait* that propose an ironic distance between Joyce and Stephen Dedalus are traced back to Hugh Kenner's "The *Portrait* in Perspective," in *James Joyce: Two Decades of Criticism,* edited by Seon Givens, Augmented Edition (New York: The Vanguard Press, 1963), pp. 132–74. The essay appeared in revised form in Kenner's *Dublin's Joyce* (London: Chatto and Windus, 1955). In recent decades such a view has become common, but there have been significant exceptions—e.g., Wayne Booth, in *The Rhetoric of Fiction* (Revised edition, Chicago: Univ. of Chicago Press, 1983), and Louis D. Rubin, Jr., in *The Teller and the Tale* (Seattle: Univ. of Washington Press, 1967). Two book-length studies of *A Portrait* similar in perspective to my own are Marguerite Harkness's *The Aesthetics of Dedalus and Bloom* (Lewisburg, Pa.: Bucknell Univ. Press, 1984) and Joseph A. Buttigieg's *"A Portrait of the Artist" in Different Perspective* (Athens, Ohio: Ohio Univ. Press, 1987). Harkness's book is the fullest account we have of the links between Stephen Dedalus's attitudes and ideas and those of the fin de siècle aesthetes, especially Wilde and Pater; it focuses on how Joyce reveals the insufficiency of Stephen's aesthetic ideas. Buttigieg too discusses Stephen's thinking about art—especially how Joyce shows the inadequacy of the formalist aesthetic ideas that Stephen is enamoured of. Buttigieg's approach to *Portrait* through "modernism" suggests an affinity between our approaches that is more apparent than real, since his view of modernism is radically different from my own. An earlier, insufficiently appreciated book is Homer Obed Brown's *James Joyce's Early Fiction: The Biography of a Form* (Cleveland: Press of Case Reserve Univ., 1972), which proposes that *Portrait* reflects Stephen's mind even in its subject-object division and in its structure. Vicki Mahaffey's lengthy discussion of *Portrait* in her *Reauthorizing Joyce* (Cambridge: Cambridge Univ. Press, 1988) also has something in common with my approach, in its emphasis on the persistent "doubleness" of Stephen's experience and on the role of "unconscious awareness" in his response to the world. James F. Carens's lengthy essay dealing comprehensively with virtually every aspect of the novel (and with a great deal of the secondary literature) is also worthy of note: *"A*

161

Portrait of the Artist as a Young Man," in *A Companion to Joyce Studies,* edited by Zack Bowen and James F. Carens (Westport, Conn.: Greenwood Press, 1984), pp. 255–359. For an overview of critical opinion on *Portrait* (and on Joyce and his works generally), see the review essays by Thomas F. Staley, "James Joyce," in *Anglo-Irish Literature: A Review of Research,* edited by Richard J. Finneran (New York: The Modern Language Association, 1976), pp. 366–435; and "James Joyce," in *Recent Research on Anglo-Irish Writers: A Supplement to Anglo-Irish Literature: A Review of Research,* edited by Richard J. Finneran (New York: The Modern Language Association, 1983), pp. 181–202. Thomas Jackson Rice's *James Joyce: A Guide to Research* (New York: Garland, 1982) is a helpful annotated secondary bibliography.

2. Literary Modernism

1. Whatever the reasons, it is obvious that while modernism continues to be discussed in scores of essays and books each year, we do not have any coherent understanding of the term. Quite the contrary, the term is used with an amazing variety and even contradictoriness, as can be seen in the remarkable array of characterizations within recent years: modernism is seen as a response to "belatedness" (Perry Meisel, *The Myth of the Modern: A Study in British Literature after 1850* [New Haven: Yale Univ. Press, 1987]); as an essentially Humanist and traditionalist attitude (Morton P. Levitt, *Modernist Survivors: The Contemporary Novel in England, the United States, France, and Latin America* [Columbus: Ohio State Univ. Press, 1987]); as an attempt to sublimate the fear of true novelty in aesthetic forms involving a "disjunctive" or "absolute" irony (Alan Wilde, *Horizons of Assent: Modernism, Postmodernism, and the Ironic Imagination* [Baltimore: Johns Hopkins Univ. Press, 1981]); as Counter-Romanticism (Ricardo J. Quinones, *Mapping Literary Modernism: Time and Development* [Princeton: Princeton Univ. Press, 1985]; as a longing for *Nostos* or return to the classical (Jeffrey M. Perl, *The Tradition of Return: The Implicit History of Modern Literature* [Princeton: Princeton Univ. Press, 1984]); as a movement that evolved through diametrically opposed attitudes on such fundamental issues as the value of tradition and of history, individualism, and the relationship between the artist and society (Michael Levenson, *A Genealogy of Modernism: A Study of English Literary Doctrine 1908–1922* [Cambridge: Cambridge Univ. Press, 1984]). Christopher Butler sees "willed dissipation or disruption, the stripping down and primitivization of the 'poetic' . . . [as] symptomatic of the emergence of Modernism as a distinct epoch in cultural history" ("The Concept of Modernism," in Susan Dick, Declan Kiberd, Dougald McMillan, and Joseph Ronsley, eds., *Essays for Richard Ellmann: Omnium Gatherum* [Montreal: McGill-Queens Univ. Press, 1989], p. 52). Lorraine Weir, in a view diametrically opposite to the one I shall be developing, "configure[s] modernity as suture across the gap of the Enlightenment" (*Writing Joyce: A Semiotics of the Joyce System* [Bloomington: Indiana Univ. Press, 1989], p. 3). As this variety shows, we humanists have no methodology for adjudicating whatever views may be proposed. We can only hope that time and discussion will effect some winnowing of the issues and the claims. For an overview of various theories of modernism, see Stanley Sultan's *Eliot, Joyce and Company* (New York: Oxford Univ. Press, 1987), chapter 5.

2. Alan Wilde refers to "the crisis of modernism, namely, the omnipresent separation of self and world" (*Horizons of Assent*, p. 151).

3. The impossibility of exorcising the merely temporal implication is reflected in statements by a number of contemporary critics. William A. Johnsen says "students of modern literature of whatever period have always justly admired the emerging artist's compulsion to be modern, to make it new. Western civilization's obsessive use of the adjectives 'modern' and 'new' to describe its current cultural artifacts has never been more prevalent than in what we call, appropriately, the Modern Century" ("Toward a Redefinition of Modernism," *boundary 2*, 2 [Spring 1974], 539). Alan Warren Friedman begins his introduction to *Forms of Modern British Fiction* (Austin: Univ. of Texas Press, 1975) by saying, "of course, every age considers itself modern" (p. 3). Alastair Fowler, in his *Kinds of Literature: An Introduction to the Theory of Genres and Modes* (Cambridge: Harvard Univ. Press, 1982) says "but it would be wrong to suppose that generic transformation is particularly modern. Or rather, that modernism itself is new" (p. 32). Morton Levitt asks, "what will they call it [Modernism] a century from now? Surely critics (possibly artists as well) will resent an appellation from the past which seems to deny the modernity of their own time" (*Modernist Survivors*, p. 4). Richard Poirier says "it is the privilege of any people at any time in history to claim that they are living in the 'modern age,' in the sense of the Latin *modo,* just now or lately, and works that by any prevailing standards prove to be unconventional or especially difficult have been called 'modernist' since at least the seventeenth century" (*The Renewal of Literature: Emersonian Reflections* [New York: Random House, 1987], p. 95). Paul de Man explores the tensions and contradictions inherent in the term in chapter VIII of *Blindness and Insight: Essays in the Rhetoric of Contemporary Criticism* (Second edition, revised. Minneapolis: Univ. of Minnesota Press, 1983), entitled "Literary History and Literary Modernity." There he says "it is perhaps somewhat disconcerting to learn that our usage of the word goes back to the late fifth century of our era and that there is nothing modern about the concept of modernity" (p. 144). Of course by modernity here de Man refers to the generic meaning of contrast with the preceding age, not to anything that we in the twentieth century would specifically designate as *our* modernity. Later in the chapter de Man draws upon the element of novelty, of the anti-historical, that literature so often involves to say "literature has always been essentially modern" (p. 151).

4. In other contexts the scope of the modern can be even broader. Paul de Man in the preceding footnote says it goes back to the fifth century. And in the twelfth and thirteenth century, some philosophers were calling for a *via moderna* to replace the *via antiqua* that had come to dominate Scholastic thinking. These advocates of the new mode were called—not entirely complimentarily—*moderni*. For a discussion that traces the roots of the idea of the modern all the way back to Alexandria, see Ernst Robert Curtius, *European Literature and the Latin Middle Ages,* (New York: Pantheon Books, 1953), esp. pp. 251–55. Frank Kermode testifies to the perennial meaning of the term when he says that "before . . . phenomena are called 'modern' there must, presumably, be a general sense of escaping from an older state of affairs, an *ancient* state of affairs. *Devotio moderna* was not only a movement for a new morality and a new piety, but a movement against pilgrimages and excessive ornament. The Moderns of the 17th century had a programme with a similar double aspect. . . . In short, the great 17th-century Modernism involved getting out from

under something, and modernist programmes have the habit of claiming that this is what they always have to undertake" (*Continuities* [New York: Random House, 1968], p. 9).

5. Morton Levitt, for example, laments outcroppings of the unfortunate "sense that Modernism is a movement to be measured in time alone" (*Modernist Survivors*, p. 247). Jeffrey R. Smitten and Ann Daghistany, the editors of *Spatial Form in Narrative* (Ithaca: Cornell Univ. Press, 1981), testify to the temptations and the complexities of the terminology when they say in their Preface " 'Modernist' refers to works written between the end of the nineteenth century and World War II—works that are experimental and often involve spatial form. 'Contemporary' designates a similar class of works written since World War II. Two additional terms are not so tied to chronology but nonetheless refer to experimental—and thus spatial-form—narratives: 'avant-garde' and 'modern' may be applied to works from various literary periods, though they always denote the common trait of narrative experiment" (p. 14). Similarly, in *The English Modernist Reader, 1910–1930* (Iowa City: Univ. of Iowa Press, 1986), editor Peter Faulkner confines himself to two decades, saying "looking back from the late twentieth century, we can see the arts of the period 1910–1930 as having a clear cultural identity [i.e., a *substantial* justification] to which the term 'Modernist' can reasonably be applied, although it was not a term used at the time" (p. 13). Still, the two-decade parameter is procrustean.

6. Maud Ellmann says "in spite of these inconsistencies, however, the notion of impersonality is crucial to modernist aesthetics, and it is more valuable to trace the logic of its contradictions than to flounder 'in the hope of straightening things out' " (*The Poetics of Impersonality* [Brighton, Sussex: The Harvester Press, 1987], p. 3; she footnotes R. P. Blackmur's essay of that title in Hugh Kenner's *T. S. Eliot: A Collection of Critical Essays* [Englewood Cliffs, N.J.: Prentice Hall, 1962], pp. 138–39). Malcolm Bradbury and James McFarlane say that "perhaps the most any account [of modernism] can offer is a personal or at least a partial version of an overwhelmingly complex phenomenon" ("The Name and Nature of Modernism," in *Modernism: 1890–1930* [Harmondsworth: Penguin Books Ltd., 1976], p. 21). Frank Kermode, in his *The Sense of an Ending: Studies in the Theory of Fiction* (New York: Oxford Univ. Press, 1967), distinguishes between two phases of modernism—W. B. Yeats's traditional modernism and Beckett's schismatic version—and Stanley Sultan in *Eliot, Joyce and Company* discusses several critics who have posited phases of modernism. Perry Meisel distinguishes "two divergent lines of High Modernism in English at large, each with considerable and enduring influences of its own," one stemming from Arnold to Eliot, the other from Pater to Joyce (*The Myth of the Modern*, p. 120).

7. Similarly, Randy Malamud, in his *The Language of Modernism* (Ann Arbor, Mich.: UMI Research Press, 1989), explicitly raises the question of whether there is "a language of modernism" (p. 4), and then pitches upon "difficulty" as its hallmark (p. 8, et passim). His criterion enables him to include Eliot and Joyce (and more surprisingly, Woolf), but causes him to exclude Hemingway and Lawrence.

8. Bruce Johnson, though he does not mention Schwartz, suggests the insufficiency of so proximate a point of departure when he says "so many names—Edwardian artists, philosophers, and psychologists such as Bergson, Bradley, William James, Nietzsche, Meinong, Brentano—are associated with this belated reaction against the Cartesian 'two worlds' that it is really quite astonishing to find so little mention of it as a background for the great narrative experiments of Modernism" ("A Modernist Noesis," in Susan Dick et al., *Essays for*

Richard Ellmann: Omnium Gatherum [Montreal: McGill-Queens Univ. Press, 1989], p. 61). I agree that we must go back at least to Hume and Locke and Descartes—and probably to Francis Bacon and to Galileo—to understand what is involved in the "crisis of modernism."

9. No texts are subjected more to indiscriminate, non-contextual quotation than *Ulysses* and *Finnegans Wake*. Even critics who recognize these as highly subtle and complex literary texts seem to presume that virtually anything in the text can be quoted as representing a sanctioned authorial perspective—i.e., Joyce's perspective—without regard to context or narrative voice or tone. Surely no critical caveat has been more ignored than Bernard Benstock's in his Foreword to Michael H. Begnal and Grace Eckley's *Narrator and Character in "Finnegans Wake"* (Lewisburg, Pa.: Bucknell Univ. Press, 1975): "every opinion and pronouncement uttered in *Finnegans Wake* must be analyzed in regard to its source. Pompous Polonius, not Prince Hamlet, cautions against borrowing and lending; evil Iago, not Othello, is the origin of the lecture on reputation. With Shakespeare and Joyce busy paring their fingernails, it is crucial for the reader to discern the actual speaker" (p. 12).

10. I discuss more fully what Robert Bellah has called "ontological individualism" (*Habits of the Heart: Individualism and Committment in American Life* [Berkeley: Univ. of California Press, 1985], p. 334) and Christopher Lasch "atomistic individualism" (*The Minimal Self: Psychic Survival in Troubled Times* [New York: W. W Norton and Company, 1984], p. 54) in the chapter entitled "The Self" in "The Roots of Modernism."

11. For example, John Blades refers (quite typically) to stream of consciousness as "one of the most characteristic narrative devices of Modernism as a whole and of Joyce's mature work in particular" (*James Joyce: "A Portrait of the Artist as a Young Man"* [London: Penguin Books, Ltd., 1991], p. 173). But as we shall see in chapter 6 below, Joyce uses this technique to subvert the inner-outer, subject-object distinction that is so characteristic of modernist thinking.

12. Levitt, *Modernist Survivors,* especially chapter 1. Levitt's point of view shows the difficulty of separating the two retrospective characterizations of modernism that I am discussing, for he sees the whole notion of postmodernism as something largely foisted upon us by theoreticians and not necessary to the discussion of contemporary literature (see especially pp. 14–18). Similarly, Gerald Graff, in his *Literature Against Itself: Literary Ideas in Modern Society* (Chicago: Univ. of Chicago Press, 1979) has a chapter entitled "The Myth of the Postmodern Breakthrough," in which he says "this chapter argues that postmodernism should not be seen as a break with romantic and modernist assumptions but rather as a logical culmination of the premises of these earlier movements" (p. 32). Analogously, Hazard Adams says that the distinction between modernism and postmodernism in criticism is "a distinction that history is unlikely to sustain" ("Yeats, Joyce, and Criticism Today," in *The Uses of the Past: Essays on Irish Culture,* edited by Audrey S. Eyler and Robert F. Garratt [London: Associated University Presses, 1988], p. 75).

13. Ihab Hassan, "Toward a Concept of Postmodernism," in *The Postmodern Turn: Essays in Postmodern Theory and Culture* (Columbus: Ohio State Univ. Press, 1987), p. 95. Harold Bloom puts a characteristically acerbic slant on this issue when he says "French poststructuralism is of course only a belated modernism, since everything from abroad is absorbed so slowly in xenophobic Paris" (*James Joyce's "Ulysses"* [New York: Chelsea House, 1987], p. 4).

14. "The Literature of Replenishment: Postmodernist Fiction," in *The Friday Book: Essays and Other Nonfiction* (New York: G. P. Putnam's Sons, 1984), p. 196. Later in this essay

Barth laments the frequent misreading of his earlier essay "The Literature of Exhaustion," saying "but a great many people—among them, I fear, Señor Borges himself—mistook me to mean that literature, at least fiction, is *kaput;* that it has all been done already; that there is nothing left for contemporary writers but to parody and travesty our great predecessors in our exhausted medium—exactly what some critics deplore as postmodernism" (p. 205). But Barth's lament seems disingenuous, for that is precisely what his earlier essay does say.

15. "Toward a Redefinition of Modernism," p. 542. Johnsen also illustrates this aspect of what he calls the "postmodern conception of Modernism" (pp. 543–44) by quoting from Renato Poggioli's *The Theory of the Avant-Garde* (Cambridge: Belknap Press of Harvard Univ. Press, 1968): "the conventions of avant-garde art, in a conscious or unconscious way, are directly and rigidly determined by an inverse relation to traditional conventions. . . . the conventions of avant-garde art are often as easily deduced as those of the academy: their deviation from the norm is so regular and normal a fact that it is transformed into a canon no less exceptional than predictable (p. 555; Johnsen cites Poggioli, p. 56). Stanley Sultan agrees that "these contemporary writers 'define themselves' by their rejection of the Modern" (*Eliot, Joyce and Company,* p. 114). Helmut Lethen in his "Modernism Cut in Half: the Exclusion of the Avant-garde and the Debate on Postmodernism" even suggests that the concept of "Modernism" "was constructed so as to form a dark background for the brilliant claims of Postmodernism. When Hassan remarks that the term 'Postmodernism' evokes what it wishes to surpass or suppress, this also means that the postmodern situation created the possibility to see Modernism as a closed and rather rigid entity. If one wants to deconstruct, one has to homogenize one's object first so that it becomes deconstructible" (in *Approaching Postmodernism: Papers Presented at a Workshop on Postmodernism, 21–23 September 1984, University of Utrecht,* edited by Douwe Fokkema and Hans Bertens [Amsterdam: John Benjamins Publishing Company, 1986] p. 233). Lethen argues that this was done mainly by ignoring and excluding the Avant-garde aspects of modernism. Brian McHale concurs with Lethen that "this strategy really is the operation by which the modernism versus postmodernism opposition has been constructed," and says "postmodernism is precisely what is 'left over' after we have crystallized out a coherent, tidily compact, homogenous modernism" ("Constructing (Post)Modernism: The Case of *Ulysses,*" *Style* 24 [Spring 1990], 13–14). He goes on to show how this has worked in the case of *Ulysses,* permitting us to see it as paradigmatic of both modernism and postmodernism. Robert Martin Adams says of the formula "postmodernist" that it "implies an awful degree of terminological desperation. Doesn't the heedless fellow who dreamed up this formula anticipate the day when we'll have worked our way into forms like post-post-post-modernist and its inevitable, infinite sequels?" ("What Was Modernism?" *Hudson Review* 31 [Spring 1978], 32). A. Walton Litz also says of the "sad term 'postmodern' " that it "testifies to the enduring energy of the modern writers and implies (like post-mortem or post-coital) that the fun is over" ("Modernist Making and Self-Making," *Times Literary Supplement,* October 10, 1986, p. 1142).

16. Malmgren, " 'From Work to Text': The Modernist and Postmodernist *Künstlerroman,*" *Novel: A Forum on Fiction* 21 (Fall 1987), 10, 11. Malmgren is drawing on Roland Barthes's *S/Z,* trans. by Richard Miller (New York: Hill and Wang, 1974).

17. Pearce, "What Joyce after Pynchon?" in Morris Beja et al., *James Joyce: The Centennial Symposium* (1986), p. 43.

18. This Western proclivity for declaring the ideas and attitudes of earlier thinkers to be outmoded—usually because of their naively accepting certain traditional values—I explore in "The Roots of Modernism" as "Foundationalism." The term suggests the tendency of each wave of avant-garde thinkers to believe that they have now got down to certain foundations—i.e., to certain hard-headed, value-free fundamental realizations—that their predecessors did not understand. But whereas it was once the thinkers of the preceding century or generation that were assailed, now it is those of the preceding decade or lustrum. (Paradoxically, the deconstructionist program's insistence that there are no foundations serves as the basis of their radical foundationalism.)

19. Kearney's discussion of *Finnegans Wake* exemplifies the non-contextual quotation referred to above in footnote 9. Not only does he persistently quote without reference to context or speaking voice, he does not locate his quotations by page number or even by chapter. And his citations involve some egregious inaccuracies: he refers to Bloom's son as Rudi, and he misquotes Stephen Dedalus in *Portrait* as coveting art's "silver womb of the imagination" (for "virgin womb").

20. Though it did not appear until this book was well underway, I owe a great deal to Charles Taylor's *The Sources of the Self: The Making of the Modern Identity* for its clarification of the issues and its confirmation that my views were essentially on the right track. Taylor's book is of great importance to anyone who wishes to understand certain confusions and contradictions in the modern climate of opinion, especially in regard to our conception of the self and to the nature and functions of language.

21. In "The Roots of Modernism" I develop a full-scale characterization of philosophical modernism; here I can provide only a bird's eye view of what I call the Modernist Syndrome.

22. From Galileo's "The Assayer" in *The Controversy of the Comets of 1618* (Philadelphia: Univ. of Pennsylvania Press, 1960), p. 309. The primary/secondary quality distinction had been adumbrated by Democritus, but his climate of opinion was not so hospitable toward the idea as was Galileo's.

23. In "The Roots of Modernism" I spend several pages exploring the absurd and self-contradictory conclusions about what an "empty" room looks like that we are led to by the Modernist Syndrome's primary quality/secondary quality, matter/mind distinction. Virginia Woolf's concern with this theme is reflected in the nature of Mr. Ramsey's "work" in *To the Lighthouse:* "whenever she [Lily Briscoe] 'thought of his [Mr. Ramsey's] work' she always saw clearly before her a large kitchen table. It was Andrew's doing. She asked him what his father's books were about. 'Subject and object and the nature of reality,' Andrew had said. And when she said Heavens, she had no notion what that meant. 'Think of a kitchen table then,' he told her, 'when you're not there' " (New York: Harcourt, Brace and Company, 1927, p. 38).

24. Bertrand Russell is quite clear-minded about this: "I accept without qualification the view that results from astronomy and geology, from which it would appear that there is no evidence of anything mental except in a tiny fragment of space-time, and the great processes of nebular and stellar evolution proceed according to laws in which mind plays no part" (*My Philosophical Development* [London: George Allen and Unwin, 1959], p. 16).

25. Such a line of thought lies behind Joseph Conrad's occasional animadversions against consciousness. For example, in a letter to Cunninghame Graham on January 31, 1898,

Conrad says "egoism is good, and altruism is good, and fidelity to nature would be the best of all, and systems could be built, and rules could be made—if we could only get rid of consciousness. What makes mankind tragic is not that they are the victims of nature, it is that they are conscious of it. To be part of the animal kingdom under the conditions of this earth is very well—but as soon as you know of your slavery the pain, the anger, the strife—the tragedy begins." And similarly to Marguerite Poradowska July (?) 20, 1894: "Man must drag the ball and chain of his individuality up to the end. It is what one pays for the infernal and divine privilege of thought." These letters are quoted in Frederick R. Karl, *Joseph Conrad: The Three Lives* (New York: Farrar, Straus and Giroux, 1979), pp. 421 and 332.

26. Christopher Butler, in "The Concept of Modernism," is getting at the same idea when he approaches modernism in terms of a "turn of the century skepticism," a growth of subjectivism, and a "skeptical withdrawal from social consensus and the morality it implied" (pp. 54, 55). He suggests also that "there are indeed overarching subjectivist and skeptical epistemological explanations of the early impulse to Modernism" (p. 56), thus indicating a link between modernism and the Pyrrhonism of Descartes and Hume.

27. Hume makes pointed acknowledgment of the limitations of the analytic, Pyrrhonic stance in his *Treatise of Human Nature* (Oxford: Clarendon Press, 1888) and his *Enquiry Concerning Human Understanding* (La Salle, Ill.: Open Court Publishing Company, 1958). In the *Treatise* he says "Shou'd it here be ask'd me, whether I sincerely assent to this argument, which I seem to take such pains to inculcate, and whether I be really one of those sceptics, who hold that all is uncertain, and that our judgment is not in *any* thing possest of *any* measures of truth and falsehood; I shou'd reply, that this question is entirely superfluous, and that neither I, nor any other person was ever sincerely and constantly of that opinion" (Book I, Part IV, section I, p. 183; see also Section XII, especially Part II, of the *Enquiry*). Charles Newman, in his *Post-Modern Aura* (Evanston, Ill.: Northwestern Univ. Press, 1985), quotes a statement of Lionel Trilling's that testifies to the gap that frequently exists between theory and experience: "I think this is the great sin of the intellectual: that he never really tests his ideas by what it would mean to him if he were to undergo the experience that he is recommending" (p. 27). My approach would shift the emphasis: the great sin of the intellectual is acquiescing in his own victimization by a schema of thought that he has engendered, but that denies his very consciousness.

28. In Hassan's *The Postmodern Turn*, p. 124. Hassan goes on to quote from Wilde's "The Critic as Artist." As Isobel Murray points out, the original title of Wilde's essay, "The True Function and Value of Criticism," "suggests that Wilde is setting out to answer Matthew Arnold's essay 'The Function of Criticism at the Present Time,' " and Murray goes on to refer specifically to Arnold's statement about seeing the "object as in itself it really is" (*Oscar Wilde* [Oxford: Oxford Univ. Press, 1989], p. 589).

29. Arnold uses the term "object" in a broad context: "Of the literature of France and Germany, as of the intellect of Europe in general, the main effort, for now many years, has been a critical effort; the endeavor, in all branches of knowledge, theology, philosophy, history, art, science, to see the object as in itself it really is" ("The Function of Criticism at the Present Time," first paragraph).

30. An intriguing analogy exists between the erosion and loss of the idea of a social or cultural psyche as a sustaining psychic medium, and the jettisoning of the idea of the aether

in physics. Both came to be seen as unnecessary hypotheses, but the passing of both also left a host of presumably "atomic" phenomena unexplained.

31. This is the claim that will be developed in later chapters about the authorial perspective in Joyce's *Portrait*—that it is best understood as simulating a social or collective psyche. In discussing this necessarily nebulous idea of a collective consciousness, I am reminded of Owen Barfield's comment that from the perspective of future centuries, one of the strangest features of modern thought will be that an age that talked so readily of a collective unconscious had no conception whatsoever of a collective consciousness. Modernist skepticism in regard to the cultural psyche is a serious, persistent stumbling block to our appreciating important aspects of Joyce's art, from *Dubliners* through *Finnegans Wake*.

32. We shall explore these issues in regard to Joyce's *Portrait* more fully in chapter 6. Suffice it for now to say that modernist critics' discomfort in the face of value judgments that cannot be attributed to a character accounts for their claims that much modernist literature is self-referential (which relieves the critics of having to come to terms with various supra-individual cultural entities), and that novels are "self-narrating" (which relieves them of dealing with the ontological implications of any words not spoken by characters).

33. I have several times quoted Levenson's phrase "evocative physical description," because it oxymoronically epitomizes the problem with his argument. That is, his implicit claim is that such unattributed, impersonal accounts are merely descriptive and objective, and thus they evade the presumptuousness of Victorian omniscience. But insofar as these accounts are "evocative" they *do* invoke values and interpretation, and we must therefore ask what perspective this interpretation represents. Otherwise, Levenson's basic point is lost. Also, Levenson's case is weakened by certain passages in *Nigger* that he does not quote or acknowledge. Quoting from the Preface he leaves out those passages that invoke less concrete or individual sensations, such as Conrad's several references to the truth that underlies every aspect of the visible universe, or to "the moral and emotional atmosphere of the *place and time*" or to "temperament, whether individual or *collective*" (my italics) all of which challenge Levenson's claim that for Conrad there is so great a gap between individual subjectivity and "externals." Similarly, his claims about the striking contrast of perspectives that we feel in the paragraph from Chapter Three of the novel are weakened by the fact that the "we" or "you," perspective has been evoked several times in immediately preceding paragraphs and sentences.

34. From a lecture "On Descartes' 'Discourse Touching the Method of Using One's Reason Rightly and of Seeking Scientific Truth' " that Huxley delivered in 1870; see his *Method and Results: Essays* (New York: D. Appleton and Co., 1896) I, 194. The tenuous nature of Huxley's faith in the uniquely human phenomenon of consciousness, however, is shown by his saying "whatever the universe may be, all we can know of it is the picture presented to us by consciousness. This picture may be a true likeness—*though how this can be is inconceivable* (Ibid., p. 178; my emphasis). The lecture testifies to the precarious ontological state of consciousness at this time, for while Huxley speaks in his opening paragraph of "the conception of the intellectual filiation of mankind" (suggesting a social psyche), he also fully accepts the Cartesian division of *res cogitans* from *res extensa* and he concurs in Descartes' idea that "the body is a machine" (Ibid., p. 188). Further, he acknowledges the impossibility of explaining how volition can effect changes in the human body—

i.e., how our *willing* it can effect the raising of our arm (pp. 187–88)—or of positing a physiological site for consciousness (pp. 188–190). Over the next few decades it would become increasingly "inconceivable" how consciousness interfaces with "the object as in itself it really is," when that object is seen as "material."

35. It is clarifying (if sobering) to see how radically our experience as introspective, reflective human beings is called into question by some modernist philosophers, and to be instructed on what "the object as in itself it really is" looks like from a naturalistic perspective. The following passage from Paul Churchland's *Matter and Consciousness: A Contemporary Introduction to the Philosophy of Mind* (Cambridge, Mass.: MIT Press, 1984) directly challenges our qualitative, introspective view of the world. Note how fully Churchland's approach depends upon the primary quality/secondary quality distinction.

> But the argument [from introspection] is deeply suspect, in that it assumes that our faculty of inner observation or introspection reveals things as they really are in their innermost nature. This assumption is suspect because we already know that our other forms of observation—sight, hearing, touch, and so on—do no such thing. The red surface of an apple does not *look* like a matrix of molecules reflecting photons at certain critical wavelengths, but that is what it is. The sound of a flute does not *sound* like a sinusoidal compression wave train in the atmosphere, but that is what it is. The warmth of the summer air does not *feel* like the mean kinetic energy of millions of tiny molecules, but that is what it is. If one's pains and hopes and beliefs do not *introspectively* seem like electrochemical states in a neural network, that may be only because our faculty of introspection, like our other senses, is not sufficiently penetrating to reveal such hidden details. Which is just what one would expect anyway. The argument from introspection is therefore entirely without force, unless we can somehow argue that the faculty of introspection is quite different from all other forms of observation. (p. 15)

36. See D. C. Stove's *Popper and After: Four Modern Irrationalists* (Oxford: Pergamon Press, 1982) on Hume's pervasive influence among contemporary philosophers.

37. Minsky makes these claims in several places: in an April 1983 panel discussion on "Has Artificial Intelligence Research Illuminated Human Thinking?," printed in Heinz R. Pagels, ed., *Computer Culture: The Scientific, Intellectual, and Social Impact of the Computer* (*Annals of the New York Academy of Sciences* 426 [November 1, 1984]); in his "Why People Think Computers Can't," in *The Computer Culture: A Symposium to Explore the Computer's Impact on Society,* edited by Denis P. Donnelly (Rutherford, N.J.: Fairleigh Dickinson Univ. Press, 1985), pp. 27–43; and in an interview with Paul Hoffman, as quoted in Hoffman's "Your Mindless Brain," *Discover* 8 (September 1987): 84–85, 87. I discuss such claims in chapter 6 of "The Roots of Modernism."

3. Joyce's Assumptions and Aims

1. Hugh Kenner claims that Joyce's "idea of what goes on in life and what should go on in fiction was so simple that he understood it at twenty-two" ("Signs on a White Field," in

Morris Beja, Philip Herring, Maurice Harmon, and David Norris, eds. *James Joyce: The Centennial Symposium* [Urbana: Univ. of Illinois Press, 1986], p. 209). W. Y. Tindall says "like Mozart, Joyce knew what he was about from the beginning" (*James Joyce's "Chamber Music,"* edited by William York Tindall [New York: Columbia Univ. Press, 1954], p. 62). Robert Scholes says "to an incredible degree, Joyce as a young man knew where he was going" (*Workshop*, p. 58), and Mary Reynolds agrees: "He knew at a very early age exactly where he was going as a writer" ("Davin's Boots: Joyce, Yeats, and Irish History," in *Joycean Occasions: Essays from the Milwaukee James Joyce Conference,* ed. Janet E. Dunleavy, Melvin J. Friedman, and Michael Patrick Gillespie [Newark, Del.: Univ. of Delaware Press, 1991], p. 223). Marvin Magalaner demurs, saying that "the picture of young Joyce, mature in his artistic infancy like Hardy's Little Father Time, will not stand investigation"—but Magalaner himself concedes "there is no question, however, that even at eighteen Joyce knew what he *wanted* to do in literature" (*Time of Apprenticeship: The Fiction of the Young James Joyce* [London: Abelard-Schuman, 1959], p. 16).

2. For example, in one letter to Stanislaus he wonders whether there is any use in continuing his novel *(Stephen Hero)* and says "certainly Georgie is the most successful thing connected with me" (postmarked January 10, 1907; *Letters* II, 206); and in another he says "for my part I have one life. I have felt lately that it is slipping from me 'like water from a muslin bag' " and "I fear that my spiritual barque is on the rocks" (February 16, 1907; *Letters,* II, 215).

3. Hans Walter Gabler, in "The Seven Lost Years of *A Portrait of the Artist as a Young Man,*" in *Approaches to Joyce's "Portrait": Ten Essays,* ed. Thomas F. Staley and Bernard Benstock (Pittsburgh: Univ. of Pittsburgh Press, 1976) says that "in essence, the novel attained the shape and structure in which we now possess it during 1912 and 1913" (p. 53), but some revision went on into 1914. See also Gabler's "Preface" to volume 9 of Michael Groden's *The James Joyce Archive* (New York: Garland Publishing, Inc., 1977), pp. vii–xi.

4. The Blake lecture—what we have of it—is printed in *CW,* pp. 214–22. The Defoe lecture was published in *Buffalo Studies* in 1964.

5. Charles Rossman concurs in this view of Joyce. He lists four ideas that he calls "convictions [Joyce] formed as a young man and that, I believe, suffused his artistic theories and creations throughout his life" ("Stephen Dedalus and the Spiritual-Heroic Refrigerating Apparatus: Art and Life in Joyce's *Portrait,*" in *Forms of Modern British Fiction,* ed. Alan Warren Friedman [Austin: Univ. of Texas Press, 1975], p. 104. The first of these is that "the basic fact of human existence is that being is *in* and *of* this world" (p. 104). Drawing upon "Drama and Life," the first "James Clarence Mangan" essay, the Aesthetic Notebooks, and *Stephen Hero,* Rossman argues convincingly that "neither Joyce nor Stephen accepts, in art or life, a metaphysical dualism that postulates two worlds, one physical and one ideal" (p. 111). Similarly, Marshall McLuhan, though he sees Joyce as involved always with polarities, does not regard him as a dualist; see his "James Joyce: Trivial and Quadrivial," in *The Interior Landscape: The Literary Criticism of Marshall McLuhan, 1943–1962,* ed. Eugene McNamara (New York: McGraw-Hill, 1969) esp. p. 30.

6. Owen Barfield points out that for Francis Bacon, that exemplar of the modern mind, "this polarity [of *actus* and *potentia*], taken for granted for more than a thousand years by some of the acutest intellects the world has ever known—this polarity has become, for Bacon, a 'frigida distinctio'—mere words!" (*Saving the Appearances: A Study in Idolatry,*

Second edition [Middletown, Conn.: Wesleyan Univ. Press, 1988], pp. 93–94). Barfield points out that "when . . . we are dealing with living organisms, our whole approach, our whole possibility of grasping *process* as such, is hamstrung by the lack of . . . a concept of the potentially phenomenal and the actually phenomenal" (p. 136).

7. "The Cubist *Portrait,*" in Staley and Benstock, *Approaches to Joyce's Portrait* (1976), p. 179).

8. Others who have argued for the importance of potentiality to Joyce's works include K. E. Robinson, who contrasts Joyce and Flaubert, saying "Joyce tends to regard experience in terms of its potentiality, Flaubert to concentrate on its inevitable inadequacy" ("The Stream of Consciousness Technique and the Structure of Joyce's *Portrait,*" *JJQ* 9 [Fall 1971], p. 76); and Charles Rossman, who lists as another of Joyce's convictions that "human identity is a temporal flux, usefully understood in terms of Aristotle's conceptions of potentiality and entelechy. Human growth is the actualization of potential through acts of will implementing conscious choice (Aristotle's *praxis*)" (Rossman, "Stephen Dedalus and the Spiritual-Heroic Refrigerating Apparatus," p. 104). Arthur Power quotes Joyce as saying, "the modern writer is far more interested in the potential than the actual" (*Conversations with James Joyce,* edited by Clive Hart [London: Millington, Ltd., 1974], p. 75).

9. I was pleased to find confirmation of these points in an essay by Charles Rossman that I came across after having myself arrived at this conclusion. In his "The Reader's Role in *A Portrait of the Artist as a Young Man,*" in *James Joyce: An International Perspective,* ed. Suheil Badi Bushrui and Bernard Benstock (Gerrards Cross: Colin Smythe, 1982), pp. 19–37), Rossman says that both the epiphany and the aesthetic theory in *Portrait* involve "basically a theory of perception" (p. 24), and he goes on to say that "Joyce and Stephen agree, at least, on their theories of perception" (p. 25).

10. I choose this text rather than *Stephen Hero* or the Notebooks because it is Joyce's "culminating" text and because it is the most fully elaborated; in terms of the philosophical issues that I am interested in, I find no important differences among the three texts. There is strong evidence in both the Pola Notebook and in *Stephen Hero* that the underlying issue is perception. The Pola Notebook deals explicitly with perception. There Joyce says "if the activity of simple perception is, like every other activity, itself pleasant, every sensible object that has been apprehended can be said in the first place to have been and to be in a measure beautiful. . . . Consequently even the most hideous object may be said to be beautiful for this reason as it is *a priori* said to be beautiful in so far as it encounters the activity of simple perception" (*CW,* p. 147). Similarly, in *Stephen Hero* Stephen says " 'imagine my glimpses at that clock as the gropings of a spiritual eye which seeks to adjust its vision to an exact focus. The moment the focus is reached [i.e., the moment the object is clearly perceived] the object is epiphanized. It is just in this epiphany that I find the third, the supreme quality of beauty' " [i.e., *quidditas*] (*SH,* p. 211). The Ballast Office clock, is not, of course, an object we think of as "beautiful." This passage in *Stephen Hero* suggested to me the device of the slide projector coming into focus.

11. David E. Jones agrees, saying "if, in defining epiphany as a sudden spiritual manifestation, Joyce intended to connote Christian or Platonic overtones, we may well wonder what Platonic elements are inherent in the vulgarity of speech and what Christian ones in a clock. It seems far more credible that 'spiritual' specifies the Aristotelian and Aquinian concept of

the immateriality of the object as it is known in the mind—especially in relation to *quidditas*" ("The Essence of Beauty in James Joyce's Aesthetics" *JJQ* 10 [Spring 1973], 303).

12. Michael Polanyi detects unformalizable elements in the most ordinary mental acts, including our every act of perception: "[Kant] says that the way our intelligence forms and applies the schema of a class to particulars 'is a skill so deeply hidden in the human soul that we shall hardly guess the secret trick that Nature here employs.' (*Critique of Pure Reason*, A.141.) We are told, in effect, that every time we speak of dogs, trees or tables in general, or else identify something as a dog, a tree or a table, we are performing a secret trick which is unlikely ever to be revealed to our understanding" ("The Unaccountable Element in Science," in *Knowing and Being: Essays by Michael Polanyi*, ed. by Marjorie Grene [Chicago: Univ. of Chicago Press, 1969], pp. 105–06). Cf. Joyce's acknowledging the artist's reliance upon "some process of the mind as yet untabulated" ("Portrait of the Artist," *Workshop*, p. 60). A lucid and thorough discussion of the problems posed for perception theories by this object quality of perceptions—i.e., by the qualitative *whatness* of each perception—is Floyd Allport's *Theories of Perception and the Concept of Structure: A Review and Critical Analysis with an Introduction to a Dynamic-Structural Theory of Behavior* (New York: John Wiley and Sons, Inc., 1955). See especially chapter 19: "The Unsolved Problem of Meaning: Perception of Object Character and Situation . . . ." Of the many perceptual theories that he surveys, Allport says "the theories give some elaborate way of accounting for almost everything about the perception of an apple except the fact that it is perceived as an *apple*" (p. 538).

13. Fritz Senn views these same phenomena from the other end—from that of the responding reader—in his "In Quest of a *nisus formativus Joyceanus*" (*Joyce Studies Annual 1990*, pp. 26–42) when he calls attention to the distinctive essence of various aspects of Joyce's works—his individual works, his characters, even the sections or chapters of his works, each of them possessing "its palpable *quidditas*," or as he calls it in the case of Stephen Dedalus, *"Stephenitas."* In a statement that testifies simultaneously to this distinctive quality of his works and to Joyce's belief in entelechy, Senn says "*A Portrait* is based on some notion, that through all vicissitudes of growing and changing Stephen Dedalus at each separate stage is what he is. In this sense, each of Joyce's works, and distinct parts thereof, have their entelechy, are what they are and nothing else" (pp. 28, 30, 30). Similarly, F. Parvin Sharpless speaks of the reader's recognizing the *"quidditas"* of various episodes in *Portrait*, such as the pandybatting scene: "One at once recognizes the objective *quidditas* of the situation as one appropriate to Stephen at his age and given his particular character" ("Irony in Joyce's *Portrait:* The Stasis of Pity," *JJQ* 4 [Summer 1967], 323).

14. I believe that the reason that Joyce did not continue to use the term *epiphany* after *Stephen Hero* was his coming to understand that the epiphany as he had earlier construed it imputed too much "activity" to the field of experience and too little to the discerning mind. At first, that is, Joyce seems to have felt that "epiphanic" experiences were as public and "objective" as simple perceptions—i.e., that they came virtually "pre-packaged." But he came later to realize that an epiphany requires an active imagination and a discerning mind. John Blades seems to suggest the same point when, discussing the absence of the term epiphany from *Portrait*, he says "whereas in *Stephen Hero* the emphasis is placed on a passive artist whose job is merely to record these moments, in *A Portrait* Stephen's idea of

the artist-priest is more active, more engaged" (*James Joyce: "A Portrait of the Artist,"* p. 116).

15. See my "Between Circle and Straight Line: A Pragmatic View of W. B. Yeats and the Occult," *Studies in the Literary Imagination* 14 (Spring 1981): 61–75. Arthur Power says that Joyce objected to the classical style of writing because "it is a form of writing which contains little or no mystery . . . and since we are surrounded by mystery it has always seemed to me inadequate" (*Conversations,* pp. 73–74). Thomas C. Singer, in his comparison of Joyce and Wittgenstein, says "what ties these two writers together above all else is their belief that the ordinary is the extraordinary, that the wonder of this world is not hidden behind any veils but is open to our view, and that language is both a revelation of this wonder and its riddle" ("Riddles, Silence, and Wonder: Joyce and Wittgenstein Encountering the Limits of Language," *ELH* 57 [Summer 1990], 462).

16. Joyce's Aesthetic Notebooks draw heavily on these two thinkers. In the opening lines of "The Holy Office" Joyce explicitly invokes Aristotle and peripatetic philosophy, and subsequently he speaks of "Those souls that hate the strength that mine has / Steeled in the school of old Aquinas" (*CW,* pp. 149–50, 152). In his review of Burnet's *Aristotle on Education,* Joyce refers to Aristotle as "one who has been wisely named 'maestro di color che sanno' " (*CW,* p. 110). Richard Ellmann says that Joyce "had great admiration for Aristotle, and demonstrated it in many ways from 1902 to 1905" (*Ulysses on the Liffey* [New York: Oxford Univ. Press, 1972], p. 12; Ellmann cites evidence from Joyce's letters and from Stanislaus' diary). That his high opinion of Aristotle continued is shown by a comment he made to George Borach in 1917: "In the last two hundred years we haven't had a great thinker. My judgment is bold, since Kant is included. All the great thinkers of recent centuries from Kant to Benedetto Croce have only cultivated the garden. The greatest thinker of all times, in my opinion, is Aristotle. Everything, in his work, is defined with wonderful clarity and simplicity. Later, volumes were written to define the same things" (in Willard Potts, ed., *Portraits of the Artist in Exile: Recollections of James Joyce by Europeans* [Seattle: Univ. of Washington Press, 1979] p. 71). In "Ireland, Island of Saints and Sages" Joyce calls Aquinas "perhaps the keenest and most lucid mind known to human history" (*CW,* p. 161). In his lecture on Blake (1912) Joyce speaks of the "immense symmetrical edifice constructed by the Angelic Doctor, St. Thomas Aquinas" (*CW,* p. 220). Christopher Butler says "his [Joyce's] philosophical allegiances are to the pre-moderns, for example to Aquinas, for even when he is subverting Catholic dogma, one can feel that so far as Stephen's aesthetic theories go, he believes that the Scholastics have at least correctly formulated the categories with which we have to think" ("Joyce, Modernism, and Post-Modernism," in Derek Attridge, ed. *The Cambridge Companion to James Joyce* (Cambridge: Cambridge Univ. Press, 1990), p. 265; Butler cites *SH,* pp. 81 ff.).

17. In "James Joyce and the Power of the Word" (in *The Classic British Novel,* ed. Howard M. Harper, Jr. and Charles Edge [Athens: Univ. of Georgia Press, 1972] pp. 183–201) I explore the artist/priest analogy in some detail, arguing that the analogy suggests that, just as the priest is the vehicle, not the originator, of the forces he embodies while conducting the Mass, so the artist necessarily uses potentialities that are inherent in reality and in the human imagination to carry out his work.

18. Gabler argues that this is probably a "Dublin" notebook, dating from the months of Joyce's visit to Dublin in 1909; see "The Seven Lost Years of *A Portrait,*" p. 52.

19. In this regard, a statement that Joyce made in a letter to Stanislaus October 18, 1906 is noteworthy: "I regret that years are going over and that I cannot follow the road of speculation which often opens before me. I think I have unlearned a great deal but I am sure I have also a great deal to learn. . . . What really is the point is: whether it is possible for me to combine the exercise of my art with a reasonably happy life" (*Letters*, II, 182). In *Ulysses*, when Stephen thinks "Dublin. I have much, much to learn" (*U*, 7.915), we sense that he means about life, not about abstract philosophical principles.

20. Arthur Power quotes Joyce as saying "though people may read more into *Ulysses* than I ever intended, who is to say that they are wrong: do any of us know what we are creating? Did Shakespeare know what he was creating when he wrote *Hamlet;* or Leonardo when he painted 'The Last Supper'?" (*Conversations*, p. 89). Elsewhere Joyce told Power "you must write what is in your blood and not what is in your brain" (*From the Old Waterford House* [London: Mellifont Press, Ltd., n.d.], p. 64). Joyce also told Power of *Ulysses* "I have tried to write naturally, on an emotional basis as against an intellectual basis. Emotion has dictated the course and detail of my book, and in emotional writing one arrives at the unpredictable which can be of more value, since its sources are deeper, than the products of the intellectual method. . . . the emotionally creative writer . . . creates a signifi-cant image in the only significant world, the world of our emotions" (*Conversations*, p. 95).

21. For Zola's strongly "empirical" view of the writer's work, see his frequently reprinted essay "The Experimental Novel."

22. The opening chapter, "Symbolism," of Wilson's *Axel's Castle: A Study in the Imagi-native Literature of 1870–1930*. (New York: Scribners, 1931) provides a lucid account of the evolution of nineteenth-century and early twentieth-century literary ideas out of the Enlight-enment milieu. Kenner says "Joyce eludes altogether the party politics of 'symbolism' and 'naturalism' " ("*Portrait* in Perspective," p. 160). Charles Rossman makes a similar point about Joyce's philosophical orientation, using the terms romanticism and realism ("Stephen Dedalus and the Spiritual-Heroic Refrigerating Apparatus," p. 110). Marguerite Harkness says "above all, we can see in Joyce's novels the conjunction of Aestheticism and Natural-ism" (*Aesthetics*, p. 200). In her more recent *"A Portrait of the Artist as a Young Man": Voices of the Text* (Boston: Twayne Publishers, 1990), Harkness says more pointedly that writers of Joyce's period "were faced with two competing notions about art"—naturalism and symbolism—and that "one task of any twentieth-century writer was to choose or to select from among these notions about art and to carve out his own practice" (p. 5); "Joyce's work clearly shows that he attempted to fuse these two traditions" (p. 6).

23. Others have preceded me not only in the idea of *Chamber Music* as apprentice work, but in the musical metaphor as well. Speaking of the manuscripts of Joyce's early poems, W. B. Yeats perspicaciously described them as the work of "a young man who is practicing his instrument, taking pleasure in the mere handling of the stops" (quoted in Ellmann, *JJ II*, p. 114). William York Tindall calls *Chamber Music* "the first trial of a method that was to produce his poetic, musically organized stories and *A Portrait of the Artist*, an even more musical work, which may be called symphonic. Without the intimate music of the poems that symphony might have lacked assurance" (*Chamber Music*, p. 58). Similarly, Max Wildi describes *Chamber Music* as "nothing more or less than finger-exercises that were to prove essential for that astonishing mastery of phrasing that one admires in Joyce's mature prose" ("James Joyce and Arthur Symons," *Orbis Litterarum* 19 [1964], 191). And a

similar idea (though a different metaphor) seems to lie behind Seamus Heaney's saying "I have often wondered about what constitutes the difference between Joyce's use of language in his poems, *Chamber Music* for example, and in his prose works, *A Portrait* or *Ulysses*. It seems to me that in the former Joyce is approaching language as a sort of ventriloquist, he remains its obedient servant, he rehearses a note caught from literature" (quoted in Richard Kearney, *Transitions,* p. 49; Heaney made the observation in a conversation with Jorge Luis Borges). What Heaney senses as ventriloquy I see as Joyce's attempting to capture the accent of the Symbolist mode. The Virgil analogy is used by John Porter Houston, who in reference to the scrupulous meanness of *Dubliners,* says that Joyce had "calculated the kind of writing that would best convey the tone he wanted at that moment, just as in the classical account Virgil chose the low style for his eclogues before attempting the middle style of the *Georgics* and the elevated manner of the *Aeneid*" (*Joyce and Prose: An Exploration of the Language of Ulysses* [Lewisburg, Pa.: Bucknell Univ. Press, 1989], p. 170). Joyce does seem to have aspired to be the great artist of his age, comparable to those named above. Steven Helmling says that "the young Joyce's ambitions as an artist were grandiose. He aspired to a world-historical role" ("Joyce: Autobiography, History, Narrative," *Kenyon Review* New Series 10 [Spring 1988], 94). R. P. Blackmur says "Joyce, like Dante, tried to read his experience through every form or mode of knowledge available to him" (*Anni Mirabeles 1921–1925: Reason in the Madness of Letters* [Washington, D.C.: Library of Congress, 1956], p. 24), and John Eglinton says that Joyce was a Dublin Dante (E. H. Mikhail, ed. *James Joyce: Interviews and Recollections* [London: Macmillan, 1990], pp. 35–36). Thomas C. Singer is even more explicit: citing Joyce's reference to Dante as "the first poet of the Europeans" (in *SH,* p. 41), and describing the Florentine as "the great synthesizer of medieval thought in verse," Singer says "indeed, at times Joyce conceived of himself as doing for the early twentieth century what Dante had done for the early fourteenth" (pp. 460–61). Magalaner in *Time of Apprenticeship* says "the youthful Joyce was fired, like Milton in 'Lycidas,' to equal or surpass his masters" (p. 17), and he reminds us of the statement from "The Day of the Rabblement" that Ibsen and Hauptmann have had their day "and the third minister will not be wanting when his hour comes. Even now that hour may be standing by the door" (in *CW,* p. 72). In his letters to Nora, Joyce was explicit about his aims: "My darling, tonight I was in the Gresham Hotel and was introduced to about twenty people and to all of them the same story was told: that I was going to be the great writer of the future in my country. All the noise and flattery around me hardly moved me. . . . O take me into your soul of souls and then I will become indeed the poet of my race" (Sept. 5, 1909; Joyce, *Selected Letters,* p. 169). A few weeks later: "Then another night I came home to your bed from the café and I began to tell you of all I hoped to do, and to write, in the future and of those boundless ambitions which are really the leading forces in my life" (Oct. 27, 1909; *Selected Letters,* p. 174).

    24. The little that we know about Joyce's other early literary endeavors conforms to such a pattern. Ellmann tells us that Joyce began a series of prose sketches entitled *Silhouettes;* from Stanislaus' recollection of one of the sketches, they were dingy and violent, smacking of naturalism (see *JJ II,* p. 50). The title, though, might well reflect Joyce's interest in Arthur Symons, in whose *Silhouettes* (1892) "poems influenced by Symons' reading of the French Symbolists and Decadents, particularly Baudelaire, make their first appearance" (Karl Beckson,

Arthur Symons: A Life [Oxford: Clarendon Press, 1987], p. 89). Joyce also began a series of poems entitled *Moods,* which Ellmann says suggests the influence of Yeats (*JJ II,* p. 50)—though Symons' *Silhouettes* contains a section of poems headed "Moods and Memories." The influence of Symons' poetry on Joyce's is suggested also by the fact that when George Russell showed some of Joyce's poems to George Moore, he (in Ellmann's words) "handed them back with the derisive *but acute* comment, 'Symons!' " (*JJ II,* p. 135; my emphasis).

25. Constantine Curran speaks of Joyce's interest in the symbolists and of how influential Symons' *The Symbolist Movement* was among Joyce's cohort; see his *James Joyce Remembered* (London: Oxford Univ. Press, 1968), pp. 31–32. Also, Gogarty makes a great deal of Joyce's quoting Rimbaud and even calls him "the hidden model whom Joyce was imitating" (Mikhail, *James Joyce: Interviews and Recollections,* p. 26). See also Max Wildi, "James Joyce and Arthur Symons," and David Hayman, *Joyce et Mallarmé* (Paris: Lettres Modernes, 1956).

26. Joyce's misgivings about aestheticism generally and certain of the Symbolist poets in particular are manifested quite early. In his childhood essay that Mason and Ellmann have titled "Force," Joyce speaks critically of the "*fin-de-siècle* sneer" (*CW,* p. 23). In "Drama and Life," he tells us "beauty is the swerga of the aesthete" (*CW,* p. 43), and in "The Day of the Rabblement" he says "an aesthete has a floating will" (*CW,* p. 71). There is explicit criticism of Baudelaire in "James Clarence Mangan" (*CW,* p. 75), of Mallarmé in "The Soul of Ireland" (*CW,* p. 104), of Huysmans in "A French Religious Novel" (*CW,* p. 123), and of Rimbaud in a letter to Stanislaus of about September 24, 1905 (*Letters,* II, 110).

27. That Joyce may have regarded these poems as exercises in a mode is suggested by a juxtaposition made by Stanislaus: "My brother wrote a few poems while he was in Paris, the last four in *Chamber Music,* which I placed at the end of it because of their sombre tone. He tried his hand, too, at dialogue in the style of Ben Jonson, not seriously but merely as an exercise. I never saw these efforts but he told me that though they were just nonsense he had caught the style. They had, he said, the true Jonsonian ring" (*MBK,* pp. 224–25).

28. See especially *Letters* II, 172 and 219, and *JJ II,* p. 260, where Ellmann tells of a long argument between Stanislaus and James over whether the book should be published, even after the proofs had been read.

29. Anglea Habermann argues that in the villanelle "Joyce closely imitated" Mallarmé's "Afternoon of a Faun," and that this "imitation of the musings of Mallarmé's faun in the description of Stephen's creative efforts is one of the means he used to define the romantic artist portrayed through Stephen" ("The Joycean Faun," *The International Fiction Review* 10 [Winter 1983]) 44).

30. Phillip F. Herring calls attention to such details as evidence of the stories' naturalism. He sees "Eveline" as "told in the naturalist tradition of Zola's *L'Assommoir* and George Moore's *Esther Waters,* one difference being that it has the more precise economy of a story by Maupassant" (*Joyce's Uncertainty Principle.* [Princeton: Princeton Univ. Press, 1987], p. 36). But I agree with Derek Attridge that the story, and the *Dubliners* collection as a whole, is far too rich and evocative to be so classified ("Reading Joyce," esp. pp. 3–10). Richard Ellmann says of *Dubliners* that in it Joyce "presented his initial indictment of Ireland, in terms of its inertness, repression and corruption"—which sounds like naturalism—but Ellmann goes on to say "yet *Dubliners* does not rest in the portrayal of decadence," and he points to three elements of possible relief: "The first is a sympathy, usually latent and unstated, for

thwarted lives. The second is the evident pleasure taken by the author in Dublin humor. . . . The third is the reserved, fastidious diction and occasional bursts of lyricism" ("The Uses of Decadence: Wilde, Yeats, Joyce," in Ellmann's *a long the riverrun: Selected Essays* [New York: Alfred A. Knopf, 1989], p. 15).

31. These comments occur in letters to Grant Richards of October 15, 1905, May 5, 1906, and June 23, 1906 respectively. See *Letters,* II, 123 and 134, and I, 64.

32. The *Athenaeum* review, for example, said "the fifteen stories given here under the collective title of *Dubliners* are nothing if not naturalistic. In some ways, indeed, they are unduly so: at least three would have been better buried in oblivion" (*CH,* I, 61).

33. Brown, *James Joyce's Early Fiction,* p. 5. Brown develops this point more fully on pp. 13 ff. M. Keith Booker says "one of the favorite pastimes of Joyce scholars in recent decades has been the development of narrative/biographical models for the progress of Joyce's career from the relatively traditional naturalism/realism of the earlier stories in *Dubliners* to the stunningly non-traditional verbal magic (black or otherwise) of *Finnegans Wake*" ("History and Language in Joyce's 'The Sisters,' " *Criticism* 33 [Spring 1991], 217); Booker goes on to show that the language in "The Sisters" is far too rich and complex to conform to such a schema. (See also the following footnote.) Karen Lawrence's *The Odyssey of Style in "Ulysses"* (Princeton: Princeton Univ. Press, 1981) pursues such a line. But most critics who see *Dubliners* as unqualifiedly naturalistic acknowledge that Joyce very quickly moved beyond this perspective—certainly by the time of *Portrait of the Artist,* perhaps by the time of "The Dead." Steven Helmling, though, sees Joyce's "naturalistic realism" as extending all the way to "*Ulysses*-before-Sirens" ("Joyce the Irresponsible," *Sewanee Review* 94 [Summer 1986], 463–64; see also pp. 451 and 468).

34. David Krause insists that *Dubliners* is far more than minimal realism: "Even in his first book, *Dubliners,* Joyce creates not an imitation but an ambience of reality, that intensification of reality which Synge in his Preface to *The Playboy* called the 'richness' of reality" ("Joyce vs. Yeats?," *Irish Literary Supplement* 9 [Fall 1990], 6). And Derek Attridge's discussion of what is implicitly involved in the text of "Eveline" shows how far beyond naturalism such an apparently simple text goes ("Reading Joyce," pp. 4–10). Similarly, M. Keith Booker's "History and Language" shows that the style of "The Sisters" is too subtle and "palinodic" to be described as naturalistic.

35. I find it interesting that Michael Patrick Gillespie says *Dubliners* demonstrates "a masterful command of the idiom of naturalistic fiction" (*Reading the Book of Himself: Narrative Strategies in the Works of James Joyce* [Columbus: Ohio State Univ. Press, 1989], p. 61)—which is quite different from saying that the book is naturalism. For fuller development of this idea that Joyce saw various styles or schools as modes of the word and wished to be able to draw upon them at will, so as to incorporate and transcend them, see my "James Joyce and the Power of the Word."

36. The subject-object perspective is of course not utterly specious; philosopher A. N. Whitehead has suggested that some such structure is probably inherent in human experience. But in the wake of Descartes' proclamation of two substances, our sense of this dichotomy has become distortive and pernicious. All human perceptions, whether Western or not, evoke differing aspects of reality—broadly speaking mental and material—but the Modernist Syndrome has severed the two, set them over against one another, and denied the reality of the mental or psychic aspect to a degree that is unparalleled in other cultures

of the world. Perhaps one measure of Joyce's success in incorporating both the "inner" and the "outer" perspectives into his novel is the number of critics who have seen the novel as *either* symbolist *or* naturalist. Joseph A. Buttigieg says that upon its publication in 1916, "there was, initially, some . . . debate as to whether it belonged to the naturalist movement or whether it represented a move into more original territory" (*"A Portrait of the Artist" in Different Perspective,* p. 13), and several of the reviews saw it as strongly naturalistic (see for example *CH,* I, 97 and I, 116). But other critics have regarded the novel as symbolist (see those cited by Buttigieg, p. 16).

37. Maurice Beebe concurs when he says "the often maligned style of the *Portrait* may thus be defended as Joyce's quite brilliant effort to show how life might have been viewed by an archetypal young artist at the turn of the century who had not yet found his own separate and unique identity" ("The *Portrait* as Portrait: Joyce and Impressionism," *Irish Renaissance Annual I* [1980], p. 29).

38. Kenner, MacCabe, and Herr are among those critics who talk as if the individual is no more than a nexus of linguistic and cultural forces; see Kenner's *"Ulysses"* (Revised edition. Baltimore: Johns Hopkins Univ. Press, 1987), p. 70; MacCabe's *James Joyce and the Revolution of the Word* (New York: Harper and Row, 1979), p. 156; and Herr's *Joyce's Anatomy of Culture* (Urbana: Univ. of Illinois Press, 1986), esp. p. 154. (See also the quotes from R. B. Kershner in Chapter 5, footnote #1.) It is not always easy to know what critics mean when they talk about Joyce's subverting the idea of the self. For example, M. Keith Booker says "one of the most important assumptions about authority that Joyce's radical practice of writing seeks to undermine is the traditional liberal-humanist notion of the autonomous self" ("The Baby in the Bathwater: Joyce, Gilbert, and Feminist Criticism." *Texas Studies in Literature and Language* 32 [Fall 1990], 454). It is not clear, though, even from the full context of Booker's remark, precisely what Joyce's presumed challenge to "autonomy" involves—whether the self's claim of utter autonomy and discreteness (a "modernist" idea that Joyce does criticize), or every vestige of coherence and volition the self might aspire to.

39. Tim Cribb says of Joyce's turning to *Ulysses* after *Portrait* and *Exiles,* "once Joyce had accomplished his revolution against the imperialism of the Cartesian mind and overthrown the reactive regime of the Romantic subjectivist he was free for the world of *Ulysses.* The unconscious is now united with the conscious mind, and both with the world and the body, through a constantly interacting dynamics that makes any systematic separation between the elements impossible" ("James Joyce: The Unconscious and the Cognitive Epiphany," in *Modernism and the European Unconscious,* ed. by Peter Collier and Judy Davies, pp. 64–78 [New York: St. Martin's, 1990], p. 73). Similarly, Carl Jung, in his *"Ulysses:* A Monologue," says of the novel, "objective and subjective, outer and inner, are so constantly intermingled that in the end, despite the clearness of the individual images, one wonders whether one is dealing with a physical or a transcendental tapeworm" (in *The Spirit in Man, Art, and Literature* [New York: Pantheon Books, 1966], p. 112).

40. Criticism of *Ulysses* has yet to take seriously the implications of the hundreds of links—linguistic, psychological, situational, mythic—that exist among the characters in *Ulysses*—especially Stephen and Bloom. Most critics either disregard these links or see them simply as a stylistic or a technical tour de force on Joyce's part whereby he embellished his artifact, ignoring the question of what these links imply about the social psyche and about

the existence of a cultural continuum that complexly involves all of us. One exception is Sheldon Brivic who deals with these correspondences in his *The Veil of Signs: Joyce, Lacan, and Perception* (Urbana: Univ. of Illinois Press, 1991), passim.

41. I develop these ideas about *Ulysses* in an unpublished essay "Self and Myth in Joyce's *Ulysses*."

42. The idea for an additional short story, about a Mr. Hunter and to be entitled "Ulysses," emerges as early as September-November of 1906—before *Dubliners* was completed or *Portrait* begun (*Letters*, II, 168, 190, 193). Joyce later spoke of *Ulysses* as "a continuation of *A Portrait of the Artist* and also of *Dubliners*" (letter to H. L. Mencken, July 7, 1915; *Letters*, I, 83). In his discussion of the French translation of *Dubliners* in 1926, Edmond Jaloux said "when the great fragments of *Ulysses* are published . . . we will be able to see the road covered by Mr. James Joyce from *Dubliners* to his extraordinary encyclopedic epic of an individual; but it is obvious that *Dubliners* was already a solid platform for advancing toward this conception" (*CH*, I, 70).

43. Carl Jung, *The Psychology of the Unconscious* (New York: Moffatt, Yard, and Co., 1916), pp. 13 ff.

44. Though I cannot develop the idea here, Joyce's sensitivity to the limitations of modernist directed thinking and his affinity for metaphoric, analogic thinking were facilitated by his Celtic roots. *Finnegans Wake* is Joyce's most Celtic book not simply in incorporating Irish history and Celtic myth and in drawing upon *The Book of Kells* as a technical model, but in its underlying perspective upon reality. (Seamus Deane emphasizes its Irishness, along different lines, in his "Joyce the Irishman," in *The Cambridge Companion to James Joyce,* ed. Derek Attridge [Cambridge: Cambridge Univ. Press, 1990], pp. 49–52.) In writing this novel, Joyce was drawing upon the same milieu that enabled Yeats to take seriously modes of thought—the occult, automatic writing, etc.—that virtually all self-respecting modernists disdained. (See my "Between Circle and Straight Line: A Pragmatic View of W. B. Yeats and the Occult.") For a variety of reasons, the Irish were resistant to Cartesian dualism and to Lockean/Humean empiricism.

45. The letter of August 14, 1927, to Harriet Shaw Weaver in which Joyce says this is in *Letters*, I, 257–58; a fuller text is printed in the *Selected Letters*, pp. 326–28.

46. Many of Joyce's statements in this vein are discussed in the first chapter of John Bishop's *Joyce's Book of the Dark: "Finnegans Wake"* (Madison: Univ. of Wisconsin Press, 1986). Bishop's book elaborates in great detail essentially the argument that I am proposing here—that reading *Finnegans Wake* requires modes of thought that the Western mind has long denigrated. I find his argument impressive, but he elides a very important distinction when he says of *Finnegans Wake* that it "represents nothing; or . . . much of it represents much the same kind of nothing that one will not remember not having experienced in sleep last night" (*Book of the Dark*, p. 43). To claim that our unremembered sleep/dream life— which is the wellspring of our non-directed thinking—amounts to nothing or has no value for the balance and well-being of our psyche, undermines our appreciation of much of what *Finnegans Wake* does for us as individuals and as a culture.

47. To be more precise, what *Finnegans Wake* provides is a literary *analogue* of non-directed thinking. For even here, in spite of Samuel Beckett's famous dictum that Joyce's writing "is not *about* something; *it is that something itself*" ("Dante . . . Bruno. Vico . . . Joyce," in *Our Exagmination Round his Factification for Incamination of Work in Progress,* by

Samuel Beckett et al. [London: Faber and Faber, 1929] p. 14), we are after all dealing with a literary-conventional simulation.

48. For a discussion of the complex issue of the status of the narrative voices in *Ulysses*, arguing that the narrative voices of certain episodes represent values very different from those of the novel as a whole, see my "Voices and Values in *Ulysses*," in *Joyce's "Ulysses": The Larger Perspective*, edited by Robert D. Newman and Weldon Thornton (London: Associated Univ. Presses, 1987), pp. 244–70.

4. The Antimodernist Implications of the *Bildungsroman*

1. *Kinds of Literature*, p. 38. Fowler elaborates: "In literary communication, genres are functional: they actively form the experience of each work of literature. . . . When we try to decide the genre of a work, then, our aim is to discover its meaning. . . . It follows that genre theory, too, is properly concerned, in the main, with interpretation" (p. 38). Fowler's book is a comprehensive and discriminating study of literary types. Though generally substantial, his account of the formation of genres (chapter 9) does not attend sufficiently to the responsiveness of genres to changing cultural conditions and philosophical currents. He does say that "modes are subject to mutability and become obsolete when the values they enshrine, or the emotions they invoke, grow alien" (p. 111), but he does not do justice to the way in which genres emerge, evolve, flourish, and decline in conjunction with changes in the underlying cultural milieu.

2. See *Aristotle on the Art of Poetry*, translated by Ingram Bywater (Oxford: The Clarendon Press, 1959), pp. 31 and 35. Alastair Fowler says "Aristotle is sometimes smiled at for saying that tragedy reached its perfection in his time. But it is true that tragedy as he knew it was complete. . . . A coherent cycle of development, it might be argued, was complete in his time. One kind of tragedy had reached the end of its life" (*Kinds of Literature*, p. 164).

3. Lengthy discussion of the nature of genre would deflect me from my main point, but let me illustrate what I mean by an ad hoc genre. Let us ask whether we could arbitrarily create a genre, such as, for example, Poems of twenty lines that are not in free verse. We could, by assiduous searching, locate a number of such poems (or write them, if need be), but it seems clear that the "genre" would be a creation of caprice and that very few meaningful generalizations about it could be made. Or consider the even more capricious "genre" of poems that begin at the top of page ten in the volume than contains them; this is a category of sorts, but a very trivial one. The point is that the human mind can conceive an endless array of categories or "genres." The question is which of these categories reflect recurrent, meaningful modes of human experience. When, for example, Aristotle describes the genre of tragedy, he is *recognizing* (not creating) a recurrent type of literature that was brought into being by certain constancies of human experience and by certain psychological/spiritual needs within his cultural milieu. For such a genre, meaningful generalizations and even normative statements are possible. Nor is this to hypostatize the genre, as if it were some preexisting form; it is simply to recognize that the genre is rooted in recurrent human needs and in enduring cultural structures.

4. I document the unfortunate effects of procrustean genre criticism in the chapter on *Riders to the Sea* in my *J. M. Synge and the Western Mind* (Gerrards Cross: Colin Smythe

Ltd., 1978), showing how often that play has been judged by the totally inappropriate standards of Aristotelian tragedy. Such criticism assumes that because Synge's play depicts unhappy events, he must have intended to write a "tragedy," but failed.

5. Martin Swales develops an essentially similar claim in his *The German Bildungsroman from Wieland to Hesse* (Princeton: Princeton Univ. Press, 1978): "I want to argue that the *Bildungsroman* genre was born in specific historical circumstances, that is, within the *Humanitätsideeal* of late eighteenth-century Germany. It is a novel form that is animated by a concern for the whole man unfolding organically in all his complexity and richness. . . . The centrality of the concept *Bildung*, of the self-realization of the individual in his wholeness, for such figures as Goethe, Schiller, and Wilhelm von Humboldt is well known. The urgency of their concern is a measure of the anguish with which they perceived the growing threat of narrowness and specialization in the society around them" (pp. 14–15). Swales's view supports my claim that the genre involves anti-empiricist/Enlightenment implications.

6. Though he says little about the picaresque and nothing about its relation to the *Bildungsroman*, Fowler does acknowledge transformations among genres. Specifically, he says that the picaresque developed "as a countergenre to escapist chivalric romance" (*Kinds of Literature*, p. 167; see also p. 175). And in a section entitled "Modal Transformation," Fowler says that "a kind's last stage by no means ends in mere extinction. For it may have generated modal transformations of other kinds" (p. 167).

7. One persistent theme of Fowler's *Kinds of Literature* is the changes of genres over time—e.g., "the character of genres is that they change" (p. 18); "all genres are continuously undergoing metamorphosis" (p. 23); "a literary genre changes with time, so that its boundaries cannot be defined by any single set of characteristics such as would determine a class" (p. 38); "in their historical development, too, the genres change continually" (p. 45); "it is time that genre theory acknowledged the historical mutability of the genres themselves, and dealt much more freely with temporal concepts" (p. 46). Similar statements occur *passim*.

8. G. B. Tennyson makes substantially the same point: "This emphasis on the primacy of *Wilhelm Meister* for the *Bildungsroman* has advantages and disadvantages. On the one hand, *Wilhelm Meister*, especially the full version, contains a God's plenty of everything, and it would be an unimaginative reader indeed who could not find just about anything he wanted in that immense and varied work. On the other hand, this very abundance mitigates against precision in the form and leads us to ask, which features in *Meister* are essential to the form and which are superfluous?" ("The *Bildungsroman* in Nineteenth-Century English Literature," in *Medieval Epic to the "Epic Theatre" of Brecht*, ed. Rosario P. Armato and John M. Spalek [Los Angeles: Univ. of Southern California Press, 1968], p. 136).

9. *Ivory Towers and Sacred Founts: The Artist as Hero in Fiction from Goethe to Joyce* (New York: New York Univ. Press, 1964), p. 260. H. M. Daleski says similarly that "Joyce's *A Portrait of the Artist* is perhaps the tightest example in English of the unifying force of the *Bildungsroman* form" (*Unities: Studies in the English Novel* [Athens: Univ. of Georgia Press, 1985], p. 171).

10. I follow Susanne Howe and Randolph Shaffner in acknowledging that the prototype—by which we mean that example that came to be virtually identified with the form—may not be the historically earliest example of the form. On Goethe's novel being " 'the seminal instance' " of the form (though not historically the first), see Shaffner, *The Apprenticeship Novel: A Study of the Bildungsroman as a Regulative Type in Western Literature*

with a Focus on Three Representatives by Goethe, Maugham, and Mann (New York: Peter Lang, 1984), p. 28, and the sources cited there. Howe develops the same point in her *Wilhelm Meister and his English Kinsmen: Apprentices to Life* (New York: Columbia Univ. Press, 1930), in a chapter entitled "Apprenticeships before *Wilhelm Meister*"; see esp. pp. 24–25.

11. In the discussion that follows, I make no distinction between the *Bildungsroman* and the *Künstlerroman*. The latter, as the name implies, involves a protagonist who is in the process of becoming an artist—usually a writer or a painter. While some critics would argue for a distinction between these two forms, I regard the *Künstlerroman* as a species of the *Bildungsroman* and find no significant differences for my purposes between them. Gregory Castle concurs, at least in regard to Joyce's *Portrait,* saying "I have subsumed the latter term *[Künstlerroman]* under the term *Bildungsroman,* for Joyce, it seems to me, is writing against the general notion of *Bildung*" ("The Book of Youth: Reading Joyce's Bildungsroman," *Genre* 22 [Spring 1989], 25). Interestingly, Maurice Beebe, in his book devoted to the *Künstlerroman, Ivory Towers and Sacred Founts,* makes few claims for the distinctiveness of the artist-novel, even taking as his first paradigm Goethe's *Wilhelm Meister,* which, as Beebe acknowledges, is "a novel in which the hero turns out to be no artist at all" (p. 33). Beebe also speaks very broadly of the artist-type when he says "it is apparent that the artist-hero, like the hero with a thousand faces, is always the same man and the conflicts he faces are essentially the same conflicts" (p. 299). On possible differences between the two modes, see Shaffner, *The Apprenticeship Novel,* pp. 13–14, and the sources cited there.

12. Daleski says "The *Bildungsroman* traces the continuity within change in a process of growth . . . " (*Unities,* p. xiii). Scholars discuss the differences implied by the various terms that have been used for modes or cognates of the genre—i.e., *Erziehungsroman, Entwicklungsroman, Selbsterziehungsroman.* The consensus seems to be that English lacks convenient qualifying terms that make these discriminations, and that the term Apprenticeship Novel is the best English approximation of what *Bildung* implies. See Shaffner, chapter 2. Marianne Hirsch posits the "confessional novel" as the counterpart of the picaresque, and in doing so, focusses nicely one characteristic trait of the "novel of formation" (her term for the *Bildungsroman*): "While the picaresque novel is turned outward toward society and the confessional novel is turned inward toward consciousness, the novel of formation maintains a peculiar balance between the social and the personal and explores their interaction. . . . The novel of formation's dual focus, inward toward the self and outward toward society, makes it one of the major fictional types of European realism" ("The Novel of Formation as Genre: Between Great Expectations and Lost Illusions," *Genre* 12 [Fall 1979] 299, 300).

13. Such claims, assuming both the continuity of the self and Joyce's belief in that continuity, are regarded askance by some contemporary critics, who would argue that Joyce disavowed such a view of the psyche, or even that *Portrait* is a parody of the traditional quest novel. Richard Kearney says that *Portrait* is "as the self-reflexive title suggests, a parody of the quest structure of the traditional bourgeoise novel" *Transitions,* p. 36), and Calvin Thomas says that "all of Joyce is a parody and subversion of [the] essentialist formulation" ("Stephen in Process/Stephen on Trial: The Anxiety of Production in Joyce's *Portrait,*" *Novel* 23 [Spring 1990], 293, fn. 24). Karen Lawrence, in a brief essay unfavorably comparing *A Portrait* with Woolf's *Jacob's Room,* suggests that Joyce's novel might have been able to subvert certain features of the traditional *Bildungsroman,* except that he "nevertheless accepts

some of the premises of that form," such as "the development of the 'self' of the protagonist," and she finds that "the basic idea of growth and development, however problematic,
is, nevertheless, ultimately accepted" ("Gender and Narrative Voice in *Jacob's Room* and *A
Portrait of the Artist as a Young Man*," in Morris Beja et al., *James Joyce: The Centennial
Symposium* (Urbana: Univ. of Illinois Press, 1986, p. 32). She concludes regrettably that "in *A
Portrait*, Joyce had not yet begun to question certain central patriarchal ideas" (p. 36),
including "identity." The thrust of my argument in succeeding chapters is that while Joyce
does take the measure of Stephen's "modernist" view of the self (and by extension of all
empiricist/Enlightenment views), he shows that the processes of individuation do exist, at a
level deeper than self-analysis can ever fathom.

14. Auspicious subconscious developmental patterns exist even in such early examples
of the genre as *Wilhelm Meister* and *The Prelude*. They are manifested in the former both in
Wilhelm's not fully comprehending the maturity that the members of the Society of the
Tower have been leading him toward, and in Goethe's refusal, in spite of Schiller's behest,
to have his hero's development illustrate "any clear-cut message which appeals to the
conceptual faculty alone" (letter from Goethe to Schiller, quoted by Swales, *The German
Bildungsroman*, p. 70). In *The Prelude* such patterns emerge in the poet's realization, in
Book Eleven, of the wrongness of his having "dragg[ed] all precepts, judgments, maxims,
creeds, / Like culprits to the bar" of cognitive judgment (lines 294–95), and of how certain
implicit aspects of his experience had "Maintained for me a saving intercourse / With my
true self" (lines 341–42). This is in keeping with the genre's implication that the psyche is far
richer than the mind can understand (in Jung's terms, that the Self can never be compre-
hended by the Ego), and that something deep within the psyche guides the personality
towards its distinctive "individuation."

15. See the comments by Daleski and by Stanislaus Joyce quoted on pp. 85–86.

16. This sympathetic quality of Joycean irony has been recognized by several critics—
e.g., S. L. Goldberg, *The Classical Temper: A Study of James Joyce's "Ulysses"* (London:
Chatto and Windus, 1961), chapter IV, esp., p. 110; F. Parvin Sharpless concurs with Goldberg's
judgment ("Irony in Joyce's *Portrait*," p. 98), as does L. A. Murillo (*The Cyclical Night: Irony
in James Joyce and Jorge Luis Borges* (Cambridge: Harvard Univ. Press, 1968), esp. pp. 24–
32 and 42 ff. K. E. Robinson says "Whereas Flaubert's irony leans toward the denigratory,
Joyce's is gentle and knowing" ("Stream of Consciousness Technique," p. 76).

17. For Jung, this process necessarily involves supra-individual elements: "As the individual is not just a single, separate being, but by his very existence presupposes a collective
relationship, it follows that the process of individuation must lead to more intense and
broader collective relationships and not to isolation." Jung sharply distinguishes individuation from "extreme individualism," which he describes as "pathological and inimical to life"
(from "Definitions," in *Psychological Types* [Princeton: Princeton Univ. Press, 1971], pp. 448–
49). (Interestingly, Joyce used the term "individuating rhythm" in his 1904 "Portrait" sketch,
to describe what the artist is trying to "liberate.") D. H. Lawrence concurs that the process of
self-realization necessarily involves subconscious forces; this is implicit in his conception of
the will, developed in chapter six of *Psychoanalysis and the Unconscious and Fantasia of
the Unconscious* (New York: Viking Press, 1960). There he describes the will as "a certain
faculty belonging to every living organism, the faculty for self-determination. It is a strange
faculty of the soul itself, for its own direction. . . . It seems as if the will were given as a great

balancing faculty, the faculty whereby automatization is *prevented* in the evolving psyche. . . . the will is the power which the unique self possesses to right itself from automatism" (pp. 47–48). I find it appropriate that Lawrence describes the role of the will as *balancing* the strivings of the psyche, implying as it does that the psyche develops by virtue of an oscillation between poles—something characteristic of the structure of the *Bildungsroman.*

5. The Structures

1. From Gaggi's *Modern/Postmodern: A Study in Twentieth-Century Arts and Ideas* (Philadelphia: Univ. of Pennsylvania Press, 1990), pp. 157–58. Gaggi is drawing upon Jonathan Culler's discussion of "the anti-humanistic implications of semiotics and structuralism, which suggest that 'the self is dissolved as its various functions are ascribed to impersonal systems that operate through it.' The individual ceases to be centered in an *a priori* 'self' but becomes instead a locus where various signifying systems intersect" (Gaggi quotes from Jonathan Culler's *The Pursuit of Signs: Semiotics, Literature, Deconstruction* [Ithaca: Cornell Univ. Press, 1981], p. 33. Chapter 2 of Culler's book discusses how the self is dissolved into the cultural nexus). R. B. Kershner's reading comes very close to eliding Joyce and Stephen into the various cultural influences and texts that act upon them. He says for example that "much of *Portrait* reflects—or embodies—Stephen's possession by the languages that surround him, and his attempts to appropriate them in turn" (*Joyce, Bakhtin, and Popular Literature: Chronicles of Disorder* [Chapel Hill: Univ. of North Carolina Press, 1989], p. 154); "For long stretches, during this phase of his development, Stephen's thoughts simply are not his own" (Ibid., p. 157); and "Stephen is a product of his listening and reading, an irrational sum of the texts, written and spoken, to which he has been exposed. . . . the very structure of his consciousness is dependent upon these texts" (Ibid., p. 162); and Kershner refers to Stephen's being " 'spoken through' even in his private thoughts, in a sort of mental ventriloquy" (Ibid., p. 164). John McGowan's discussion of the self, in "From Pater to Wilde to Joyce: Modernist Epiphany and the Soulful Self," *Texas Studies in Literature and Language* 32 (Fall 1990): 417–45, sees modern and postmodern conceptions of the self as involving either a heroic self created ex nihilo, or a denial of the constraints of selfhood; he posits no healthy alternative, and he presumes that Stephen's heroic view of the self is sanctioned by Joyce. (For other critics who would dissolve the self into its linguistic and cultural components, see the citations of Hugh Kenner's *"Ulysses,"* Colin MacCabe's *James Joyce and the Revolution of the Word,* and Cheryl Herr's *Joyce's Anatomy of Culture* in Chapter 3, footnote 38.)

2. Richard Ellmann also cites this observation of Stanislaus' and says "for *A Portrait of the Artist as a Young Man* is in fact the gestation of a soul, and in the metaphor Joyce found his new principle of order" (*JJ II,* pp. 296–97). He goes on to describe the unfolding of Stephen's character in keeping with this metaphor. Fritz Senn also stresses the developmental and process-oriented aspects of the novel in his *"A Portrait:* Temporal Foreplay," *Etudes Irlandaises* No. 12 (December 1987): 65–73.

3. "Strings in the Labyrinth: Sixty Years with Joyce's *Portrait,*" in *Approaches to Joyce's "Portrait": Ten Essays,* ed. Thomas F. Staley and Bernard Benstock, (Pittsburgh: Univ. of

Pittsburgh Press, 1976), p. 20. Maurice Beebe, in *Ivory Towers and Sacred Founts,* speaks pointedly of "the structure of the novel, which is identical with the development of Stephen . . . " (p. 268).

4. Since virtually every discussion of Stephen's character, including those of various psychological motifs, involves the novel's structure, a review of the critical literature relevant to this issue would survey a large proportion of what has been written about it. (As early as 1964 Robert J. Andreach apologized for offering yet another discussion of the novel's structure, in his *Studies in Structure* [New York: Fordham Univ. Press, 1964].) The discussions that I have found most provocative or helpful are the following (chronologically listed): Hugh Kenner, "The *Portrait* in Perspective" (1948, 1955); Dorothy Van Ghent, *The English Novel: Form and Function* (New York: Rinehart and Company, 1953); Grant H. Redford, "The Role of Structure in Joyce's *Portrait,*" *Modern Fiction Studies* 4 (Spring 1958): 21–30; Robert J. Andreach, *Studies in Structure* (1964); David Hayman, "*A Portrait of the Artist as a Young Man* and *L'Education Sentimentale:* The Structural Affinities," *Orbis Litterarum* 19 (1964): 161–75; J. E. Hardy, "Joyce's *Portrait:* The Flight of the Serpent," in *Man in the Modern Novel,* pp. 67–81 (Seattle: Univ. of Washington Press, 1964); Thomas Van Laan, "The Meditative Structure of Joyce's *Portrait," JJQ* 1 (Spring 1964): 3–13; Evert Sprinchorn, "A Portrait of the Artist as Achilles," in *Approaches to the Twentieth-Century Novel,* ed. John Unterrecker (New York: Crowell, 1965), pp. 9–50; Sidney Feshbach, "A Slow and Dark Birth: A Study of the Organization of *A Portrait of the Artist as a Young Man," JJQ* 4 (Summer 1967): 289–300; Lee T. Lemon, " '*A Portrait of the Artist as a Young Man*': Motif as Motivation and Structure," *Modern Fiction Studies* 12 (Winter 1967–68): 441–52; K. E. Robinson, "Stream of Consciousness Technique" (1971); H. O. Brown, *James Joyce's Early Fiction* (1972); Diane Fortuna, "The Labyrinth as Controlling Image in Joyce's *A Portrait,*" *Bulletin of the New York Public Library* 76 (1972): 120–80; William A. Gordon, "Submission and Autonomy: Identity Patterns in Joyce's *Portrait,*" *Psychoanalytic Review* 61 (Winter 1974–75): 535–55; Bernard Benstock, "A Light from Some Other World: Symbolic Structures in *A Portrait of the Artist as a Young Man,*" in *Approaches to Joyce's "Portrait,"* ed. Thomas F. Staley and Bernard Benstock (Pittsburgh: Univ. of Pittsburgh Press, 1976), pp. 185–211; Hans Walter Gabler, "The Seven Lost Years of *A Portrait*" (1976); J. Delbaere-Garant, "From the Moocow to Navelless Eve: The Spiral Growth of Stephen Dedalus," *Revue des langues vivantes [Tijdschrift Voor Levende Talen]* 43 (1977): 131–41; Jon Lanham, "The Genre of A Portrait of the Artist as a Young Man and 'the rhythm of its structure,' " *Genre* 10 (1977): 77–102; Sheldon Brivic, *Joyce Between Freud and Jung* (Port Washington, N.Y.: Kennikat Press, 1980); Thomas E. Connolly, "Kinesis and Stasis: Structural Rhythm in Joyce's Portrait," *Irish Renaissance Annual* II (1981): 166–84; Rita Di Guiseppe, "The Mythos of Irony and Satire in Joyce's Portrait," *Quaderni di Lingue e Letterature* 6 (1981): 33–48; Margaret Church, "How the Vicociclometer Works: The Fiction of James Joyce," in *Structure and Theme: "Don Quixote" to James Joyce* (Columbus: Ohio State Univ. Press, 1983), pp. 135–67; Richard Peterson, "Stephen and the Narrative of A Portrait of the Artist as a Young Man," in *Work in Progress: Joyce Centenary Essays,* ed. Richard F. Peterson, Alan M. Cohn, and Edmund L. Epstein (Carbondale: Southern Illinois Univ. Press, 1983), pp. 15–29; John Paul Riquelme, *Teller and Tale in Joyce's Fiction: Oscillating Perspectives* (Baltimore: Johns Hopkins Univ. Press, 1983); J. F. Carens, "Portrait" (1984); B. L. Reid, "Gnomon and Order in Joyce's *Portrait,*" *Sewanee Review* 92 (1984): 397–420; Marguerite Harkness, *Aesthetics* (1984); Elliott

B. Gose, Jr., "Destruction and Creation in *A Portrait of the Artist as a Young Man*," *JJQ* 22 (Spring 1985): 259–70; Joseph A. Buttigieg, *"A Portrait of the Artist" in Different Perspective* (1987); Gerald Doherty, "From Encounter to Creation: The Genesis of Metaphor in A Portrait of the Artist as a Young Man" *Style* 21 (Summer 1987): 219–36; and Phillip Herring, *Joyce's Uncertainty Principle* (1987). While I do not agree with all of these claims for structural patterns in the novel, neither do I feel that they necessarily contradict one another, for Joyce has woven innumerable overlapping and intersecting structural patterns into Stephen's development.

5. I might pose this first point as a question: Can we, in this quintessential *Bildungsroman*, discover any aspect of the novel's structure that is not simultaneously an aspect of Stephen's psyche? In the subsequent discussion of the novel's style, we shall see how difficult it is to discover any image, even any metaphor or simile, that we can regard simply as part of an artifactual design of the novel or an authorial perspective, and that does not in some way enter either into Stephen's "individual" psyche, or form some part of his cultural psyche. This issue involves interesting problems about the relationship between the unity of an aesthetic work and that of the individual psyche. For example, since the protagonist's self is still in process of formation even as the work ends, is there not an inherent discrepancy between the structures of the novel and those of Stephen's psyche? Must not the structures of the novel "round out" at the end in a way that those of the self cannot? Phillip F. Herring points to this problem when he says "the form [of *Portrait*] must therefore be incomplete or indeterminate because its autobiographical aspect can never catch up with its fictional denouement, or Joyce might have shown us Stephen beginning to write the work of which he is the subject" (*Joyce's Uncertainty Principle*, p. 172). R. B. Kershner also touches upon these issues: "in a book as dependent upon the protagonist's consciousness as is *Portrait* we find it difficult to ascribe the 'shape' of a chapter or an episode either to the impress of Stephen's consciousness in the organization that he imparts to his experience, on the one hand, or to the aesthetic intention of Joyce, on the other. . . . Nonetheless, there are areas, such as those involving the structure of the entire book, in which it is not practical to ascribe the primary role to the protagonist, whose mind, language, and sense of structure are in continual change" (*Joyce, Bakhtin, and Popular Literature*, p. 153). Not surprisingly, some critics have claimed that *Portrait* is written by Stephen—however baffling that may be to common sense; see J. P. Riquelme, *Teller and Tale in Joyce's Fiction*, pp. 51 ff., and K. E. Robinson, who proposes that the first 164 pages of the novel are "recollection," the subsequent pages Joyce's authorial presentation ("Stream of Consciousness Technique," p. 63)—an idea endorsed by Jon Lanham, "The Genre of *A Portrait of the Artist*," pp. 100–01. In the next chapter we will discuss the tendency, noted by Dorrit Cohn, in her *Transparent Minds: Narrative Modes for Presenting Consciousness in Fiction* (Princeton: Princeton Univ. Press, 1978), to treat novels that skillfully employ narrated monologue as if they had no narrator. Herring's objection, though, overlooks both the unaccountable degree to which the self does have considerable "unity" at every stage of its progressive unfolding, and the capacity of a literary work to project its structures beyond its ending. One study that proposes a pattern in the novel that it seems could hardly apply to Stephen's psyche is that of Evert Sprinchorn ("A Portrait of the Artist as Achilles"), who argues that there is a regular pattern of inverse repetition throughout the novel, by virtue of which sections 1, 2, 3, 4, etc. throughout the first half of the novel are recapped in opposite

order in the latter half, 4, 3, 2, 1. (The text of *Portrait* in which Sprinchorn discovers this pattern has seventeen "sections" rather than the nineteen of the 1964 text edited by Chester G. Anderson. For Sprinchorn's defense of his choice of text, see footnote #7 of his essay.) But there is some such structure in Stephen's psyche, though not so symmetrically, insofar as the "mature" Stephen goes back over his youthful experiences, trying to re-read or re-make them. Richard F. Peterson develops the salutary point that the narrative of *Portrait*, including such things as the cycles of the seasons, has an existence apart from Stephen's subjectivity, such that even when he thinks mistakenly about things, he nonetheless must perceive the ineluctable reality of this world around him. As Peterson puts it, "the reason for the undeniable movement of the seasons and the irresistable rhythm of tides within and without in *A Portrait* is to assure us that the body of reality has its own identity" ("Stephen and the Narrative of *A Portrait*," p. 27). I very much concur, but would stress that this body of reality is experienced by Stephen not as "inert matter," but as a public psychic entity—not "subjective" (in the sense of residing solely within Stephen), but psychic nonetheless.

6. Lee Lemon recognizes this implication and suggests that Joyce's use of motifs as motivating elements in Stephen's psyche necessarily involves very implicit stimuli. See Lemon, "Motif as Motivation and Structure," pp. 43, 44, 51.

7. Perhaps the most assiduous Freudian reading is Chester G. Anderson's "Baby Tuckoo: Joyce's 'Features of Infancy,' " in *Approaches to Joyce's "Portrait": Ten Essays,* ed. Thomas F. Staley and Bernard Benstock (Pittsburgh: Univ. of Pittsburgh Press, 1976), 135–69. While I do concur with psychoanalytical readings in seeing Stephen's psyche as involving subconscius elements, there are crucial differences between such approaches and my own: they ascribe undue importance to sexuality, they presume the forces or patterns they explore to be virtually deterministic, and they do not see the dynamics that they discuss as an integral part of a larger, positive process of "individuation." Other psychoanalytical readings of the novel include William A. Gordon's "Submission and Autonomy"—an intelligent, perspicacious essay), Calvin Thomas's "Stephen in Process/Stephen on Trial," and Sheldon Brivic's *The Veil of Signs*.

8. As we have already seen (Chapter 3, footnote #37), Maurice Beebe has defended Joyce's style as a brilliant effort to show how the typical young artist of his time viewed the world ("*Portrait* as Portrait," p. 29). I am claiming that this veridicality necessarily extends to the structure of the novel, since that structure is an expression of his underlying view of reality.

9. I had used this figure for the novel's structure in class discussions long before coming across B. L. Reid's similar description. Reid says "the action of chapter 1 [which he sees as a paradigm of the whole] can be crudely abstracted as an inclined plane slanting upward, beginning low and moving gradually then suddenly high. That is a coarse graph of the whole action of the novel, and it works for each of the five parts" ("Gnomon and Order," p. 406). Later Reid says " . . . one sees a succession of five inclined planes slanting from low to high. The eye . . . then tends to draw a mental dotted vertical line from each high end to the following low beginning" (p. 420). In my figure, the declining line slopes gradually and crosses the ascending one at about mid-chapter, to suggest that each successive approach erodes gradually as the next one arises.

10. Chiasmus as a structural element of the novel has been proposed by several critics, on various scales. Gabler ("The Seven Lost Years of A Portrait") and, more extensively,

Sprinchorn ("A Portrait of the Artist as Achilles"), have described the larger structures of the book in these terms; Eliott B. Gose, Jr. has explored it on the level of phrase and sentence, and as it enters into Stephen's creative process itself. Gose sees chiasmic statements as attempts to balance inner and outer in Stephen's experience ("Destruction and Creation in *A Portrait*," p. 259). Hugh Kenner briefly discusses chiasmus on several levels in his Introduction to the Signet edition of *Portrait* (New York: Penguin Books USA Inc., 1991).

11. It may be questionable whether so ordinary, unimagistic a term as "the fellows" constitutes a psychological "motif" for Stephen, but these words are doubtless associated unpleasantly with the bewildering social forces the young boy is subjected to at this time. A glance at Leslie Hancock's *Word Index to James Joyce's "Portrait of the Artist"* (Carbondale and Edwardsville: Southern Illinois Univ. Press, 1967) shows the great preponderance of *fellow, fellow's,* and *fellows* in chapter I. And most occurrences of these words in subsequent chapters strongly carry the theme of social demands upon Stephen. For example, Mr. Dedalus says of the Jesuits, "those are the fellows that can get you a position" (p. 71). And in the single paragraph that involves most of the uses of these words after Chapter I, Mr. Dedalus, in Cork, advises his son, whatever he does to "mix with gentlemen," and says, "when I was a young fellow I tell you I enjoyed myself. I mixed with fine decent fellows" and the words occur five more times in this paragraph of quintessentially social, paternal advice (pp. 91–92). But by now it is obvious to Stephen how inappropriate and ineffectual such advice is. This flurry of *fellow* and *fellows* signals an important juncture in Stephen's turning his back on such social demands.

12. I have labeled this approach to life sensuous rather than sensual to suggest that the "inner" forces acting on Stephen at this time are not confined to sexuality. Here it is his belly that is counseling him. The word *counseled* invokes the motif of voices, which itself reflects Stephen's inner/outer predisposition, in that some of the voices that Stephen hears he regards as representing private needs, others public demands. Here he construes his belly as expressing a demand of his inner sensuosity. Interestingly, Stephen in *Portrait* never manifests the extreme modernist disjunction that would regard his body as outer, as alien to his self. The various somatic motifs of blood, heart, belly, are all read as aspects of Stephen's self. (In *Stephen Hero* we are at one point told "His body disturbed him and he adopted the expedient of appeasing it by gentle promenading" [*SH,* p. 69].) A more reflective Stephen in *Ulysses* does not feel so comfortable with his body and cannot so easily identify it with his self. He is aware of the decay of his teeth (*U,* 3.494), for which Mulligan mocks him (*U,* 1.708 and 1.412), and in Wandering Rocks, listening to the whirr of the dynamos in the powerhouse in Fleet Street, Stephen refuses to identify his self with either the outer or the inner: "Throb always without you and the throb always within. . . . I between them. Where? Between two roaring worlds where they swirl, I" (*U,* 10.822–824). Regarding the body as outer or alien does occur in certain quintessentially modernist literary characters—Kafka's Gregor Samsa, who becomes a cockroach, or Sartre's Roquentin, whose hand becomes an alien object.

13. The sincerity—or at least the depth—of Stephen's social feeling is called into question by the image of the ants, and even more by an image two paragraphs earlier of "the sound of softly browsing cattle as the other boys munched their lunches tranquilly" (p. 125).

14. Stephen's unwitting reliance upon the Church in a variety of ways—most obviously his conception of the artist as a "priest of eternal imagination" (p. 221)—offers a tangible

and persistent example of the novel's irony in regard to Stephen's presumed self-understanding. Stephen's debt to the church extends, however, not merely to abstract theological concepts, but to more implicit ways in which his very self (which he increasingly regards as a thing of his own making) is structured by the images, presuppositions, and attitudes of the church. James Carens says that even Stephen's gestures in chapters III and IV are institutional, devotional gestures ("The Motif of Hands in *A Portrait of the Artist as a Young Man*," *Irish Renaissance Annual II* (1981), 150; as an illustration, see *P*, p. 158.21–27). Stephen's simplistic subject/object dichotomy causes him to underestimate the continuing influence of the church on him once he has formally broken with it. Unable, that is, to understand the impossibility of separating inner from outer, he fails to see that while you can take the boy out of the church, you cannot so easily take the church out of the boy. Interestingly, in *Stephen Hero*, this realization is explicitly present in Stephen's own inner monologue, in the passage where Stephen hears the "embassy of nimble pleaders": "was it anything but vanity which urged him to seek out the thorny crown of the heretic while the entire theory, in accordance with which his entire artistic life was shaped, arose most conveniently for his purpose out of the mass of Catholic theology?" (*SH*, p. 205); and later in the same passage "can you be fatuous enough to think that simply by being wrong-headed you can recreate entirely your mind and temper or can clear your blood of what you may call the Catholic infection?" (*SH*, p. 206). The Stephen of *Portrait* is not so perspicacious on these points.

15. Others have acknowledged (though not *explained*) this predilection in Stephen. Marguerite Harkness says "Joyce is more precise and careful in his analysis of Aestheticism than of naturalism or realism because it is, for him, simultaneously the more attractive and the more dangerous tendency" (*Aesthetics*, p. 44). Charles Rossman says that Stephen in *Portrait* is "alienated from external reality" and "fluctuates between distorted perceptions of the outer world, scorn of it, and open flight from it," and that "eventually, a persistent gulf opens between the subjective world and the outer world, and Stephen soon prefers the 'adventure of the mind' " ("Stephen Dedalus and the Spiritual-Heroic Refrigerating Apparatus," pp. 114, 116).

16. B. L. Reid says of Stephen in chapter II, "he longs to meet his *anima*, his mystic salvatory female spirit . . . " ("Gnomon and Order," p. 407). Marguerite Harkness verges on a similar insight when she says "Each time that [Stephen] has accepted an order of his own making [i.e., what I am calling internal], he has 'seen' a woman" (*Aesthetics*, p. 27). Hugh Kenner also posits the similarity of odd and even numbered chapters, but does not pursue it along these lines; see *Dublin's Joyce*, pp. 123, 129). Another expression of this identification of the depths of Stephen's psyche with the female is that whenever Joyce refers to Stephen's soul he uses the feminine pronoun. For example, in the passage that we looked at above Stephen reflects on "the remoteness of his soul from what he had hitherto imagined her sanctuary" (p. 161). And just before the climactic beach passage, "His soul had arisen from the grave of boyhood, spurning her graveclothes" (p. 170), or a few pages later, "his soul was loosed of her miseries" (p. 176). For a good discussion of the uses to which Stephen puts women, see Suzette Henke, "Stephen Dedalus and Women: A Portrait of the Artist as a Young Misogynist," in *Women in Joyce*, ed. Suzette Henke and Elaine Unkeless (Urbana: Univ. of Illinois Press, 1982), pp. 82–107.

17. Hugh Kenner long ago said matter of factly, "the climax of the book is of course Stephen's ecstatic discovery of his vocation at the end of chapter IV" (*Dublin's Joyce*,

p. 131). David Hayman says of the "bird-girl passage" that "most critics consider [it] the novel's climax" ("Daedalean Imagery in *A Portrait*," in *Hereditas: Seven Essays on the Modern Experience of the Classical*, ed. Frederick Will (Austin: Univ. of Texas Press, 1964), p. 51), and Diarmuid Sheehan, in a recent Exemplar Notes publication on *Portrait* that is largely a mirror of critical opinion says of this scene "this is the climax of the novel" (*James Joyce's "A Portrait of the Artist as a Young Man"* [Ashbourne, Co. Meath: Exemplar Publications, Ltd., n.d.], p. 2).

18. Evert Sprinchorn, for example, begins his long essay on *Portrait* acknowledging that most readers feel "a sense of disappointment arising from the last chapter" ("A Portrait of the Artist as Achilles," p. 9), and trying to account for this feeling. John Edward Hardy finds in the chapter "an effect of falling-off that needs to be explained," and seriously asks "why did Joyce not end the novel with the triumphant vision of mortal beauty? Why doesn't Stephen simply take flight immediately in full glory?" And he finds "a distinct weakening of the heroic character in the final episodes" ("Joyce's *Portrait*," pp. 78–79). Hugh Kenner, who is very severe on Stephen, calls chapter V a "suspended chord" and says "there remains a moral ambiguity (how seriously are we to take Stephen?) which makes the last forty pages painful reading" (*Dublin's Joyce*, p. 121). Arno Heller more or less concurs, detecting in the last chapter a "complete change of tone and narrative texture [that] has led to a series of controversial interpretations which call for a reconsideration of the novel" ("Ambiguous Equilibrium: Joyce's *A Portrait* Reconsidered," *Literatur in Wissenschaft und Unterricht* 11 [1978], 34), and finding in Joyce's attitude toward Stephen in chapter V at best an "ambiguous equilibrium" (p. 39). A more imaginative and contrived explanation for the change that we feel at this point in the novel is offered by Jon Lanham—namely, that Stephen's own persona had narrated the novel until late in chapter IV, but then evaporates, and "the absence of this buffering personality wholly sympathetic to young Stephen is clearly felt in chapter V" ("The Genre of *A Portrait*," p. 101). (Marguerite Harkness rather surprisingly calls this chapter "the funniest in Joyce's novel" [*Portrait: Voices of the Text*, p. 77].) While I feel the negative qualities that these critics are troubled by, and I myself am arguing that some such difference is effected in Stephen by his aspiration to self-determination, I nonetheless find a great deal about the Stephen of chapter V to admire, to sympathize with, and even to like. He is several times shown to be vulnerable, wavering, self-critical. Consider for example his withdrawing the barb that his mind sends at MacAlister (pp. 193–94); his confusion about the tundish/funnel matter (pp. 188–89); his criticism of his own attempt to think of E———— C———— in sensual terms (p. 233); and his April 15 diary entry (which we shall look at later). His least appealing moments involve public scenes, when Stephen is concerned about the image he is projecting.

19. I will not review the extensive literature on the villanelle; briefly, I see it as an effete symbolist effusion on Stephen's part, not without some skill, but reflecting a pallid, callow sense of reality, very much in keeping with his subjectivist orientation. We know that Joyce wrote the villanelle much earlier, destroyed most of his juvenile verse, and disavowed even what he later published, and that in *Stephen Hero* the "Vilanelle of the Temptress" is referred to as "some ardent verses" inspired by a "trivial incident" (*SH*, p. 211).

20. I disagree, that is, with Maurice Beebe's view that this is a "theory of aesthetics propounded by Joyce through Stephen" ("The *Portrait* as Portrait," p. 14), and agree with those earlier critics who have argued that the function of the theorizing is dramatic—i.e.,

that it characterizes Stephen. S. L. Goldberg says of the aesthetic theory that "its force in the novel is not so much philosophical as dramatic," and that it "serves to reveal not so much the nature of art as the nature of Stephen Dedalus; and to miss this, or to attempt to assess Joyce's work by the theory as he there presents it, is inevitably to distort his artistic achievement" (*Classical Temper,* p. 43). Charles Rossman says "Everyone agrees that Stephen's discourse on Shakespeare in *Ulysses* reveals more about Stephen than Hamlet; yet that the same is true of Stephen's aesthetics in the earlier novels has gone relatively unappreciated" ("Stephen Dedalus and the Spiritual-Heroic Refrigerating Apparatus," p. 102). Richard F. Peterson takes this same tack, saying "more than anything else Stephen's theories reflect his personal ordeals in the novels" ("Stephen's Aesthetics: Reflections of the Artist or the Ass?" *JJQ* 17 [Summer 1980] 427). Ben Forkner's unpublished Ph.D. dissertation, "Stephen Dedalus: Verbal Consciousness and the Birth of an Aesthetic" (University of North Carolina at Chapel Hill, 1975), makes an extensive case for regarding Stephen's theories dramatically.

21. That Joyce felt an obligation to include in his books aspects of life he may not personally have approved of is suggested by a story Italo Svevo tells: "Dedalus is loose-spoken, while Joyce one day called me to task because I allowed myself to make a rather free joke. 'I never say that kind of thing,' said he 'though I write it.' So it seems that his own books cannot be read in his presence" (E. H. Mikhail, *James Joyce: Interviews and Recollections,* p. 47).

22. James Naremore discusses Stephen's turning to art as an escape from sordid circumstances and says of this passage describing Stephen's morning walk that Stephen is "meditating on art in order to ward off reality" ("Consciousness and Society in *A Portrait of the Artist,*" in *Approaches to Joyce's "Portrait": Ten Essays* [1976], ed. Thomas F. Staley and Bernard Benstock, p. 121). But what Naremore does with this insight is strange. Though he sees that Joyce is taking Stephen's measure in the novel, he ends by claiming ambiguously that while "Joyce could learn to criticize his life . . . he could not change his entire consciousness and become another man" (p. 133). In effect he judges that Joyce was "untaught by the wisdom he has written or by the laws he has revealed," as Stephen says of Shakespeare in *Ulysses* (9.477).

23. The fullest discussion of Stephen's debts to Pater, Wilde, Yeats, and Aestheticism in general is Marguerite Harkness's *Aesthetics* (1984), which shows how debilitating the effects of Aestheticism are on Stephen. John McGowan's "From Pater to Wilde to Joyce" is not concerned with influences so much as with modernist and post-modernist conceptions of the self in these three writers. His discussion of Joyce is vitiated by his presuming that Stephen Dedalus' "willful heroic self that is created ex nihilo" (p. 418) expresses Joyce's own view.

24. S. L. Goldberg quotes this passage as reflecting "the first glimmering of Stephen's maturity . . . and even a significant touch of *self*-irony" (*Classical Temper,* pp. 110–11). F. Parvin Sharpless sees this passage as an example of Stephen's having succeeded in moving from "kinetic involvement through detachment to pity" in his relationships with women ("Irony in Joyce's *Portrait,*" pp. 104–5). James Carens, by contrast, says of Stephen's "Now I call that friendly, don't you?" "Stephen's only sign of maturity is the cynicism with which he mocks the gesture" [of her farewell handshake] ("Motif of Hands," p. 152).

6. The Verbal Simulation of Stephen's Psychic Milieu

1. Predictably, Joyce's presentation of Stephen's consciousness in *Portrait* has been the object of a great deal of critical commentary. I have drawn most on the following discussions: Robert S. Ryf, *A New Approach to Joyce: The "Portrait of the Artist" as a Guidebook* (Berkeley: Univ. of California Press, 1962), pp. 94–97; Derek Bickerton, "James Joyce and the Development of Interior Monologue," *Essays in Criticism* 18 [1968]: 32–46; Robinson, "Stream of Consciousness" (1971); Anthony Burgess, *Joysprick: An Introduction to the Language of James Joyce* (London: Andre Deutsch, 1973); Erwin R. Steinberg, *The Stream of Consciousness and Beyond in "Ulysses"* (Pittsburgh: Univ. of Pittsburgh Press, 1973); Nancy G. Wilds, "Style and Auctorial Presence in *A Portrait of the Artist as a Young Man*," *Style* 7 (Winter 1973): 39–55; William A. Gordon, "Submission and Autonomy" (1974–75); Jerry Allen Dibble, "Stephen's Esthetic and Joyce's Art: Theory and Practice of Genre in *A Portrait of the Artist as a Young Man, Journal of Narrative Technique* 6 (Winter 1976): 29–40; Dorrit Cohn, *Transparent Minds* (1978); Tanya Reinhart, "Reported Consciousness and Point of View: A Comparison between Joyce's *Stephen Hero* and *A Portrait of the Artist as a Young Man*," *PTL: A Journal for Descriptive Poetics and Theory of Literature* 4 (January 1979): 63–75; David Jauss, "Indirect Interior Monologue and Subjective Narration in *A Portrait of the Artist as a Young Man*," *Par Rapport: A Journal of the Humanities* 3–4 (1980–81): 45–52; Shari Benstock, "The Dynamics of Narrative Performance: Stephen Dedalus as Storyteller," *ELH* 49 (Fall 1982): 707–38; James Michels, "The Role of Language in Consciousness: A Structuralist Look at 'Proteus' in *Ulysses*," *Language and Style* 15 (Winter 1982): 23–32; Christine O'Neill-Bernhardt, "Narrative Modes for Presenting Consciousness," a paper read at the James Joyce Symposium in Monte Carlo in 1990; Brian McHale, "Constructing (Post)Modernism" (1990); Naomi Segal, "*Style indirect libre* to Stream-of-Consciousness: Flaubert, Joyce, Schnitzler, Woolf," in *Modernism and the European Unconscious,* ed. Peter Collier and Judy Davies (New York: St. Martin's, 1990), pp. 94–114; and Katie Wales, *The Language of James Joyce* (New York: St. Martin's Press, 1992).

2. Joyce's awareness of the difference in this respect between his work and Dujardin's is shown in his statement to Valery Larbaud that "In that book *[Les Lauriers]* the reader finds himself established, from the first lines, in the thought of the principal personage, and the uninterrupted unrolling of that thought, replacing the usual form of narrative, conveys to us what this personage is doing or what is happening to him" (*JJ II,* pp. 519–20). Burgess acknowledges the "implausibility" that this sheer interiority creates in Dujardin's text, and shows that Joyce's more skillful use of mediated stream-of-consciousness in *Ulysses* smoothly blends inner and outer, so that "it is not really possible to separate the observed from the observer" (*Joysprick,* pp. 50–51). Another work that Joyce might have learned from is Arthur Symons' "A Prelude to Life" (1905), which is concerned with the tensions between the character's consciousness and the outer world, and with the limitations of the narrator's self-understanding, but which presents those themes awkwardly because of the first-person mode of presentation; see Karl Beckson's "Symons' 'A Prelude to Life,' Joyce's *A Portrait,* and the Religion of Art," *JJQ* 15 (Spring 1978): 222–28 (the story, by the way, briefly presents a girl named Emma). Dorrit Cohn makes the point that "in figural novels especially, where the narration of external reality is intimately related to subjective perception, there is no

clear borderline between the external and the internal scene" (*Transparent Minds*, p. 49). Later she argues that one reason that writers prefer the less direct technique of narrated monologue is that it achieves "a seamless junction between narrated monologues and their narrative context." Quoting as an example the passage in *Portrait* in which Stephen makes his confession, Cohn says "note how . . . the text weaves in and out of Stephen's mind without perceptible transitions, fusing outer with inner reality, gestures with thoughts, facts with reflections. . . . By employing the same basic tense for the narrator's reporting language and the character's reflecting language, two normally distinct linguistic currents are made to merge" (Ibid., p. 103).

3. The chameleonic quality of the narrative voice in Joyce's novels has been commented on by many critics and has driven some to strange strategems—including the idea that *Portrait* is written by Stephen, or that *Ulysses* writes itself. That is, critics faced with the undeniable presence of some voice, some perspective, other than that of a first person narrator, and yet not finding a tangible persona as in Mann or James, do not know what to make of this presence—especially since they are sure that Joyce disdained the traditional omniscient narrator and the accessory values that it seems to imply. R. B. Kershner wrestles with this issue in a long paragraph and concludes "the words are Stephen's, only slightly less so than if he had spoken them aloud. If we must specify a source, it is the language of his own future consciousness, which is to be formed in part by the 'subversive authors' (*P*, p. 78) from whom his verbal style will derive" (*Joyce, Bakhtin, and Popular Literature*, p. 161). It strains credulity less to say that the narrative voice represents the social psyche. Susan Snaid Lanser shows a similar confusion over the status of the speaking voice in *Portrait*, claiming that the novel has a "persona" whose personality shapes the text, but who is hardly present in the reader's mind: "the fictional world is presented through the mediation of a narrator. While this narrator does not declare his presence as a *persona*, in the text, his language—his 'personality'—shapes the text," and she goes on to say that "the discreet narrator is probably barely present in the reader's mind"; but on the next page she tells us that "Joyce as declared persona exists nowhere in the text" ("Stephen's Diary: The Hero Unveiled," *JJQ* 16 [Summer 1979], 418, 419). John Blades devotes an irresolute chapter to this question and tentatively proposes that "it is tempting to regard the anonymous narrator as Stephen Dedalus himself" (*James Joyce: "A Portrait of the Artist,"* p. 139). Dorrit Cohn in her *Transparent Minds* specifically criticizes this tendency to elide the distance between narrator and character in third-person presentations: "But to speak simply of a *single* presence (perspective, voice, etc.) is even more misleading: for one then risks losing sight of the difference between third- and first-person narration; and before long the protagonists of figural novels ([Joyce's] Stephen, [Kafka's] K., [James's] Strether) become the 'narrators' of their own stories" (p. 112). John Paul Riquelme's *Teller and Tale in Joyce's Fiction* and Shari Benstock's "Who Killed Cock Robin? The Sources of Free Indirect Style in *Ulysses*," *Style* 14 (Summer 1980): 259–73, are prime examples of such elision. Riquelme proposes that Stephen is the author of *Portrait* (for other similar opinions, see above, chapter 5, fn. 5). Benstock talks as if *Ulysses* produced itself, saying "the technical devices that collectively become the means for rendering plot and establishing tone and point of view are generated from subject matter and context rather than imposed from above (or behind) by an authorial presence hovering close to the narrative product," and more specifically of Aeolus, "these headlines arise in the text of *Ulysses* as they do in most newspapers, from the context of

the day's news" ("Who Killed Cock Robin?" pp. 261, 271). The same idea of a book that in effect writes itself is pursued in Shari and Bernard Benstock, "The Benstock Principle," in *The Seventh of Joyce,* ed. Bernard Benstock (Bloomington: Indiana Univ. Press, 1982), pp. 10–21.

4. Richard F. Peterson found this statement among Gorman's unpublished notes for his biography of Joyce. See "More Aristotelian Grist for the Joycean Mill," *JJQ* 17 (Winter 1980), 213.

5. Similarly, Silvio Gaggi says "the relationship between language, thought, and reality is clearly complex and understood only to a small degree; furthermore, the fact that we understand *in language* suggests that the attempt of language to understand language can never be wholly successful. As human beings it may be necessary for us to content our-selves with a forever partial, imperfect, and sometimes contradictory notion of what is. Still the assumption that language is somehow the sole or primary determiner of human reality, or the suggestion that it is in no way or very little accountable to something outside itself, has no more justification than a naive realism that assumes linguistic concepts are always perfectly correlated with natural divisions existing in the universe" (*Modern/Postmodern,* pp. 171–72). Gaggi later makes another perspicacious comment about language: "the view of language as a merely tautological structure—hermetically isolated from a world separate and inaccessible—and the belief that language always determines the world more than the world determines language are as irrational as a naive realism that assumes that the structures and categories of language mirror exactly the structures and categories of the world. The latter position is certainly simplistic, but the former leads to self-contradiction and an inevitable divorce between one's intellectual existence and one's social, ethical, and political life" (*Modern/Postmodern,* p. 186).

6. For example, Randy Malamud in *The Language of Modernism* (1989) says that "*Dubliners* is reality without consciousness" (p. 135), but that finally "Joyce's achievement is to equate language exactly with consciousness" (p. 150). In a different vein, Karen Lawrence argues that in his early works Joyce exhibits what she regards as a naive "faith . . . in the ability of language to capture reality" (*Odyssey of Style,* pp. 18–19), but that by the time of *Ulysses,* he had come to a relativistic position: "as the narrative norm is abandoned during the course of the book and is replaced by a series of styles, we see the arbitrariness of all styles" (p. 9). For quotations from critics who see Joyce as a linguistic relativist, see pp. 266–67, footnote # 15, of my "Voices and Values in *Ulysses.*" Colin MacCabe, however, says "many critics have complained that Joyce's last book marks a major change from his earlier work and that his interest in language had become a self-indulgent aberration. But such criticism ignores the fact that from his earliest work, Joyce was obsessed with language, with its structure and its effects." In this same context, speaking of *Finnegans Wake,* MacCabe says "Joyce's claim for his method was that it enabled the *articulation of areas of experience* which were barred from conventional language and plot" ("An Introduction to *Finnegans Wake,*" in *James Joyce: New Perspectives,* ed. Colin MacCabe, [Bloomington: Indiana Univ. Press, 1982], p. 30); the words that I have emphasized clearly regard language as distinguish-able from experience—a point I shall develop more fully shortly. See also the quote from Keith Booker above, in footnote # 33 in chapter 3. As that footnote shows, other critics have argued that even *Dubliners* involves a wonderfully subtle interplay of language, mind, and cultural milieu.

7. Roland McHugh observes that "nearly every *Finnegans Wake* sentence observes the formalities of English syntax" (*Annotations to "Finnegans Wake"* [Baltimore: Johns Hopkins Univ. Press, 1980], p. v), and Derek Attridge says "syntactic stability is characteristic of the *Wake,* and it often helps in the unpacking of a passage to trace the bare trellis on which the luxuriant verbiage is hung" ("Reading Joyce," p. 12).

8. Denis Donoghue, in an observation that presumes the different "structures" that I have described, says "the fact that you can't have a green rose is conceded ten pages later [in *Portrait*] and resolved by the reflection that 'perhaps somewhere in the world you could.' But Stephen's feeling does not allow itself to be curbed by botany, green roses grow in language when you want them to grow there. 'O, the green wothe botheth': I read this as a pure act of the imagination, effected by recourse to possibilities secreted in language alone and not in nature. Such blossoms grow profusely in the field of nonsense, the wildest field of language" (*The Sovereign Ghost: Studies in Imagination* [Berkeley: Univ. of California Press, 1976], p. 57).

9. For fuller development of these claims about Joyce's views on language, and how the early pages of *Portrait* illustrate these interrelationships, see my "James Joyce and the Power of the Word."

10. While this passage has attracted the attention of a number of commentators, none has attended carefully to the discrimination that Stephen intends by the locutions "better than . . . less pleasure from . . . than from." Vicki Mahaffey does say the passage shows that "Stephen is aware of the different reflective capacities of language, although he prefers its ability to reflect an individual private world to its panoramic particularization of the public one," and that his "preference is clearly symptomatic of his overall limitations: he favors a personal over a shared reality" (*Reauthorizing Joyce,* p. 62).

11. Such opinions, however, are heard frequently in Joyce criticism. For example, Marilyn French says "in *Finnegans Wake,* language and reality become one. One is not expressive of the other, it *is* the other" ("Joyce and Language," *JJQ* 19 [Spring 1982], 254). Randy Malamud says "Joyce's achievement is to equate language exactly with consciousness" (*Language of Modernism,* p. 150; cf. also p. 5). (Cf. also Beckett's famous statement about *Finnegans Wake,* quoted above, Chapter 3, footnote # 47.). Katie Wales says that "language for Joyce is not simply a transparent medium of reality but that reality itself. . . . Those readers of *Ulysses* and *Finnegans Wake* who look for the 'real world' beyond the complex words and structural technicalities of the texts will continually be thwarted" (*The Language of James Joyce,* p. 67). But in her subsequent discussion of the styles of Joyce's works Wales persistently assumes quite the opposite. She talks repeatedly about Joyce's methods of mimesis, especially in regard to thought presentation, and she pointedly says that "since thought is not only verbal but non-verbal, such a style must inevitably be 'symbolic' in its attempt to suggest the chains of visual images and memories, as well as other mental stimuli such as sensations, feelings, etc." (Ibid., pp. 72–73). It is interesting that working novelist Anthony Burgess consistently presumes that Joyce uses language to *represent* something (cf. *Joysprick,* pp. 17, 50, 52; the passage from p. 50 is quoted below in footnote 14). In his comparison of the views on language of Joyce and Wittgenstein, David A. White says (perhaps naively, in view of Joycean criticism) "now surely neither reader nor writer (Joyce included) is under the illusion that language is a *substitute* for life, that we actually live in and through the blotches of ink on the page"; he concludes that "for all his experimentation and seeming

obsession with verbal expertise Joyce should not be convicted of disregarding life and replacing it with the maniacal joys of verbal self-abuse" ("Joyce and Wittgenstein," *JJQ* 12 [Spring 1975], pp. 300, 303). Thomas C. Singer, in another essay comparing Joyce and Wittgenstein, concurs in this view but places the emphasis a bit differently: "What ties these two writers together above all else is their belief that the ordinary is the extraordinary, that the wonder of this world is not hidden behind any veils but is open to our view, and that language is both a revelation of this wonder and its riddle" ("Riddles, Silence, and Wonder," p. 462). Later in the same paragraph, Singer quoting Wittgenstein, says, "indeed, 'the existence of language itself' is one way in which 'the world as a miracle' shows itself."

12. If Joyce thought that language and reality were identical, why he was so worried about thunderstorms (*Letters,* II, 160), or explosions (*Letters,* II, 197), or physical weakness (*Letters,* II, 164)? If these phenomena were sheerly linguistic, surely Joyce of all people could simply have conjured them away.

13. D. H. Lawrence is quite explicit about this in *Aaron's Rod* (Cambridge: Cambridge Univ. Press, 1988), in a passage of several pages that describes one of Aaron's life crises. At one point Lawrence says "thoughts something in this manner ran through Aaron's subconscious mind as he sat in the strange house. He could not have fired it all off at any listener, as these pages are fired off at any chance reader. Nevertheless there it was, risen to half-consciousness in him" (p. 163). And shortly thereafter, Lawrence goes on "in his own powerful but subconscious fashion Aaron realized this. He was a musician. And hence even his deepest *ideas* were not word-ideas, his very thoughts were not composed of words and ideal concepts. They too, his thoughts and his ideas, were dark and invisible, as electric vibrations are invisible no matter how many words they may purport. If I, as a word-user, must translate his deep conscious vibrations into finite words, that is my own business. I do but make a translation of the man. He would speak in music. I speak with words. . . . Don't grumble at me then, gentle reader, and swear at me that this damned fellow wasn't half clever enough to think out all these smart things, and realize all these fine-drawn-out subtleties. You are quite right, he wasn't, yet it all resolved itself in him as I say, and it is for you to prove that it didn't" (p. 164).

14. Joyce's very skill in using language to simulate a wide range of psychic phenomena has invited confusion in regard to the processes he is simulating. As Anthony Burgess says of Leopold Bloom's thoughts about breakfast, "reading, we are convinced that this is how thoughts flow through the mind, and we forget that most of our inner life, especially when it is concerned with elemental matters like bodily wants, is preverbal. Desiring ham and eggs for breakfast, we experience sensations of appetite, memories of the mixed taste of salt, albumen and fat, and perhaps even erect a brief image of the frying pan with the food sizzling in it. But we do not say to ourselves: 'Ham and eggs, yes.' Joyce is working in a verbal medium and has to contrive a verbal equivalent for the preverbal flow" (*Joysprick,* p. 50).

15. C. S. Lewis raises such objections to the stream of consciousness technique in his *Preface to "Paradise Lost"* (New York: Oxford Univ. Press, 1961), saying that introspection itself inherently distorts consciousness, and that "the moment you put it [unfocused consciousness] into words you falsify it" (pp. 135–36). But this objection is valid only if the writer claims he or she is presenting the whole truth about consciousness; Lewis's objection applies to all of literature, for whenever we put *any* aspect of life into mere words, we

"falsify" it. Erwin R. Steinberg discusses various opinions and confusions among early commentators on *Ulysses* about the question of how veridical such techniques are. But some of the comments that he quotes, including some by Joyce, do not involve the claims of veridicality that Steinberg imputes to them. (See his *The Stream of Consciousness and Beyond in Ulysses,* especially sections 1 and 2 [pp. 3–28].) Most literary critics agree these modes of psychological presentation are conventional and psychic activity is not coterminous with language; Steinberg makes a great deal of these points, and he argues again in his 1982–83 article that "the stream of consciousness novelist can not present or reproduce a stream ot consciousness but can only suggest or simulate one" ("The Stream-of-Consciousness Technique in the Novel: Simulating a Stream of Concurrencies," *Imagination, Cognition and Personality* 2 (1982–83), 243). Child psychologist Joseph Church repeatedly deals with the relation of thought to language in *Language and the Discovery of Reality: A Developmental Psychology of Cognition* (New York: Random House, 1961), especially in chapter 6, "Language and Thinking"; his view is that many modes of thought are not coterminous with language. Dorrit Cohn recognizes that unconscious aspects of the psyche lie beyond the reach of language, but she overstates her claim that Joyce cannot, when he relies upon the character's own language to convey his psychic processes, evoke any supra-linguistic mental effects or any simultaneity of various mental processes (*Transparent Minds,* pp. 79, 86, 87). An interesting case in this regard is James Michels' "The Role of Language in Consciousness." For the most part Michels claims that all thought and consciousness are verbal, and that therefore the text offers not a simulation but a "veracious representation of consciousness" (p. 24); that "Stephen's thought cannot and does not exist apart from the signifier"; and that "the orders of language determine the organization of experience and the self. Indeed, we can no longer think of the mind as possessed of contents on any level" (pp. 28–29 and p. 31). But his subsequent analysis of the stream of consciousness in Proteus is so subtle that it demonstrates levels and modes of consciousness in Stephen beneath those carried by words, involving perceptions, images, and even an "ironic mode" (p. 30). Those who would identify thought or consciousness with language should reflect on the following questions: 1) How do new words, new linguistic structures that involve new discriminations, ever arise if thought is identical and coterminous with language? 2) When we speak of a person's having an ironic or a sentimental bent of mind, we know that such a temperamental bias manifests itself in his vocabulary, his language, but do we believe that even his very temperamental bias is "linguistic?" That is, does someone who is by nature ironic always have the word IRONY in his mind, or do such temperamental biases involve something "pre-linguistic?" 3) A child who is just prior to acquiring language nevertheless is conscious and has a large array of sensations, perceptions, intentions, inferences, and thoughts. If language and consciousness or language and thought are co-terminous, how can we explain such phenomena?

16. Apropos of this, Robert Ryf sees no true stream of consciousness in *Portrait,* saying that "the closest approximation of the technique to be found anywhere in the novel" is in the diary entries. But he acknowledges that in those entries "the flux is insufficiently undifferentiated, and the associations are too overtly directed and unified—in short, one dimensional" (*A New Approach to Joyce,* p. 96). John Blades simply uses the term stream of consciousness to refer to the technique of *Portrait*—and "interior monologue" to describe *Ulysses* and *Finnegans Wake*—apparently without awareness of its inappropriateness (e.g.,

James Joyce: "A Portrait of the Artist," pp. 62 and 133 ff.). K. E. Robinson does the same, referring, however, to "a loss in immediacy rooted in a presentation which is not in the first person" ("Stream of Consciousness," p. 64). Several other commentators acknowledge this in one way or another. Dorrit Cohn discusses the "complex relationship [that] exists between techniques and levels of consciousness. Most generally, one can say that the more direct the technique, the more evidently verbal the activity of the mind, and therefore the more clearly conscious the mind that is exposed" (*Transparent Minds,* p. 139). (Strangely, Tanya Reinhart in a puzzling article argues just the opposite; see her "Reported Consciousness and Point of View," p. 66). David Jauss focuses on the difference in immediacy that he finds between chapter I of the novel and the last four chapters and criticizes Joyce sharply for the inappropriateness of presentation in these last four chapters. Arguing that the first chapter uses a technique approaching stream of consciousness (what Jauss calls indirect interior monologue) that does permit immediacy, Jauss faults Joyce for abandoning this technique after chapter I. From that point on, Jauss says, "the narrator no longer presents Stephen's thought processes—he tells us of them" ("Indirect Interior Monologue," p. 48). Jauss claims that this indirect mode of presentation of the last four chapters (which he calls subjective narration) is "inappropriate to [Joyce's] subject matter and style" (Ibid., p. 52). But Jauss's claim that Joyce "presents" Stephen's thought processes less in the later chapters is demonstrably wrong; the greater immediacy he feels in chapter I is probably a function of the distinctively child-like quality of Stephen's thought, and of our sympathy with this young, vulnerable boy.

17. Speaking generally of the style in which a narrator mimics the speech and thought patterns of a character, Attridge says "this device goes by many names—free indirect discourse, narrated monologue, empathetic narrative, *style indirect libre, erlebte Rede*—and is perhaps best regarded as a cluster of techniques ranging from precisely recoverable thoughts to a slight coloring of the narrator's style by that of the character" ("Reading Joyce," p. 29, fn. 3). I agree that in the hands of a skillful writer, these techniques involve such a continuous psychic spectrum that all categorizations are ultimately unsatisfactory. (Erwin R. Steinberg's "The Stream-of-Consciousness Technique in the Novel" proposes a schema of six gradations—p. 246.)

18. Cohn says that there are only four such passages in the novel—three claimed by Derek Bickerton, plus the villanelle (Cohn, *Transparent Minds,* p. 276, fn. # 20, citing Bickerton, "James Joyce and the Development of Interior Monologue"). What Bickerton is illustrating is "direct interior monologue"—which is not identical with Cohn's quoted monologue—and he is vague about his three instances in *Portrait:* "once in a conventional soliloquy, once (and the pretext is significant) in the diary extracts that close the novel, once, and that briefly and almost unnoticeably, in the normal course of the narrative itself" (Bickerton, pp. 40–41). But the diary doesn't qualify even technically—though first person, it is past tense—and it has an utterly different psychological status than spontaneous interior monologue, being highly reflective, and written (cf. the "21 *March, morning*" entry). I find in *Portrait* five passages illustrating Cohn's quoted monologue: pp. 70.1–70.4; 86.27–86.29; 92.32–92.35; 189.30–189.36; 193.35–194.4. While Cohn has technical justification for counting the villanelle as quoted monologue, it is, like the diary entries, an anomalous example, since it is so reflective and so well shaped. My count of five does not include a number of sentences embedded within Cohn's other modes which come much closer to the feel of

interior monologue than do the diary or the villanelle. The presence of such embedded sentences (which she herself obviously does not regard as quoted monologue) is another reason that her schema is not particularly useful with *Portrait*. As an example of such a sentence, consider "Nice mother!" (p. 9.20).

19. There is some vagueness and discrepancy in Cohn's account of the language of narrated monologue. In her introduction she says that narrated monologue "reproduces verbatim the character's own mental language" (p. 14), and this austere criterion seems consistent with her later saying that the test of narrated monologue is that it can readily be translated into interior monologue (pp. 100–101). But she also says that narrated monologue renders a "character's thought in his own idiom" (p. 100)—a vaguer and more flexible standard that would not necessarily permit of direct translation into interior monologue. In any event, there are many passages in *Portrait* that indubitably reflect Stephen's idiom— which would seem to put them closer to narrated monologue than to psycho-narration—but that are not verbatim representations of his consciousness.

20. R. B. Kershner has made a similar point about this paragraph—"the sentences become smoothly and increasingly 'internal' "—but he regards this as problematic—as an acute instance of the "difficulty in ascertaining the epistemological status of the book's narration" (*Joyce, Bakhtin, and Popular Literature*, p. 160).

21. Ruth vonPhul's analysis of this passage involving Stephen and the dean (" 'The Last Word in Stolentelling,' " *Modern British Literature* 1 [Fall 1976]: 3–21) is an amazing display of literary-cultural contextualization, involving layers upon layers of material that would seem to constitute a veritable cultural psyche, simulated by the text. She finds within and behind this scene use of Epictetus' *Discourses*, Kierkegaard, Matthew and Thomas Arnold, Father Darlington (the real-life dean), Gerard Manley Hopkins's poems, and *King Lear*.

22. For example, Cohn illustrates how, in a passage from the Proteus episode of *Ulysses*, "the elements of the reported scene . . . activate the associations of Stephen's thoughts" to achieve a twofold result: "a purely subjective expression of *internal* happenings, and a blending of objective and subjective viewpoints on *external* happenings" (*Transparent Minds*, p. 72).

23. Strangely, Cohn assumes that "the early Joyce" of *Portrait*, who employs narrated monologue, had a more sophisticated view of the nature of thought than the later Joyce of *Ulysses*, who resorts to quoted monologue—cf. Cohn, *Transparent Minds*, p. 108. Cohn's misreading of Joyce's attitude toward thought and language in *Ulysses* is grounded in her erroneous presumption that quoted monologue is not a literary convention, but is literally mimetic of our interior language—of endophasy (see Cohn, pp. 76–98, esp. pp. 77–78, 86–87, 88–89).

24. The novel contains numerous instances of *felt* or *feeling* in a non-tactile sense; those instances that explicitly indicate vague or unclear mental processes include "he felt confused" (p. 112.5); "he had felt the slight changes in his house" (p. 64.22); "The ambition which he felt astir at times" (p. 64.24).

25. Homer Obed Brown quotes this "Masked Memories" sentence, saying of it, "the world in Stephen's mind always exceeds his understanding of it in a way that is apparent to the reader even when it is not to Stephen. Stephen himself is aware of this fact at one point" (*James Joyce's Early Fiction*, p. 126). Similarly, John Edward Hardy has said "all along, actually, much has been going on in the novel, in his own thoughts and emotions, which

Stephen is not aware of, or at any rate can never be supposed in a position to interpret" ("Joyce's *Portrait*," pp. 79–80). Other critics have testified in various ways to Stephen's psychic processes exceeding his awareness and understanding. See for example David E. Jones's "Spatial Relations in Joyce's *Portrait*," *Ball State University Forum* 17 (Autumn 1976): 37–40; Michael H. Levenson's "Stephen's Diary in Joyce's *Portrait*—The Shape of Life," *ELH* 52 (Winter 1985): 1017–35; and Vicki Mahaffey's *Reauthorizing Joyce*, esp. pp. 54–55. Similarly, William A. Gordon, in "Submission and Autonomy," distinguishes between two modes of discourse in the presentation of Stephen's psyche—what he calls "sub-thinking," and rational thought. Of the first he says that it "is a unified field of feeling-thought as it arises in response to experience. In effect, Stephen is not thinking, a controlled ego activity, but responding, with his thoughts and feelings recorded in complex, often contradictory images." The second mode "is that of ego-controlled abstract thought, especially in his aesthetic theories" (p. 537). See also footnote 32, below.

26. H. M. Daleski claims that the noose image—which was proposed by Kenner—is in the author's mind, not Stephen's (*Unities*, p. 176). Its status is problematic since the text does not explicitly involve the word *noose;* the closest we come is that the director is "slowly dangling and looping the cord of the other blind" (p. 153.34). But if the director's action can conjure a noose image in the mind of the reader, it can do so in the mind of Stephen— though not necessarily consciously. The skull image is explicit (p. 154.6), and there are enough similarities between this interview and that with Father Conmee in chap. I, where a skull is quite prominent (pp. 56.24, 56.28, 58.3), to make the image a very likely one for Stephen's (semi)conscious mind. For similar questions about the bird imagery on Clongowes playing field, see chapter 7, footnote 4. But the heuristic assumption that all such images are on some level "available" to Stephen is justified by the fact that the overall tenor of the novel's style, from chapter to chapter, is so fully attuned to and reflective of Stephen's psyche.

27. Hancock's *Word Index* lists seven instances of cave(s) or cavern(s), thirteen of echo(-es) (-ed) (seven of them within this section of Chapter IV, pp. 153–64). Some of these instances of cave/cavern are unambiguously a part of Stephen's consciousness—e.g., pp. 62.31, 68.7, 249.33. This last one is particularly subtle in terms of its borderline "consciousness-status," in that it occurs in a dream that Stephen then writes out in his diary. Vicki Mahaffey says of this scene with the director, "as Stephen talks with the director, 'the caves of his mind' are beseiged with numerous apparitions the meaning of which he fails to grasp" (*Reauthorizing Joyce*, p. 91). She discusses for several pages (89–93) the allusive reverberations of the cave image from Yeats, from Shelley ("the dim caves of human thought," in *Prometheus Unbound*, I, 559), and from Plato, assuming that this archetypal imagery serves to enrich Stephen's psyche, even while he is not fully aware of it.

28. The phrase "as if by magic" to describe how these memories arise is particularly interesting in light of Yeats's 1901 essay "Magic," which Joyce doubtless knew: it was included in Yeats's *Ideas of Good and Evil* (1905), which was in Joyce's Trieste library. There Yeats articulates three of his own doctrines that involve the social or collective psyche: "(1) That the borders of our mind are ever shifting, and that many minds can flow into one another, as it were, and create or reveal a single mind, a single energy. (2) That the borders of our memories are as shifting, and that our memories are a part of one great memory, the memory of Nature herself. (3) That this great mind and great memory can be evoked by

symbols" (*Essays and Introductions* [New York: Collier Books, 1968], p. 28). Yeats goes on to emphasize the capacity of the imagination to "move of itself and to bring before me vivid images that, though never too vivid to be imagination . . . had yet a motion of their own, a life I could not change or shape" (p. 29). Craig Carver, in his "James Joyce and the Theory of Magic," *JJQ* 15 (Spring 1978): 201–14) agrees that Joyce knew this essay by Yeats (p. 207); he explores Joyce's broader interest in the topic—especially the idea of a Universal Memory.

29. Another passage involving an expanded moment occurs in Stephen's talk with the dean of studies, between phrases spoken by the dean. See pp. 188.37–189.20.

30. Marguerite Harkness adds another dimension to this: "What is curious about Stephen's choice here is that this is the line [from Nash] Yeats quoted as representative of true symbolism in 'The Symbolism of Poetry'; Stephen cannot even, initially, manage to refer to his artistic ancestors accurately" (*Portrait: Voices of the Text*, p. 72).

31. There are many other passages in the novel that involve Stephen's experiencing his mind as having virtually its own activity, or being beyond his control. These include p. 83.4–6 (spontaneous memory); p. 91.12 (the riot of his mind); pp. 92.36–93.1 (inability to evoke memories); p. 99.30–32 (cries rush forth); p. 136.32–33 (can't evoke memories); p. 137.20 ff. (desires not to see and hear images, but must); p. 151.22 (surprised at how easily imperfections affect him). Another interesting example that requires the fuller context of the Irish shadow complex for its appreciation occurs when Stephen surprises himself by depicting Davin's hands in the story of an incestuous union that he imagines; see pp. 150–51 ff.

32. Other critics have seen the great extent to which Stephen's psychic life is beyond his conscious control. John McGowan uses the passage about Stephen's misremembering Nash's line as an illustration of Stephen's "lack of control over his thoughts and emotions" ("From Pater to Wilde to Joyce," p. 440). McGowan cites several instances of "the transience of [Stephen's] emotions," as part of his broader claim that "Stephen's pretensions to autonomy will be ironized by all those features of the novel that indicate how completely Stephen is immersed in and influenced by the world he longs to escape" (p. 439). (The other passages that he cites as examples of transience of emotions are p. 82.23–28 and p. 149.21–28.) Richard Ellmann earlier made a similar point about the ironizing effect of Stephen's various forms of dependence upon his would-be autonomy: "Although Stephen Dedalus in both *Stephen Hero* and *A Portrait* assumes his isolation, he surrounds himself with friends and family to whom he can confide it. When he rebels he hastens to let them know of his rebellion so that he can measure their response to it. He searches for disciples who must share his motives vicariously. As he demands increasing allegiance from them, step by step, he brings them to the point where they will go no further, and their refusal, half-anticipated, enables him to feel forsaken and to forsake them. He buys his own ticket for Holyhead, but claims to have been deported. Yet his mother prepares his clothing for the journey; she at any rate does not break with him. Of this young man it may be safely predicted that he will write letters home" (*JJ II*, p. 292; this passage was in the 1959 edition, p. 302).

33. "Stephen's Diary in Joyce's *Portrait*," p. 1024. While I agree with the gist of Levenson's statement, I disagree with his quasi-structuralist attribution of "knowledge" to the words themselves. The active agent here is Stephen's subconscious psyche, not the medium of language per se. Similarly, while Levenson's positing of a "linguistic unconscious" points in a very interesting direction, I would argue that the active agent is the collective conscious or unconscious, not language itself.

7. Motif/Complex/Allusion

1. An early perspicacious essay on the importance of motifs in the psychology and structure of the novel is Lee Lemon's "Motif as Motivation and Structure" (1966–67). Bernard Benstock provides a fairly comprehensive discussion of motifs in the novel in his "A Light from Some Other World." Baruch Hochman's "Joyce's *Portrait* as Portrait," *The Literary Review* 22 (Fall 1978): 25–55 also develops an insightful discussion of how various motifs work in the novel, illustrated through the bird and cow images. Articles have been written on many individual motifs; see for example Barbara Seward's "The Artist and the Rose," *Univ. of Toronto Quarterly* 26 (January 1947), 180–90; Diane Fortuna's "The Labyrinth as Controlling Image" (1972); James F. Carens's "Motif of Hands" (1981); and Steven R. Centola's " 'The White Peace of the Altar': White Imagery in James Joyce's *A Portrait of the Artist as a Young Man*," *South Atlantic Review* 50 (November 1985): 93–106. The most extensive discussions of the bird motif are Ronald Bates's "The Correspondence of Birds to Things of the Intellect," *JJQ* 2 (Summer 1965): 281–90; David Hayman, "Daedalian Imagery" (1964); Donald J. Foran's "A Mirror Held Up to Stephen," *JJQ* 4 (Summer 1967): 301–9; Lee Lemon (above), and Bernard Benstock (above).

2. An interesting confirmation of how many elements of the novel enter into Stephen's psyche emerged several years ago when John B. Smith began his dissertation on the motif-structure of *Portrait of the Artist,* later published as *Imagery and the Mind of Stephen Dedalus: A Computer-Assisted Study of Joyce's "A Portrait of the Artist as a Young Man"* (Lewisburg, Pa.: Bucknell Univ. Press, 1980). Since his work studied the frequency of occurrence of each image or motif in the novel, we had to determine which elements of the book were images or motifs—i.e., were meaning-bearing—and which were merely details—i.e., the "furniture" necessary to the novel's presentation. Scrutinizing the language of the novel with this question in mind, we found it had no details, only motifs! The novel, that is, so fully reflects the psyche of Stephen Dedalus that virtually every verbal element carries psychological freight.

3. In addition to these more or less conscious elements the episode may involve "mythic" contexts Stephen cannot yet be aware of that come into play as his acculturation develops. Hugh Kenner is not the only one to suggest that the eagles "evoke Prometheus and gnawing guilt" (*Dublin's Joyce,* p. 116), and Edmund L. Epstein (among others) sees the eagles as involving an allusion to Proverbs 30:17, which says that "the eye that mocketh at his father and that despiseth the labor of his mother in bearing him, let the ravens of the brook pick it out, and the young eagles eat it"; see Edmund L. Epstein's *The Ordeal of Stephen Dedalus: The Conflict of Generations in James Joyce's "A Portrait of the Artist as a Young Man"* (Carbondale and Edwardsville: Southern Illinois Univ. Press, 1971), p. 34. Epstein quotes the Douay version; the King James version is only slightly different: "The eye that mocketh at his father, and despiseth to obey his mother, the ravens of the valleys shall pick it out, and the young eagles shall eat it." Since Dante voices this line, she may well have apprised the young rebel of the biblical context.

4. K. E. Robinson concurs that the image of the ball as bird arises from Stephen's projection, saying "he has an uneasy and guilty feeling as he fails to take part to the full in the game. And the ball beomes unconsciously associated with the eagle, which, Dante says, 'will come and pull out his eyes' " ("Stream of Consciousness," p. 68). Here again the

question arises of how consciously an image exists in the boy's mind. R. B. Kershner asks of this image, "But is the bird image Stephen's? And if so, are we to assume he is conscious of this?" (*Joyce, Bakhtim, and Popular Literature*, p. 161). That the bird image is in some sense Stephen's (rather than just an authorial simile) is shown by the way that he recalls this event: "That was a long time ago then out on the playgrounds in the evening light, creeping from point to point on the fringe of his line, a heavy bird flying low through the grey light" (pp. 21–22). But Joyce's persistent point is that conscious and unconscious, private and public, cannot be sharply divided.

5. David Hayman has noted that Father Dolan "combines ornithic and human attributes" ("Daedalian Imagery," p. 42.) Another implicit reference to Father Dolan as an eagle in this passage occurs in his warning to the class that he "will be in tomorrow. . . . Tomorrow and tomorrow and tomorrow, said the prefect of studies. Make up your minds for that. Every day Father Dolan"—thus echoing the daily punishment of Prometheus by the eagles of Zeus. Interestingly, Fr Bruce Bradley, S.J., in his *James Joyce's Schooldays* (New York: St. Martin's Press, 1982), notes references in the 1890 school paper *The Rhetorician*, to Father Daly's (the original of Father Dolan) "eagle spectacles in the study" (p. 70). Bradley also presents photographs of Daly in 1887–1888 and in 1914, and points out that "Joyce's description of the prefect of studies in *A Portrait* fits Fr Daly in old age much better that the Fr Daly he would actually have known" (p. 71). The younger Fr Daly has dark hair; the elder is bald with a fringe of grey hair. Once again, life imitates Joyce's art.

6. Lee Lemon makes a similar point, noting that after his decision against the church and his mock-baptism, Stephen transforms what had been an unpleasant and threatening image of the bird into something positive, and that before this "Stephen's actions are derivative rather than creative" ("Motif as Motivation and Structure," p. 48). Lemon, however, sees no irony in Stephen's presumption of self-definition, and does not discuss the Icarus image at the novel's end.

7. Since Harry Levin's *James Joyce: A Critical Introduction* (1941; Revised edition. New York: New Directions, 1960), many critics have argued that this final diary entry does involve irony, and have several have pointed to the passage in Scylla and Charybdis. Joseph A. Buttigieg says that Stephen "remains totally blind to the fact that Icarus fell into the waters, and that he, too, is bound to undergo a similar fall" (*"A Portrait" in Different Perspective*, p. 72; the idea is repeated on pp. 74 and 75). Other scholars have found ironic aspects to the Daedalus/Icarus allusions even earlier in the novel. John Frederick Nims sees an irony in the phrase "a hawklike man flying sunward above the sea" that occurs in the midst of Stephen's exultation at the end of chapter IV, saying that "in the framework of the myth this is a highly ironic reference: an image not so much of triumph as of death. For in the myth the sun is a destructive force; it melts the wax that holds the wing together and precipitates Icarus into the sea in which Breughal paints him vanishing" ("Dedalus in Crete," in *Dedalus on Crete: Essays on the Implications of Joyce's "Portrait"* [Los Angeles: Immaculate Heart College, 1956], pp. 81–82). And J. S. Atherton traces an ironic aspect to the myth even earlier in the text, pointing out that the Latin phrase Stephen is quizzed about by one of his father's friends in Cork (*P,* p. 94) "was used by Robert Greene as the title of a poem, advising the reader to shun envy and ambition, which has as its second line, 'Proud Icarus did fall he soared so high' " (Atherton's edition of *Portrait of the Artist* [London: Heinemann Educational Books Ltd., 1964], p. 244). Marguerite Harkness not only sees the final line as an

Icarus allusion, she points out the shift of meaning of the image from the end of *Potrait* to Mulligan's ballad in the first episode of *Ulysses*. She also quotes the Scylla and Charybdis passage, seeing it as "totally a reversal of Stephen's associaton of himself with birds in *A Portrait*" (*Aesthetics*, p. 139). By far the most extensive discussion of the Daedalian-labyrinthine material in the novel is that of Diane Fortuna ("The Labyrinth as Controlling Image"); her explanation of the bird-girl's crane-like features as deriving from Minoan myth and her thus being "a type of Ariadne" (p. 157) is distinctive and interesting. Other discussions include those of Jean Paris (*James Joyce par lui-même* [Paris: Éditions du Seuil, 1957], pp. 100–19), David Hayman ("Daedalean Imagery," 1964), and Donald Gutierrez's "The Labyrinth in Myth, Reality, Modern Fiction," in *The Maze in the Mind and the World: Labyrinths in Modern Literature* [Troy, N.Y.: Whitston Pub. Co., 1985], esp. pp. 12–20. Fritz Senn's "close reading" of the Ovidian epigraph, "The Challenge: *'ignotas animum'* (An Old-Fashioned Close Guessing at a Borrowed Structure)," *JJQ* 16 [Fall 1978/Winter 1979]: 123–34 is fascinating.

8. Jungian Marie-Louise von Franz warns against taking the term "shadow" to have only dark implications. She quotes Jung as saying "The shadow is simply the whole unconscious," and von Franz describes it as "simply a 'mythological' name for all that within me of which I cannot directly know" (*Shadow and Evil in Fairy Tales* [Irving, Texas: Spring Publications, Inc., 1980] p. 5).

9. *Stephen Hero* contains some passages involving Irishness, but there the theme is presented more explicitly and less subtly. See especially *SH*, pp. 238, 239, and 242–44.

10. As a part of his discussion of Stephen's attitudes toward the Irish race, Bernard Benstock points out how this story awakens and revivifies Stephen's childhood memories (*James Joyce: The Undiscovered Country* [New York: Barnes and Noble, 1978] pp. 16 ff. Nehama Aschkenasy makes the interesting suggestion that Davin's story incorporates both the story of Jael and Sisera in Judges 4 and 5, and the "strange woman" who is discussed in Proverbs, especially Proverbs 7:6–23. Aschkenasy suggests also that Stephen's image of the peasant woman as a "batlike soul" invokes the figure of Lilith; see "Biblical Females in a Joycean Episode: The 'Strange Woman' Scene in James Joyce's A Portrait of the Artist as a Young Man," *Modern Language Studies* 15 (Fall 1985), 38.

11. This, then, is another diary passage that resurrects earlier feelings and images, probably quite unknown to Stephen, as noted by Michael Levenson in "Stephen's Diary in Joyce's *Portrait*." Levenson does not note this conjunction, but instead suggests (not very convincingly) that the April 14 entry links up with Stephen's early fear of the eagles bringing retribution. Anthony Roche sees John Alphonsus Mulrennan as "scarcely disguising the figure of John Millington Synge" (" 'The Strange Light of Some New World': Stephen's Vision in 'A Portrait,' " *JJQ* 25 [Spring 1988], p. 330). Interestingly, Mary Reynolds argues that his knowledge of Synge and his works made Joyce more realistic and tough-minded about the Irish peasantry, and she points out that Davin's story "parallels, in form and substance," Synge's *The Shadow of the Glen,* which Joyce had seen performed in 1903 ("Davin's Boots," p. 230).

12. Another instance of Stephen's equating Irishness with cultural crudity is shown in his phrase "a race of clodhoppers!" (p. 249) to refer to those who played "O Willie, we have missed you" soon after the death of William Ewart Gladstone. J. S. Atherton says that William Blake—mentioned in the preceding lines—comes under the same condemnation because

his father was an Irishman originally named O'Neill, so that Stephen considers him Irish (Atherton's edition of *Portrait,* p. 256). Discussing Joyce's own attitude toward Irishness and the Irish would be a topic to itself, but it is worth noting that his feelings were ambivalent and his recorded statements range from saying that "the present race in Ireland is backward and inferior" and Ireland is "a country destined by God to be the everlasting caricature of the serious world" (*CW,* pp. 166, 168), to his saying that the Irish were "the most intelligent, most spiritual, and most civilized people in Europe" (*JJ II,* p. 259, and *Letters* II, 202). It is also noteworthy, given the next to last sentence of the novel, that Joyce said "in time, perhaps there will be a gradual reawakening of the Irish conscience" (*CW,* p. 169), and that he said in a letter to Nora (postmarked August 22, 1912) that "I am one of the writers of this generation who are perhaps creating at last a conscience in the soul of this wretched race" (*Letters* II, 311).

13. Stephen could not of course proclaim the meaning of his name as he does at this point without having learned of the Daedalus myth somewhere along the way, and it is interesting to speculate about Stephen's relationship with his name as he grows up. He has long known that it was a strange name—both Nasty Roche and Athy at Clongowes told him that (pp. 9, 25)—but Joyce tells us nothing of what went on in Stephen's mind as he learned about and came gradually to comprehend who Daedalus was. This and other allusive, mythic contexts that Stephen gradually becomes "aware of" raise the question of how the individual's acculturation to such material takes place; just as Wittgenstein rejected the atomic, word-by-word view of language acquisition in favor of a more global process, Joyce shows that acculturation of the "individual psyche" is not simply a matter of the child's learning to recognize discrete names and stories. See Thomas C. Singer, "Riddles, Silence, and Wonder," pp. 468–69; Singer says that "perhaps the central thesis of [Wittgenstein's] *Philosophical Investigations* [is] that the child learns language as a form of life" (p. 469).

14. For a fuller development of this point and citation of earlier critics who have discussed it, see above, pp. 144–45 and footnote 7 of this chapter.

15. For more on the sympathetic quality of Joyce's irony, see above p. 79 and footnote 16 of Chapter 4.

16. Fritz Senn says "all of Joyce's characters, just like us, play roles, better or worse. Joyce, moreover, puts them into scripts they never know of" (" 'Stately, plump,' for example: Allusive Overlays and Widening Circles of Irrelevance," *JJQ* 22 [Summer 1985], 349).

17. The implications of Stephen's discussion of Shakespeare are developed in my unpublished essay "Self and Myth in Joyce's *Ulysses.*" We see evidence of Stephen's more complex view of the self not only in his exploratory attitude toward the Shakespeare material that he develops, but in his sensitive, empathetic reflections on the relationship between Sergeant and himself, and even in his quoting Goethe's proverb, "Beware of what you wish for in youth because you will get it in middle life" (*U,* 9.451).

18. From "Freud and the Future," in *Freud, Goethe, Wagner* (New York: Alfred A. Knopf, 1937), pp. 31–32.

Bibliography

Adams, Hazard. "Yeats, Joyce, and Criticism Today." In *The Uses of the Past: Essays on Irish Culture,* edited by Audrey S. Eyler and Robert F. Garratt, pp. 64–78. London: Associated University Presses, 1988. Reprinted in Adams' *Antithetical Essays in Literary Criticism and Liberal Education* (Florida State Univ. Press, 1990), pp. 144–59.

Adams, Robert Martin. "What Was Modernism?" *Hudson Review* 31 (Spring 1978): 19–33.

Allport, Floyd H. *Theories of Perception and the Concept of Structure: A Review and Critical Analysis with an Introduction to a Dynamic-Structural Theory of Behavior.* New York: John Wiley and Sons, Inc., 1955.

Anderson, Chester G. "Baby Tuckoo: Joyce's 'Features of Infancy.' " In Staley and Benstock, *Approaches to Joyce's "Portrait"* (1976), 135–69.

———. *Word Index to James Joyce's "Stephen Hero."* Ridgefield, Conn.: Ridgefield Press, 1958.

Andreach, Robert J. *Studies in Structure.* New York: Fordham Univ. Press, 1964.

Angeli, Diego. "An Italian Comment on *A Portrait.*" In Deming, *James Joyce: The Critical Heritage* (1970), I, 114–16.

Aristotle. *Aristotle on the Art of Poetry.* Translated by Ingram Bywater, with a Preface by Gilbert Murray. Oxford: The Clarendon Press, 1959.

Aschkenasy, Nehama. "Biblical Females in a Joycean Episode: The 'Strange Woman' Scene in James Joyce's *A Portrait of the Artist as a Young Man.*" *Modern Language Studies* 15 (Fall 1985): 28–39.

Attridge, Derek, ed. *The Cambridge Companion to James Joyce.* Cambridge: Cambridge Univ. Press, 1990.

———. "Reading Joyce." In Attridge, *The Cambridge Companion to James Joyce* (1990), pp. 1–30.

Barfield, Owen. *Saving the Appearances: A Study in Idolatry.* Second edition. Middletown, Conn.: Wesleyan Univ. Press, 1988.

Barth, John. *The Friday Book: Essays and Other Nonfiction.* New York: G. P. Putnam's Sons, 1984. This contains updated, self-annotated versions of Barth's essays "The Literature of Exhaustion" (1967) and "The Literature of Replenishment" (1979).

Barthes, Roland. *S/Z.* Translated by Richard Miller. New York: Hill and Wang, 1974.

Bates, Ronald. "The Correspondence of Birds to Things of the Intellect." *JJQ* 2 (Summer 1965): 281–90.

Beckett, Samuel. "Dante . . . Bruno. Vico . . . Joyce." In *Our Exagmination Round his Factification for Incamination of Work in Progress,* 1–22, by Samuel Beckett et al. London: Faber and Faber, 1929.

Beckson, Karl. *Arthur Symons: A Life.* Oxford: Clarendon Press, 1987.

———. "Symons' 'A Prelude to Life,' Joyce's *A Portrait,* and the Religion of Art." *JJQ* 15 (Spring 1978): 222–28.

Beebe, Maurice. *Ivory Towers and Sacred Founts: The Artist as Hero in Fiction from Goethe to Joyce.* New York: New York Univ. Press, 1964.

———. "The *Portrait* as Portrait: Joyce and Impressionism." *Irish Renaissance Annual I* (1980): 13–31.

Begnal, Michael H. and Grace Eckley. *Narrator and Character in "Finnegans Wake."* Lewisburg, Pa.: Bucknell Univ. Press, 1975. Foreword by Bernard Benstock.

Beja, Morris, ed. *James Joyce: Dubliners and A Portrait of the Artist as a Young Man: A Casebook.* London: Macmillan, 1973.

Beja, Morris, Philip Herring, Maurice Harmon, and David Norris, eds. *James Joyce: The Centennial Symposium.* Urbana: Univ. of Illinois Press, 1986.

Bellah, Robert, et al. *Habits of the Heart: Individualism and Committment in American Life.* Berkeley: Univ. of California Press, 1985.

Benstock, Bernard. *James Joyce: The Undiscovered Country.* New York: Barnes and Noble, 1978.

———. "A Light from Some Other World: Symbolic Structures in *A Portrait of the Artist as a Young Man.*" In Staley and Benstock, *Approaches to Joyce's "Portrait"* (1976), pp. 185–211.

Benstock, Shari. "The Dynamics of Narrative Performance: Stephen Dedalus as Storyteller." *ELH* 49 (Fall 1982): 707–38.

———. "Who Killed Cock Robin? The Sources of Free Indirect Style in *Ulysses.*" *Style* 14 (Summer 1980): 259–73.

Benstock, Shari, and Bernard Benstock. "The Benstock Principle." In *The Seventh of Joyce,* edited by Bernard Benstock, pp. 10–21. Bloomington: Indiana Univ. Press, 1982.

Bickerton, Derek. "James Joyce and the Development of Interior Monologue." *Essays in Criticism* 18 (1968): 32–46.

Bidwell, Bruce, and Linda Heffer. *The Joycean Way: A Topographic Guide to "Dubliners" and "A Portrait of the Artist as a Young Man."* Dublin: Wolfhound Press, 1981. With Maps and Photographs.

Bishop, John. *Joyce's Book of the Dark: "Finnegans Wake."* Madison: Univ. of Wisconsin Press, 1986.

Blackmur, R. P. *Anni Mirabeles 1921–1925: Reason in the Madness of Letters.* Washington, D.C.: Library of Congress, 1956.

———. "In Hope of Straightening Things Out." In *T. S. Eliot: A Collection of Critical Essays,* ed. Hugh Kenner, pp. 136–48. Englewood Cliffs, N.J.: Prentice Hall, 1962.

Blades, John. *James Joyce: "A Portrait of the Artist as a Young Man."* London: Penguin Books, Ltd., 1991. Penguin Critical Studies.

Bloom, Harold, ed. *James Joyce's "A Portrait of the Artist as a Young Man."* New York: Chelsea House, 1988. Modern Critical Interpretations. N.B.: Bloom's "reprints" delete all footnotes from the essays.

———, ed. *James Joyce's "Ulysses."* New York: Chelsea House, 1987. Modern Critical Interpretations. N.B.: Bloom's "reprints" delete all footnotes from the essays.

Booker, M. Keith. "The Baby in the Bathwater: Joyce, Gilbert, and Feminist Criticism." *Texas Studies in Literature and Language* 32 (Fall 1990): 446–67.

———. "History and Language in Joyce's 'The Sisters.' " *Criticism* 33 (Spring 1991): 217–33.

Booth, Wayne. *The Rhetoric of Fiction.* Revised edition. Chicago: Univ. of Chicago Press, 1983. First edition published in 1961.

Bradley, Bruce. *James Joyce's Schooldays.* New York: St. Martin's Press, 1982. Foreword by Richard Ellmann.

Bradbury, Malcolm, and James McFarlane. *Modernism: 1890–1930.* Harmondsworth: Penguin Books Ltd., 1976.

Brivic, Sheldon. *Joyce Between Freud and Jung.* Port Washington, N.Y.: Kennikat Press, 1980.

———. *The Veil of Signs: Joyce, Lacan, and Perception.* Urbana: Univ. of Illinois Press, 1991.

Brown, Homer Obed. *James Joyce's Early Fiction: The Biography of a Form.* Cleveland: Press of Case Reserve Univ., 1972.

Buckley, Jerome H. *Season of Youth: The Bildungsroman from Dickens to Golding.* Cambridge: Harvard Univ. Press, 1974.

Burgess, Anthony. *Joysprick: An Introduction to the Language of James Joyce.* London: Andre Deutsch, 1973.

Bushrui, Suheil Badi, and Bernard Benstock, eds. *James Joyce: An International Perspective.* Gerrards Cross, Bucks.: Colin Smythe, 1982.

Butler, Christopher. "The Concept of Modernism." In Dick et al., *Essays for Richard Ellmann: Omnium Gatherum* (1989), pp. 49–59, 443–44.

———. "Joyce, Modernism, and Post-Modernism." In Attridge, *The Cambridge Companion to James Joyce* (1990), pp. 259–82.

Buttigieg, Joseph A. *"A Portrait of the Artist" in Different Perspective.* Athens, Ohio: Ohio Univ. Press, 1987.

Butler, Samuel. *The Way of All Flesh.* First pub. 1903. New York: The New American Library, 1960. A Signet Classic edition.

Byrne, J. F. *Silent Years: An Autobiography with Memoirs of James Joyce and Our Ireland.* New York: Farrar, Straus and Young, 1953.

Calinescu, Matei. *Five Faces of Modernity: Modernism, Avant-Garde, Decadence, Kitsch, Postmodernism.* Second edition. Durham, N.C.: Duke Univ. Press, 1987.

Carens, James. "The Motif of Hands in *A Portrait of the Artist as a Young Man.*" *Irish Renaissance Annual II* (1981), 139–57.

———. "*A Portrait of the Artist as a Young Man.*" In *A Companion to Joyce Studies,* edited by Zack Bowen and James F. Carens, pp. 255–359. Westport, Conn.: Greenwood Press, 1984.

Carver, Craig. "James Joyce and the Theory of Magic. *JJQ* 15 (Spring 1978): 201–14.

Castle, Gregory. "The Book of Youth: Reading Joyce's Bildungsroman." *Genre* 22 (Spring 1989): 21–40.

Centola, Steven R. " 'The White Peace of the Altar': White Imagery in James Joyce's *A Portrait of the Artist as a Young Man.*" *South Atlantic Review* 50 (November 1985): 93–106.

Church, Joseph. *Language and the Discovery of Reality: A Developmental Psychology of Cognition.* New York: Random House, 1961.

Church, Margaret. "How the Vicociclometer Works: The Fiction of James Joyce." In *Structure and Theme: "Don Quixote" to James Joyce,* pp. 135–67. Columbus: Ohio State Univ. Press, 1983. The portion of the chapter devoted to *Portrait* is revised from an essay that appeared in Staley and Benstock, *Approaches to Joyce's "Portrait"* (1976).

Churchland, Paul M. *Matter and Consciousness: A Contemporary Introduction to the Philosophy of Mind.* Cambridge, Mass.: MIT Press, 1984.

Citino, David. "Isaac Watts and 'The Eagles Will Come and Pull Out his Eyes.' " *JJQ* 13 (Summer 1976): 471–73.

Cohn, Dorrit. *Transparent Minds: Narrative Modes for Presenting Consciousness in Fiction.* Princeton: Princeton Univ. Press, 1978.

Connolly, Thomas E. "Kinesis and Stasis: Structural Rhythm in Joyce's *Portrait.*" *Irish Renaissance Annual II* (1981): 166–84. An earlier version appeared in *University Review* (Dublin) 3 (1966): 21–30.

———, ed. *Joyce's "Portrait": Criticisms and Critiques.* New York: Appleton-Century-Crofts, 1962.

Conrad, Joseph. *The Nigger of the "Narcissus."* (1897) New York: Doubleday, Page and Company, 1916.

Cribb, Tim. "James Joyce: The Unconscious and the Cognitive Epiphany." In *Modernism and the European Unconscious,* edited by Peter Collier and Judy Davies, pp. 64–78. New York: St. Martin's, 1990.

Culler, Jonathan. *The Pursuit of Signs: Semiotics, Literature, Deconstruction.* Ithaca: Cornell Univ. Press, 1981.

Curran, C. P. *James Joyce Remembered.* London: Oxford Univ. Press, 1968.

Curtius, Ernst Robert. *European Literature and the Latin Middle Ages.* Trans. by Willard R. Trask. New York: Pantheon Books, 1953. Bollingen Series no. 36. Originally published in 1948.

Daleski, H. M. "The Double Bind of Consciousness: *A Portrait of the Artist as a Young Man.*" In *Unities: Studies in the English Novel,* pp. 171–88. Athens: Univ. of Georgia Press, 1985.

Deane, Seamus. "Joyce's Irishness." In Attridge, *The Cambridge Companion to James Joyce* (1990), pp. 31–53.

Delbaere-Garant, J. "From the Moocow to Navelless Eve: The Spiral Growth of Stephen Dedalus." *Revue des langues vivantes [Tijdschrift Voor Levende Talen]* 43 (1977): 131–41.

de Man, Paul. "Literary History and Literary Modernity." In *Blindness and Insight: Essays in the Rhetoric of Contemporary Criticism,* pp. 142–65. Second edition, revised. Minneapolis: Univ. of Minnesota Press, 1983.

Deming, Robert H., ed. *James Joyce: The Critical Heritage.* 2 vols. New York: Barnes and Noble, 1970.

Dibble, Jerry Allen. "Stephen's Esthetic and Joyce's Art: Theory and Practice of Genre in *A Portrait of the Artist as a Young Man. Journal of Narrative Technique* 6 (Winter 1976): 29–40.

Dick, Susan, Declan Kiberd, Dougald McMillan, and Joseph Ronsley, eds. *Essays for Richard Ellmann: Omnium Gatherum.* Montreal: McGill-Queens Univ. Press, 1989.

Di Guiseppe, Rita. "The Mythos of Irony and Satire in Joyce's *Portrait.*" *Quaderni di Lingue e Letterature.* 6 (1981): 33–48.

Doherty, Gerald. "From Encounter to Creation: The Genesis of Metaphor in *A Portrait of the Artist as a Young Man,*" *Style* 21 (Summer 1987): 219–36.

Donoghue, Denis. *The Sovereign Ghost: Studies in Imagination.* Berkeley: Univ of California Press, 1976. Chapter 2, "The Sovereign Ghost" (pp. 35–83), is a revised and expanded version of the W. P. Ker Memorial Lecture in 1974, separately published that same year as *Imagination.*

Ellmann, Maud. *The Poetics of Impersonality.* Brighton, Sussex: The Harvester Press, 1987.

Ellmann, Richard. *James Joyce.* Revised edition. New York: Oxford Univ. Press, 1982.

———. *Ulysses on the Liffey.* New York: Oxford Univ. Press, 1972.

————. "The Uses of Decadence: Wilde, Yeats, Joyce." In *a long the riverrun: Selected Essays*, pp. 3–17. New York: Alfred A. Knopf, 1989.

Epstein, Edmund L. *The Ordeal of Stephen Dedalus: The Conflict of Generations in James Joyce's "A Portrait of the Artist as a Young Man."* Carbondale and Edwardsville: Southern Illinois Univ. Press, 1971.

Faulkner, Peter, ed. *The English Modernist Reader, 1910–1930*. Iowa City: Univ. of Iowa Press, 1986.

Feshback, Sidney. "A Slow and Dark Birth: A Study of the Organization of *A Portrait of the Artist as a Young Man*." *JJQ* 4 (Summer 1967): 289–300.

Foran, Donald J. "A Mirror Held Up to Stephen." *JJQ* 4 (Summer 1967): 301–09.

Forkner, Benjamin Sands. "Stephen Dedalus: Verbal Consciousness and the Birth of an Aesthetic." Ph.D. diss., University of North Carolina at Chapel Hill, 1975.

Fortuna, Diane. "The Labyrinth as Controlling Image in Joyce's *A Portrait*." *Bulletin of the New York Public Library* 76 (1972): 120–80.

Fowler, Alistair. *Kinds of Literature: An Introduction to the Theory of Genres and Modes*. Cambridge: Harvard Univ. Press, 1982.

Franz, Marie-Louise von. *Shadow and Evil in Fairy Tales*. Irving, Texas: Spring Publications, 1980.

French, Marilyn. "Joyce and Language." *JJQ* 19 (Spring 1982): 239–55.

Friedman, Alan Warren. "The Once and Future Age of Modernism: An Introduction." In Friedman, *Forms of Modern British Fiction* (1975), pp. 3–15.

————, ed. *Forms of Modern British Fiction*. Austin: Univ. of Texas Press, 1975.

Gabler, Hans Walter. "The Christmas Dinner Scene, Parnell's Death, and the Genesis of *A Portrait of the Artist as a Young Man*." *JJQ* 13 (Fall 1975): 27–38.

————. "Preface." In Groden, *The James Joyce Archive*, vol 9 (1977), vii–xi.

————. "The Seven Lost Years of *A Portrait of the Artist as a Young Man*." In Staley and Benstock, *Approaches to Joyce's "Portrait"* (1976), pp. 25–60.

————. "Towards a Critical Text of James Joyce's *A Portrait of the Artist as a Young Man*." *Studies in Bibliography* 27 (1974): 1–53.

Gaggi, Silvio. *Modern/Postmodern: A Study in Twentieth-Century Arts and Ideas*. Philadelphia: Univ. of Pennsylvania Press, 1990.

Galilei, Galileo, et al. *The Controversy on the Comets of 1618*. Translated by Stillman Drake and C. D. O'Malley. Philadelphia: Univ. of Pennsylvania Press, 1960.

Geckle, George L., "Stephen Dedalus as Lapwing: A Symbolic Center of *Ulysses*." *JJQ* 6 (Winter 1968): 104–14.

Gifford, Don. *Joyce Annotated: Notes for "Dubliners" and "A Portrait of the Artist as a Young Man."* Second edition, Revised and Enlarged. Berkeley: Univ. of California Press, 1982.

Gilbert, Stuart. *James Joyce's "Ulysses": A Study*. Revised edition. New York: Vintage Books, 1955.

Gillespie, Michael Patrick. *James Joyce's Trieste Library: A Catalogue of Material at the Harry Ransom Humanities Research Center The University of Texas at Austin.* Austin: Harry Ransom Humanities Research Center, 1986.

————. *Reading the Book of Himself: Narrative Strategies in the Works of James Joyce.* Columbus: Ohio State Univ. Press, 1989.

Goldberg, S. L. *The Classical Temper: A Study of James Joyce's "Ulysses."* London: Chatto and Windus, 1961.

Gordon, William A. "Submission and Autonomy: Identity Patterns in Joyce's *Portrait.*" *Psychoanalytic Review* 61 (Winter 1974–75): 535–55.

Gose, Elliott B. Jr. "Destruction and Creation in *A Portrait of the Artist as a Young Man.*" *JJQ* 22 (Spring 1985): 259–70.

Graff, Gerald. *Literature Against Itself: Literary Ideas in Modern Society.* Chicago: Univ. of Chicago Press, 1979.

Groden, Michael. General Editor. *The James Joyce Archive.* 63 volumes. New York: Garland Publishing, Inc., 1977, 1978. Volumes 7–10 relate to *Portrait.*

Gutierrez, Donald. "The Labyrinth in Myth, Reality, Modern Fiction." In *The Maze in the Mind and the World: Labyrinths in Modern Literature,* pp. 1–28; discusses *Portrait* esp. on pp. 12–20. Troy, N.Y.: Whitston Pub. Co., 1985.

Habermann, Angela. "The Joycean Faun." *The International Fiction Review.* 10 (Winter 1983): 44–47.

Hancock, Leslie. *Word Index to James Joyce's "Portrait of the Artist."* Carbondale and Edwardsville: Southern Illinois Univ. Press, 1967.

Hardy, John Edward. "Joyce's *Portrait:* The Flight of the Serpent." In *Man in the Modern Novel,* pp. 67–81. Seattle: Univ. of Washington Press, 1964.

Harkness, Marguerite. *The Aesthetics of Dedalus and Bloom.* Lewisburg, Pa.: Bucknell Univ. Press, 1984.

————. *"A Portrait of the Artist as a Young Man": Voices of the Text.* Boston: Twayne Publishers, 1990.

Hassan, Ihab. *The Postmodern Turn: Essays in Postmodern Theory and Culture.* Columbus: Ohio State Univ. Press, 1987. Includes "Toward a Concept of Postmodernism," pp. 84–96, and "The Critic as Innovator: A Paracritical Strip in X Frames," pp. 118–46.

Hayman, David. "Daedalean Imagery in *A Portrait.*" In *Hereditas: Seven Essays on the Modern Experience of the Classical,* edited by Frederick Will, pp. 31–54. Austin: Univ. of Texas Press, 1964.

————. *Joyce et Mallarmé.* 2 vols. Paris: Lettres Modernes, 1956.

————. *"A Portrait of the Artist as a Young Man and L'Education Sentimentale:* The Structural Affinities." *Orbis Litterarum* 19 (1964): 161–75.

Heller, Arno. "Ambiguous Equilibrium: Joyce's *A Portrait* Reconsidered." *Literatur in Wissenschaft und Unterricht* 11 (1978): 32–41.

Helmling, Steven. "Joyce: Autobiography, History, Narrative." *Kenyon Review* New Series 10 (Spring 1988): 91–109.

———. "Joyce the Irresponsible." *Sewanee Review* 94 (Summer 1986): 450–70.

Henke, Suzette. "Stephen Dedalus and Women: A Portrait of the Artist as a Young Misogynist." In *Women in Joyce,* edited by Suzette Henke and Elaine Unkeless, pp. 82–107. Urbana: Univ. of Illinois Press, 1982.

Herr, Cheryl. *Joyce's Anatomy of Culture.* Urbana: Univ. of Illinois Press, 1986.

Herring, Phillip. *Joyce's Uncertainty Principle.* Princeton: Princeton Univ. Press, 1987.

Hirsch, Marianne. "The Novel of Formation as Genre: Between Great Expectations and Lost Illusions." *Genre* 12 (Fall 1979): 293–311.

Hochman, Baruch. "Joyce's *Portrait* as Portrait." *The Literary Review* 22 (Fall 1978): 25–55.

Hoffman, Paul. "Your Mindless Brain." *Discover* 8 (September 1987): 84–85, 87.

Houston, John Porter. *Joyce and Prose: An Exploration of the Language of Ulysses.* Lewisburg, Pa.: Bucknell Univ. Press, 1989.

Howe, Susanne. *Wilhelm Meister and his English Kinsmen: Apprentices to Life.* New York: Columbia Univ. Press, 1930.

Hughes, H. Stuart. *Consciousness and Society.* Brighton: Harvester Press, 1979.

Hume, David. *An Enquiry Concerning Human Understanding.* (1748) La Salle, Ill.: Open Court Publishing Company, 1958.

———. *A Treatise of Human Nature.* (1739) Edited by L. A. Selby-Bigge. Oxford: Clarendon Press, 1888.

Huxley, Thomas H. "On Descartes' 'Discourse Touching the Method of Using One's Reason Rightly and of Seeking Scientific Truth' " [1870]. In *Method and Results: Essays,* pp. 166–98. New York: D. Appleton and Co., 1896.

James Joyce Quarterly. "*Portrait* Issue." 4 (Summer 1967): 249–356.

Jauss, David. "Indirect Interior Monologue and Subjective Narration in *A Portrait of the Artist as a Young Man.*" *Par Rapport: A Journal of the Humanities* 3–4 (1980–81): 45–52.

Johnsen, William A. "Joyce's *Dubliners* and the Futility of Modernism." In McCormack and Stead, *James Joyce and Modern Literature* (1982), pp. 5–21.

———. "Toward a Redefinition of Modernism," *boundary 2,* 2 (Spring 1974): 539–56.

Johnson, Bruce. "A Modernist Noesis." In Dick et al., *Essays for Richard Ellmann: Omnium Gatherum* (1989), pp. 60–70, 444.

Jones, David E. "The Essence of Beauty in James Joyce's Aesthetics." *JJQ* 10 (Spring 1973): 291–311.

———. "Spatial Relations in Joyce's *Portrait.*" *Ball State University Forum.* 17 (Autumn 1976): 37–40.

Joyce, James. *The Critical Writings of James Joyce*. Edited by Ellsworth Mason and Richard Ellmann. New York: Viking Press, 1959.

———. "Daniel Defoe." *Buffalo Studies* 1 (December 1964): 1–27. Translated and edited by Joseph Prescott.

———. *Dubliners*. Edited by Robert Scholes and A. Walton Litz. New York: Viking Press, 1969. The Viking Critical Edition.

———. *James Joyce in Padua*. Edited, Translated, and Introduced by Louis Berrone. New York: Random House, 1977.

———. *James Joyce's "Chamber Music."* Edited by William York Tindall. New York: Columbia Univ. Press, 1954.

———. *Letters of James Joyce*. Three volumes. Vol. I edited by Stuart Gilbert (1957); vols. II and III edited by Richard Ellmann. New York: Viking Press, 1966.

———. "A Portrait of the Artist." In Scholes and Kain, *The Workshop of Daedalus* (1965), pp. 60–68; also printed in Anderson's Viking Critical Edition of *A Portrait*.

———. *A Portrait of the Artist as a Young Man*. Edited by Chester G. Anderson. New York: Viking Press, 1968. The Viking Critical Edition.

———. *A Portrait of the Artist as a Young Man*. Edited by J. S. Atherton. London: Heinemann Educational Books Ltd., 1964. Modern Novels Series.

———. *A Portrait of the Artist as a Young Man*. Introduction by Hugh Kenner. New York: Penguin Books USA Inc., 1991. The Signet Classic edition.

———. *Selected Letters of James Joyce*. Edited by Richard Ellmann. New York: Viking Press, 1975.

———. *Stephen Hero*. Edited by Theodore Spencer, John J. Slocum, and Herbert Cahoon. New York: New Directions, 1963.

———. *Ulysses*. The Corrected Text, edited by Hans Walter Gabler et al. New York: Random House, 1984.

Joyce, Stanislaus. *My Brother's Keeper: James Joyce's Early Years*. Edited by Richard Ellmann. New York: Viking Press, 1958.

———. *The Complete Dublin Diary of Stanislaus Joyce*. Edited by George H. Healey. Ithaca: Cornell Univ. Press, 1971.

Jung, Carl. "Definitions." In *Psychological Types*, pp. 408–86. Princeton: Princeton Univ. Press, 1971. Volume 6 of the *Collected Works*.

———. *The Psychology of the Unconscious*. Translated by Beatrice M. Hinkle. New York: Moffatt, Yard, and Co., 1916. This work appeared in German in 1911–12 as *Wandlungen und Symbole der Libido*, and a revised version, *Symbols of Transformation*, is volume five of Jung's *Collected Works*.

———. "*Ulysses*: A Monologue." In *The Spirit in Man, Art, and Literature*, pp. 109–34. New York: Pantheon Books, 1966. Volume 15 of the *Collected Works*.

Karl, Frederick R. *Joseph Conrad: The Three Lives*. New York: Farrar, Straus and Giroux, 1979.

Kearney, Richard. *Transitions: Narratives in Modern Irish Culture.* Dublin: Wolf-hound Press, 1988.

Kenner, Hugh. "The Cubist Portrait." In Staley and Benstock, *Approaches to Joyce's "Portrait"* (1976), pp. 171–84.

———. *Dublin's Joyce.* London: Chatto and Windus, 1955.

———. "The *Portrait* in Perspective." In *James Joyce: Two Decades of Criticism,* edited by Seon Givens, pp. 132–74. Augmented Edition. New York: The Vanguard Press, 1963. The first edition appeared in 1948.

———. "Signs on a White Field." In Beja et al., *James Joyce: The Centennial Symposium* (1986), pp. 209–19.

———. *"Ulysses."* Revised edition. Baltimore: Johns Hopkins Univ. Press, 1987.

Kermode, Frank. *Continuities.* New York: Random House, 1968.

———. *The Sense of an Ending: Studies in the Theory of Fiction.* New York: Oxford Univ. Press, 1967.

Kershner, R. B. *Joyce, Bakhtin, and Popular Literature: Chronicles of Disorder.* Chapel Hill: Univ. of North Carolina Press, 1989.

Krause, David. "Joyce vs. Yeats?" *Irish Literary Supplement* 9 (Fall 1990): 5–7.

Lanham, Jon. "The Genre of *A Portrait of the Artist as a Young Man* and 'the rhythm of its structure.' " *Genre* 10 (1977): 77–102.

Lanser, Susan Snaider. "Stephen's Diary: The Hero Unveiled." *JJQ* 16 (Summer 1979): 417–23.

Lasch, Christopher. *The Minimal Self: Psychic Survival in Troubled Times.* New York: W. W. Norton and Company, 1984.

Lawrence, D. H. *Aaron's Rod.* (1922) Edited by Mara Kalnins. Cambridge: Cambridge Univ. Press, 1988.

———. *Psychoanalysis and the Unconscious and Fantasia of the Unconscious.* (1921) New York: Viking Press, 1960.

Lawrence, Karen. "Gender and Narrative Voice in *Jacob's Room* and *A Portrait of the Artist as a Young Man.*" In Beja et al., *James Joyce: The Centennial Symposium* (1986), pp. 31–38.

———. *The Odyssey of the Style in "Ulysses."* Princeton: Princeton Univ. Press, 1981.

Lemon, Lee T., *"A Portrait of the Artist as a Young Man:* Motif as Motivation and Structure." *Modern Fiction Studies* 12 (Winter 1966–67): 439–50. Reprinted in Schutte, *Twentieth Century Interpretations of "A Portrait of the Artist as a Young Man"* (1968), pp. 41–52.

Lethen, Helmut. "Modernism Cut in Half: the Exclusion of the Avant-garde and the Debate on Postmodernism." In *Approaching Postmodernism: Papers Presented at a Workshop on Postmodernism, 21–23 September 1984, University of Utrecht,* edited by Douwe Fokkema and Hans Bertens, pp. 233–38. Amsterdam: John Benjamins Publishing Company, 1986.

Levenson, Michael H. *A Genealogy of Modernism: A Study of English Literary Doctrine 1908-1922.* Cambridge: Cambridge Univ. Press, 1984.

———. "Stephen's Diary in Joyce's *Portrait*—The Shape of Life." *ELH* 52 (Winter 1985): 1017–35.

Levin, Harry. *James Joyce: A Critical Introduction.* (1941) Revised edition. New York: New Directions, 1960.

Levitt, Morton P. "Joyce versus Joyce: Moderns and Post-Moderns." In *Modernist Survivors: The Contemporary Novel in England, the United States, France, and Latin America,* pp. 3–21, 257–58. Columbus: Ohio State Univ. Press, 1987.

Lewis, C. S. *A Preface to "Paradise Lost."* New York: Oxford Univ. Press, 1961.

Litz, A. Walton. "Modernist Making and Self-Making." *Times Literary Supplement,* October 10, 1986, p. 1142. [Review of six books on modernism.]

Lucente, Gregory L. "D'Annunzio's *Il fuoco* and Joyce's *Portrait of the Artist:* From Allegory to Irony." *Italica* 57 (Spring 1980); 19–33.

MacCabe, Colin. "An Introduction to *Finnegans Wake.*" In *James Joyce: New Perspectives,* edited by Colin MacCabe, pp. 29–41. Bloomington: Indiana Univ. Press, 1982.

———. *James Joyce and the Revolution of the Word.* New York: Harper and Row, 1979.

McCormack, W. J., and Alistair Stead, eds. *James Joyce and Modern Literature.* London: Routledge and Kegan Paul, 1982.

McGowan, John. "From Pater to Wilde to Joyce: Modernist Epiphany and the Soulful Self." *Texas Studies in Literature and Language* 32 (Fall 1990): 417–45.

McHale, Brian. "Constructing (Post) Modernism: The Case of *Ulysses.*" *Style* 24 (Spring 1990): 1–21.

McHugh, Roland. *Annotations to "Finnegans Wake."* Baltimore: Johns Hopkins Univ. Press, 1980.

McLuhan, Marshall. "James Joyce: Trivial and Quadrivial." In *The Interior Landscape: The Literary Criticism of Marshall McLuhan, 1943–1962,* pp. 23–47. Edited by Eugene McNamara. New York: McGraw-Hill, 1969. This essay first appeared in 1953.

Magalaner, Marvin. *Time of Apprenticeship: The Fiction of the Young James Joyce.* London: Abelard-Schuman, 1959.

Mahaffey, Vicki. *Reauthorizing Joyce.* Cambridge: Cambridge Univ. Press, 1988.

Malamud, Randy. *The Language of Modernism.* Ann Arbor, Mich.: UMI Research Press, 1989.

Malmgren, Carl D. " 'From Work to Text': The Modernist and Postmodernist *Künstlerroman.*" *Novel: A Forum on Fiction* 21 (Fall 1987): 5–28.

Mann, Thomas. "Freud and the Future." In *Freud, Goethe, Wagner,* pp. 3–45. New York: Alfred A. Knopf, 1937.

Meisel, Perry. *The Myth of the Modern: A Study in British Literature after 1850.* New Haven: Yale Univ. Press, 1987.

Michels, James. "The Role of Language in Consciousness: A Structuralist Look at 'Proteus' in *Ulysses.*" *Language and Style* 15 (Winter 1982): 23–32.

Mikhail, E. H., ed. *James Joyce: Interviews and Recollections.* Foreword by Frank Delaney. London: Macmillan, 1990.

Minsky, Marvin. "Why People Think Computers Can't." In *The Computer Culture: A Symposium to Explore the Computer's Impact on Society,* pp. 27–43. Edited by Denis P. Donnelly. Rutherford, N.J.: Fairleigh Dickinson Univ. Press, 1985.

Mitchell, Breon. "*A Portrait* and the *Bildungsroman* Tradition." In Staley and Benstock, *Approaches to Joyce's "Portrait"* (1976), pp. 61–76.

Morris, William E., and Clifford A. Nault, Jr. *Portraits of an Artist: A Casebook on James Joyce's "A Portrait of the Artist as a Young Man."* New York: Odyssey Press, Inc., 1962.

Murillo, L. A. *The Cyclical Night: Irony in James Joyce and Jorge Luis Borges.* Cambridge: Harvard Univ. Press, 1968.

Murray, Patrick. *Companion to "A Portrait of the Artist as a Young Man."* Dublin: The Educational Company, 1990.

Naremore, James. "Consciousness and Society in *A Portrait of the Artist.*" In Staley and Benstock, *Approaches to Joyce's "Portrait"* (1976), pp. 113–34.

———. "Style as Meaning in *A Portrait of the Artist.*" *JJQ* 4 (Summer 1967): 331–42.

Newman, Charles. *The Post-Modern Aura: The Act of Fiction in an Age of Inflation.* Evanston, Ill.: Northwestern Univ. Press, 1985.

Nims, John Frederick. "Dedalus in Crete." In *Dedalus on Crete: Essays on the Implications of Joyce's "Portrait,"* pp. 75–88. Los Angeles: Immaculate Heart College, 1956.

Noon, William T., S.J. *Joyce and Aquinas.* New Haven: Yale Univ. Press, 1957.

O'Faolain, Sean. "Commentary." In James Joyce, *A Portrait of the Artist as a Young Man.* New York: The New American Library, 1954, pp. [i–iv], 200–02.

O'Neill-Bernhard, Christine. "Narrative Modes for Presenting Consciousness." A paper read at the James Joyce Symposium in Monte Carlo in 1990.

The Oxford English Dictionary. Second Edition. 20 volumes. Oxford: Clarendon Press, 1989.

Pagels, Heinz R., ed. *Computer Culture: The Scientific, Intellectual, and Social Impact of the Computer. Annals of the New York Academy of Sciences* 426 (November 1, 1984). Contains a panel discussion: "Has Artificial Intelligence Research Illuminated Human Thinking?" involving Hubert L. Dreyfus, John McCarthy, Marvin L. Minsky, Seymour Papert, and John Searle, pp. 138–60.

Paris, Jean. *James Joyce par lui-même.* Paris: Éditions du Seuil, 1957. Écrivains de Toujours.

Peake, C. H. *James Joyce: The Citizen and the Artist.* Stanford: Stanford Univ. Press, 1977.

Pearce, Richard. "What Joyce After Pynchon?" In Beja et al., *James Joyce: The Centennial Symposium* (1986), pp. 43–46.

Perl, Jeffrey M. *The Tradition of Return: The Implicit History of Modern Literature.* Princeton: Princeton Univ. Press, 1984.

Peterson, Richard F. "More Aristotelian Grist for the Joycean Mill." *JJQ* 17 (Winter 1980): 213–16.

———. "Stephen's Aesthetics: Reflections of the Artist or the Ass?" *JJQ* 17 (Summer 1980): 427–33.

———. "Stephen and the Narrative of *A Portrait of the Artist as a Young Man.*" In *Work in Progress: Joyce Centenary Essays,* edited by Richard F. Peterson, Alan M. Cohn, and Edmund L. Epstein, pp. 15–29. Carbondale: Southern Illinois Univ. Press, 1983.

Poggioli, Renato. *The Theory of the Avant-Garde.* Cambridge: Belknap Press of Harvard Univ. Press, 1968.

Poirier, Richard. "Modernism and its Difficulties." In *The Renewal of Literature: Emersonian Reflections,* pp. 95–113 et passim. New York: Random House, 1987.

Polanyi, Michael. "The Unaccountable Element in Science." In *Knowing and Being: Essays by Michael Polanyi,* edited by Marjorie Grene, pp. 105–20. Chicago: Univ. of Chicago Press, 1969.

Potts, Willard. "Stephen Dedalus and 'Irrland's Split Little Pea.' " *JJQ* 27 (Spring 1990): 559–75.

———, ed. *Portraits of the Artist in Exile: Recollections of James Joyce by Europeans.* Seattle: Univ. of Washington Press, 1979.

Power, Arthur. *Conversations with James Joyce.* Edited by Clive Hart. London: Millington, Ltd., 1974.

———. *From the Old Waterford House.* London: Mellifont Press, Ltd., n.d.

Quinones, Ricardo J. *Mapping Literary Modernism: Time and Development.* Princeton: Princeton Univ. Press, 1985.

Radford, F. L. "Dedalus and the Bird Girl: Classical Text and Celtic Subtext in *A Portrait.*" *JJQ* 24 (Spring 1987): 253–74.

Ranald, Margaret Loftus. "Stephen Dedalus's Vocation and the Irony of Religious Ritual." *JJQ* 2 (Winter 1965): 97–102.

Redford, Grant H., "The Role of Structure in Joyce's *Portrait.*" *Modern Fiction Studies* 4 (Spring 1958): 21–30. Reprinted in Connolly, *Joyce's "Portrait": Criticisms and Critiques* (1962) and Morris and Nault, *Portraits of an Artist: A Casebook* (1962).

Reid, B. L. "Gnomon and Order in Joyce's *Portrait.*" *Sewanee Review* 92 (1984): 397–420.

Reinhart, Tanya. "Reported Consciousness and Point of View: A Comparison between Joyce's *Stephen Hero* and *A Portrait of the Artist as a Young Man*." *PTL: A Journal for Descriptive Poetics and Theory of Literature* 4 (January 1979): 63–75.

Reynolds, Mary T. "Davin's Boots: Joyce, Yeats, and Irish History." In *Joycean Occasions: Essays from the Milwaukee James Joyce Conference,* edited by Janet E. Dunleavy, Melvin J. Friedman, and Michael Patrick Gillespie, pp. 218–34. Newark, Del.: Univ. of Delaware Press, 1991.

Rice, Thomas Jackson. *James Joyce: A Guide to Research.* New York: Garland, 1982.

Riquelme, John Paul. "*Stephen Hero, Dubliners,* and *A Portrait of the Artist as a Young Man:* Styles of Realism and Fantasy." In Attridge, *The Cambridge Companion to James Joyce* (1990), pp. 103–30.

———. *Teller and Tale in Joyce's Fiction: Oscillating Perspectives.* Baltimore: Johns Hopkins Univ. Press, 1983.

Robinson, K. E. "The Stream of Consciousness Technique and the Structure of Joyce's *Portrait*." *JJQ* 9 (Fall 1971): 63–84.

Roche, Anthony. " 'The Strange Light of Some New World': Stephen's Vision in *'A Portrait.'* " *JJQ* 25 (Spring 1988): 323–32.

Rogers, Judy Robinson. "The Evolution of the Bildungsroman." Ph.D. diss., University of North Carolina at Chapel Hill, 1973.

Rossman, Charles. "The Reader's Role in *A Portrait of the Artist as a Young Man*." In Bushrui and Benstock, *James Joyce: An International Perspective* (1982), pp. 19–37.

———. "Stephen Dedalus and the Spiritual-Heroic Refrigerating Apparatus: Art and Life in Joyce's *Portrait*." In Friedman, *Forms of Modern British Fiction* (1975), pp. 101–31.

Rubin, Louis D, Jr. "A Portrait of a Highly Visible Artist." In *The Teller and the Tale,* pp. 141–67. Seattle: Univ. of Washington Press, 1967.

Russell, Bertrand. *My Philosophical Development.* (1917) London: George Allen and Unwin, 1959.

Ryf, Robert S. *A New Approach to Joyce: The "Portrait of the Artist" as a Guidebook.* Berkeley: Univ. of California Press, 1962.

Scholes, Robert, and Richard M. Kain. *The Workshop of Daedalus: James Joyce and the Raw Materials for "A Portrait of the Artist as a Young Man."* Evanston: Northwestern Univ. Press, 1965.

Schutte, William M., ed. *Twentieth Century Interpretations of "A Portrait of the Artist as a Young Man."* Englewood Cliffs, N.J.: Prentice-Hall, Inc., 1968. Schutte's "Introduction" is pp. 1–14.

Schwartz, Sanford. *The Matrix of Modernism: Pound, Eliot, and Early Twentieth-Century Thought.* Princeton: Princeton Univ. Press, 1985.

Segal, Naomi. *"Style indirect libre* to Stream-of-Consciousness: Flaubert, Joyce, Schnitzler, Woolf." In *Modernism and the European Unconscious,* edited by Peter Collier and Judy Davies, pp. 94–114. New York: St. Martin's, 1990.

Senn, Fritz. "The Challenge: *'ignotas animum'* (An Old-Fashioned Close Guessing at a Borrowed Structure)." *JJQ* 16 (Fall 1978/Winter 1979): 123–34.

———. "In Quest of a *nisus formativus Joyceanus.*" In *Joyce Studies Annual 1990,* edited by Thomas Staley, pp. 26–42.

———. *"A Portrait:* Temporal Foreplay." *Etudes Irlandaises* No. 12 (December 1987): 65–73.

———. " 'Stately, plump,' for example: Allusive Overlays and Widening Circles of Irrelevance." *JJQ* 22 (Summer 1985): 347–54.

Seward, Barbara. "The Artist and the Rose." *Univ. of Toronto Quarterly* 26 (January 1947), 180–90. Reprinted in Schutte, *Twentieth Century Interpretations of "A Portrait of the Artist as a Young Man"* (1968), pp. 53–63.

Shaffner, Randolph. *The Apprenticeship Novel: A Study of the Bildungsroman as a Regulative Type in Western Literature with a Focus on Three Representatives by Goethe, Maugham, and Mann.* New York: Peter Lang, 1984.

Sharpless, F. Parvin. "Irony in Joyce's *Portrait:* The Stasis of Pity." *JJQ* 4 (Summer 1967): 320–30. Reprinted in Schutte, *Twentieth Century Interpretations of "A Portrait"* (1968), pp. 96–106.

Sheehan, Diarmuid. *James Joyce's "A Portrait of the Artist as a Young Man."* Ashbourne, Co. Meath: Exemplar Publications, Ltd., n.d.

Singer, Alan. "The Metaphors of Fiction." In *A Metaphorics of Fiction: Discontinuity and Discourse in the Modern Novel,* pp. 23–45. Tallahassee: Florida State Univ. Press, 1983.

Singer, Thomas C. "Riddles, Silence, and Wonder: Joyce and Wittgenstein Encountering the Limits of Language." *ELH* 57 (Summer 1990): 459–84.

Smith, John B. *Imagery and the Mind of Stephen Dedalus: A Computer Assisted Study of Joyce's "Portrait of the Artist as a Young Man."* Lewisburg, Pa.: Bucknell Univ. Press, 1980.

Smitten, Jeffrey R., and Ann Daghistany, eds. *Spatial Form in Narrative.* Ithaca: Cornell Univ. Press, 1981.

Sosnoski, James J. "Reading Acts and Reading Warrants: Some Implications for Readers Responding to Joyce's Portrait of Stephen." *JJQ* 16 (Fall 1978/Winter 1979): 43–63.

Sprinchorn, Evert. "A Portrait of the Artist as Achilles." In *Approaches to the Twentieth-Century Novel,* edited by John Unterrecker, pp. 9–50. New York: Crowell, 1965.

Staley, Thomas F. *An Annotated Critical Bibliography of James Joyce.* New York: St. Martin's Press, 1989.

———. "James Joyce." In *Anglo-Irish Literature: A Review of Research,* edited by Richard J. Finneran, pp. 366–435. New York: The Modern Language Association, 1976.

———. "James Joyce." In *Recent Research on Anglo-Irish Writers: A Supplement to Anglo-Irish Literature: A Review of Research,* edited by Richard J. Finneran, pp. 181–202. New York: The Modern Language Association, 1983.

———. "Strings in the Labyrinth: Sixty Years with Joyce's *Portrait.* In Staley and Benstock, *Approaches to Joyce's "Portrait"* (1976), pp. 3–24.

Staley, Thomas F., and Bernard Benstock, eds. *Approaches to Joyce's "Portait": Ten Essays.* Pittsburgh: Univ. of Pittsburgh Press, 1976.

Steinberg, Erwin R. "The Bird-Girl in *A Portrait* as Synthesis: The Sacred Assimilated to the Profane." *JJQ* 17 (Winter 1980): 149–63.

———. *The Stream of Consciousness and Beyond in "Ulysses."* Pittsburgh: Univ. of Pittsburgh Press, 1973.

———. "The Stream-of-Consciousness Technique in the Novel: Simulating a Stream of Concurrencies." *Imagination, Cognition and Personality* 2 (1982–83): 241–49.

Stove, D. C. *Popper and After: Four Modern Irrationalists.* Oxford: Pergamon Press, 1982.

Sullivan, Kevin. *Joyce Among the Jesuits.* New York: Columbia Univ. Press, 1958.

Sultan, Stanley. *Eliot, Joyce and Company.* New York: Oxford Univ. Press, 1987.

Swales, Martin. *The German Bildungsroman from Wieland to Hesse.* Princeton: Princeton Univ. Press, 1978.

Taylor, Charles. *Sources of the Self: The Making of the Modern Identity.* Cambridge: Harvard Univ. Press, 1989.

Tennyson, G. B. "The *Bildungsroman* in Nineteenth-Century English Literature." In *Medieval Epic to the "Epic Theatre" of Brecht,* edited by Rosario P. Armato and John M. Spalek, pp. 135–46. Los Angeles: Univ. of Southern California Press, 1968.

Thomas, Calvin. "Stephen in Process/Stephen on Trial: The Anxiety of Production in Joyce's *Portrait.*" *Novel* 23 (Spring 1990): 282–302.

Thornton, Weldon. "Between Circle and Straight Line: A Pragmatic View of W. B. Yeats and the Occult." *Studies in the Literary Imagination* 14 (Spring 1981): 61–75.

———. "James Joyce and the Power of the Word." In *The Classic British Novel,* edited by Howard M. Harper, Jr. and Charles Edge, pp. 183–201. Athens: Univ. of Georgia Press, 1972.

———. *J. M. Synge and the Western Mind.* Gerrards Cross: Colin Smythe Ltd., 1979.

———. "The Roots of Modernism: A Study in Cultural Temperament." Unpublished typescript. Pp. 378.

――――. "Self and Myth in Joyce's *Ulysses*." Unpublished typescript. Pp. 32.

――――. "Voices and Values in *Ulysses*." In *Joyce's "Ulysses": The Larger Perspective*, edited by Robert D. Newman and Weldon Thornton, pp. 244–70. London: Associated University Presses, 1987.

Tindall, William York. *Forces in Modern British Literature 1885–1956*. New York: Vintage Books, 1956.

Unkeless, Elaine. "Bats and Sanguivorous Bugaboos." *JJQ* 15 (Winter 1978): 128–33.

Van Ghent, Dorothy. *The English Novel: Form and Function*. New York: Rinehart and Company, 1953.

Van Laan, Thomas. "The Meditative Structure of Joyce's *Portrait*." *JJQ* 1 (Spring 1964): 3–13.

vonPhul, Ruth. " 'The Last Word in Stolentelling.' " *Modern British Literature* 1 (Fall 1976): 3–21. "Corrigenda," 2 (Spring 1977), 117.

Wales, Katie. *The Language of James Joyce*. New York: St. Martin's Press, 1992.

Weathers, Winston. "A Portrait of the Broken Word." *JJQ* 1 (Summer 1964): 27–40.

Weir, Lorraine. *Writing Joyce: A Semiotics of the Joyce System*. Bloomington: Indiana Univ. Press, 1989.

White, David A. "Joyce and Wittgenstein." *JJQ* 12 (Spring 1975): 294–304.

Wilde, Alan. *Horizons of Assent: Modernism, Postmodernism, and the Ironic Imagination*. Baltimore: Johns Hopkins Univ. Press, 1981.

Wilde, Oscar. *Oscar Wilde*. Edited by Isobel Murray. Oxford: Oxford Univ. Press, 1989. Oxford Authors Edition.

Wildi, Max. "James Joyce and Arthur Symons." *Orbis Litterarum* 19 (1964): 187–93.

Wilds, Nancy G. "Style and Auctorial Presence in *A Portrait of the Artist as a Young Man*." *Style* 7 (Winter 1973): 39–55.

Wilson, Edmund. *Axel's Castle: A Study in the Imaginative Literature of 1870–1930*. New York: Scribners, 1931.

Woolf, Virginia. *To the Lighthouse*. New York: Harcourt, Brace and Company, 1927.

Yeats, W. B. "Magic." In *Essays and Introductions*, pp. 28–52. New York: Collier Books, 1968.

Index

The Antimodernism of Joyce's *Portrait of the Artist as a Young Man*
was composed in 10 on 13 Garamond Light on a Mergenthaler Linotronic 303
by Partners Composition;
with display type set in Centaur
by Dix Type;
printed by sheet-fed offset of 50-pound, acid-free Natural Hi Bulk,
Smyth-sewn and bound over binder's boards in Holliston Roxite B,
and notch bound with paper covers printed in 2 colors
by Braun-Brumfield, Inc.;
and published by
Syracuse University Press
Syracuse, New York 13244-5160

Richard Fallis, *Series Editor*

Irish Studies presents a wide range of books interpreting important aspects of Irish life and culture to scholarly and general audiences. The richness and complexity of the Irish experience, past and present, deserves broad understanding and careful analysis. For this reason, an important purpose of the series is to offer a forum to scholars interested in Ireland, its history, and culture. Irish literature is a special concern in the series, but works from the perspectives of the fine arts, history, and the social sciences are also welcome, as are studies that take multidisciplinary approaches.

Selected titles in the series include: